MW00951738

MESSENGER OF THE HOLY

MESSENGER *OF THE* HOLY

GUIDANCE FROM A SPIRITUAL MESSENGER ON LIVING, GRIEVING AND GROWING

Michael Olin-Hitt, Ph.D.

To Jonathan

Blessings for your insights & inspiration

[illegible]

BALBOA. PRESS
A DIVISION OF HAY HOUSE

Balboa Press books may be ordered through booksellers or by contacting:

Balboa Press
A Division of Hay House
1663 Liberty Drive
Bloomington, IN 47403
www.balboapress.com
1 (877) 407-4847

Print information available on the last page.

ISBN: 978-1-5043-7377-7 (sc)
ISBN: 978-1-5043-7376-0 (hc)
ISBN: 978-1-5043-7378-4 (e)

Library of Congress Control Number: 2017902198

Balboa Press rev. date: 03/15/2017

I will pour out my spirit on all
flesh;
your sons and your daughters
shall prophesy,
your old men shall dream
dreams,
and your young men shall see
visions.

Joel 2:28

I count the grains of sand on the beach and measure the sea; I understand the speech of the gods and hear the voiceless.

The Oracle of Delphi

The Spirit of Wisdom is but one, yet can do everything; herself unchanging. She makes all things new; age after age she enters into holy souls, and makes them God's friends and prophets.

Wisdom of Solomon 7:27–28

Behold, a sacred voice is calling you; all over the sky a sacred voice is calling.

Black Elk Speaks

To Jennifer, my spiritual companion and beloved wife.

In honor of my mother, Donna June Wert, who pointed the way.

The previous edition of this book was published in a slightly different form by Council Oak Books in 2007 under the title *The Word of God Upon My Lips*.
The Appendix, "The Braided Way," was oritinally published in *Kindred Spirit*, Summer 2016 Edition.

Publishers have generously given permission to use extended quotations from the following copyrighted works:

Excerpts from *Meditation and the Bible* and *Meditation and Kabbalah* by Arey Kaplan with permission of Red Wheel/Weiser, Newburyport, MA and San Francisco, CA.

Excerpts from *The Prophets* by Abraham Heschel, copyright 1962 by Abraham Heschel, with permission from HarperCollins Publishers.

All quotes from the Bible are taken from the New Revised Standard Version, used by permission of the publisher; copyright 1989 by the National Council of the Churches of Christ in the United States of America, New York City, NY.

Contents

INTRODUCTION

The Shaman, the Prophet, the Oracle and the Channel

In 1998 I decided to take contemplative prayer seriously, but I was not prepared for the way the Holy would break into my body and mind.

While praying in October of that year, I was literally knocked to the floor. I was flooded with spiritual energy. My body shook with tremors, but my mind was perfectly clear. I knew that something holy was entering me, and I knew I had to surrender.

I felt a doorway open in the hollow of my chest, just below my heart. I felt as though my spirit was standing at this doorway, and beyond it was the expanse of all that is. Over the next few months, I concentrated my prayer time on this internal portal to the Holy, and my prayers deepened. I began to sense the heavy presence of the Spirit around me, even in me. My hands shook, my stomach muscles quaked, my arms and shoulders trembled.

On December 17, 1998, a spiritual presence came over me. The tremors in my body became intense. They seemed involuntary, yet I knew I had surrendered my body and mind willingly. I was held within myself by a soothing yet strong force, and I could not control any part of my own body. I stopped breathing. My awareness expanded, as if my consciousness were no longer confined to my mind. I was both intensely alert to the energies coursing through my physical body, yet released to an expansive awareness far beyond that body. The spiritual presence entered me through my chest, then rose into my neck. My throat tensed. My face contorted. My breathing returned. A long inhale filled my lungs. Then I began to speak, not of my own will. The first words spoken through me were, "Holiness, holiness, holiness. Be calm and center in. The Holy is upon you."

Such was my initiation into the intermediary experience known throughout history by the shaman, the prophet, the oracle and the channel.

Gradually, I learned that I could enter this mystical state of awareness at will, and this spiritual messenger—identified to me as a "Spirit of the Holy"—would enter me, gently take control of my body (especially my breathing and throat) and speak through my voice. I began to call this spiritual guide "the Messenger of the Holy" or "the Messenger" for short. The wisdom from these prophetic sessions presented a depth and complexity beyond my awareness, and my wife, an United Methodist minister, discovered she could ask questions and receive startling answers from the spiritual messenger who spoke through me. These answers were communicated through my voice, my vocabulary, and my cultural framework, but the wisdom came from beyond me. In short, I learned to surrender my voice and my mind to a spiritual messenger, who used them as tools to mold wisdom lessons. I've received messages on many vital topics, such as prayer, human suffering, the voice of God, the reality and roles of heavenly messengers, and the dawn of a new spiritual awareness.

The experience of becoming a host to a spiritual messenger has been known cross-culturally and throughout time. It has been understood as the journey of the shaman, the voice of the prophet, the advice of the oracle and—most recently—the guidance of the channel or psychic. However, to gain training and support for the intensity of this intermediary experience, it is necessary to have a culture that both accepts and values the ability. Sadly, such guidance is not available to most people in developed countries.

When sacred energy first shook my body and a spiritual messenger began to enter my mind, I had no framework to understand what was happening. I had been raised around artists and theologians, so I was quite open and curious about creative inspiration, sacred influence and spiritual perception. I was an English Professor and writer with a background in Native American literature. I had a respect for biblical studies and an open mind about religious diversity. However, none of this background informed me about the intermediary experiences of the shaman, prophet, oracle or channel. In short, I was intellectually curious, spiritually willing, but culturally ill-prepared for the intensity of the spiritual energy and wisdom that would shake me into paralysis, overcome my body, expand my consciousness and utilize my voice.

It became clear to me that to understand and embrace this sacred ability, I had to choose a framework and in so doing I would also choose a community in which to practice the gift. Because the learning curve was steep and the development of the ability was swift and risky, I first gravitated toward my home faith of Christianity. However, as you will see in this book, the Messenger of the Holy was always nudging me beyond the confines of any single faith perspective. The Messenger was accepting of my Christian framework and utilized it to open the door to a spiritual universe that embraces all faith traditions. Eventually, the Messenger taught me the perspective of the Braided Way, in which all faiths are viewed as strands in a unified braid of spiritual revelations and experiences.

But I am getting ahead of my story.

What you will witness in this book is the beginning of my spiritual journey. At the time, I was a progressive Christian who dove into the mystical depths of the Judeo-Christian perspective to find a framework to understand and utilize a startling, life-changing spiritual experience. What I discovered is a rich tradition of mystics and prophets. However, I also learned the difficulties of being a mystic in an organized institution, which resists change and seeks to regulate direct revelation. Over time, I began to branch out to gain further understanding and awareness of my intermediary experiences. Finally, I am convinced that all people have a spiritual gift and purpose, but some have a heightened sensitivity to the spirit realm. I have adopted a term by Marcus Borg to describe these gifted ones as "spirit people."

Spirit People

Spiritual gifts and spiritual perceptions are common, but our culture offers very few frameworks to discuss, explore and develop these abilities. Often, through the spiritual discipline of a faith tradition, people have mystical experiences in prayer, meditation or ceremonies. However, these mystical experiences can "come upon" a person without invitation, training or background. The temporary and powerful perception of the Holy can be intimidating, confusing and life-changing, whether it comes in dreams, visions, spiritual energy, intuitive knowledge, sense perception or alternate states of awareness.

While an intimate connection to the spiritual realm is the birthright of every human being, there are those among us who have a heightened sensitivity or gift for the reception of spiritual energies, perceptions and wisdom. These "spirit people" are gifted healers, visionaries, inspired artists, "priests" and teachers with the abilities to usher others into sacred awareness.

In his book *Meeting Jesus Again for the First Time*, Marcus Borg offers a view of these gifted spirit people.

> Spirit persons are known cross-culturally. They are people who have vivid and frequent subjective experiences of another level or dimension of reality. These experiences involve momentary entry into nonordinary states of consciousness and take a number of different forms. Sometimes there is a vivid sense of momentarily seeing into another layer of reality; these are visionary experiences. Sometimes there is the experience of journeying into that other dimension of reality; this is the classic experience of the shaman. Sometimes there is a strong sense of another reality coming upon one, as in the ancient expression "The Spirit fell upon me." Sometimes the experience is of nature or an object within nature momentarily transfigured by "the sacred" shining through it. Bushes burn without being consumed; the whole earth is seen as filled with the glory of God (where glory means "radiant presence"). The world is perceived in such a way that previous preceptions seem nothing more than blindness.

While the gifts of spirit people are varied and wondrous, I want to focus on the ability of spiritual intermediaries, which is the category of my own gift. In today's culture, the most widely-known term for my prophetic experience is "deep-trance channeling."

The Channel

While people have had intermediary experiences since the dawn of human consciousness, the term "channeling" came into use as a description of intermediary activity during the mid 20th Century. Beginning in the mid 19th Century in America, a movement known as spiritism or spiritualism gained popularity, and the gift of mediumship was explored and encouraged at this time. A "medium" is one who is able to speak with spirits, and it is an ancient gift mentioned in almost every culture. Around the turn of the 20th Century, the medium gift became intertwined with the "psychic." Edgar Cayce was one of the first popular psychics, and we now recognize his gift as deep-trance channeling; however, during his life he was known as the "sleeping prophet." From the 1920's until his death in 1945, Cayce provided readings for people, in which he would enter into a trance state and allow a spiritual messenger to speak through him. At first, these readings focused on physical health issues, but they gradually included issues of spiritual development and knowledge. The term "channeling" did not become popular until 1972 when Jane Roberts first published her channeled material from an entity known as Seth. Since then, there have been many published channelers, who enter into various levels of trance in order to give voice to messengers of a stunning variety of sources. Some of the popular channelers include Esther Hicks for Abraham, Lee Carrol for Kryon, and Darryl Anka for Bashar. In addition, the popular work *A Course in Miracles* is reported to be channeled material.

The problem I had with the culture of channeling was that it seemed ungrounded to me. I am drawn to the ancient traditions, and the channeling framework was an outgrowth of the 19th and 20th-Century when open thinkers were moving away from historical spiritual traditions. In addition, the wide variety of sources for channelers—including angels, ascended masters, aliens, God, Jesus, various saints, multi-dimensional beings and famous deceased people—made me skeptical. Certainly, my own intermediary experiences made me open to the whole concept of channeling, but I needed a more ancient grounding for my personal journey.

The Shaman

Shamanism is arguably the most ancient form of religion. The term *saman* of the Tungus people of Siberia means "one who is excited, moved, raised" and was first applied to the Turks and Mongols. Today, a shaman identifies healers, mystics and spiritual leaders of indigenous, usually tribal religions. In shamanic traditions, the gifted person often enters into an altered state of consciousness during a ritual in order to convey spiritual healing, guidance or dream interpretation. A shaman, then, is a tribal representative to the spiritual realm.

As a scholar of Native American literature, I had been exposed to many stories and accounts of shamanic journeys, trances and healings. The most notable is the book *Black Elk Speaks*, in which the Lakota holy man, Black Elk, goes on a spiritual journey and receives an apocalyptic vision for his people, just before the end of the Lakota tribal culture and the beginning of reservation life in the latter years of the 19th Century.

The gifts of intermediary states and spiritual communication are within the roles of the shaman; however, I did not feel that I had direct access to the shamanic traditions of the world. I have since come to know many shamanic teachers, but at the time of my own spiritual awakening, I did not yet have the resources to explore shamanism beyond scholarly interest. As far as I knew, there was no community a white guy in Ohio could enter to receive support and guidance for shamanic experiences.

I realized that within the ancient ways of Hinduism, Buddhism, Shamanism, Judaism, Christianity, Islam and Bahai there were thousands of years of guidance about intermediary experience, so I decided to dive into the mystical tradition of my spiritual home: Christianity.

The Prophet

In the Judeo-Christian tradition, the experience of receiving spiritual wisdom from the divine is known as prophecy. The Bible provides many examples of prophetic experiences, in addition to guidance for how to test and share the wisdom of prophetic revelations.

Prophecy is not limited to revealing the future. Prophecy is often about what is happening right now in regard to the work and Way of God in the contemporary moments of our lives. The prophetic messages I receive are focused on the practical patterns of living in the Holy Way in the midst of our very human moments and struggles. As such, the sessions can be categorized as wisdom teachings.

In the Old Testament, prophetic experience takes several forms. Some prophets, like Samuel, hear the voice of God, as in the story in which the young Samuel first hears God call his name at night. At other times, the prophetic experience includes visions when a prophet is shown holy wisdom, as in the cases of Ezekiel and Zechariah. Often such visions include the presence of an angel or messenger of God who interprets the visions. In some cases the prophet actually speaks the word of God. Jeremiah says, "Then the Lord put out his hand and touched my mouth; and the Lord said to me 'Now, I have put my words in your mouth'" (Jer. 1:9). King David uses a similar phrase while on his deathbed: "The Spirit of the Lord speaks through me; his word is upon my tongue" (II Sam. 23:2). Such biblical descriptions of the Spirit of God putting words in the mouth or on the tongue of the prophet were of great interest to me because of the similarity to my own experience.

For a complete parallel to my experience of prophecy, I looked to the prophet Daniel. The Angel Gabriel comes to Daniel to interpret his prophetic visions, and Daniel records the experience quite vividly: "My strength left me, and my complexion grew deathly pale, and I retained no strength. Then I heard the sound of his words; and when I heard the sound of his words, I fell into a trance, face to the ground. But then a hand touched me and set me trembling on my hands and knees" (Dan. 10:8–11). From the trembling to the trance-like state and physical paralysis, Daniel's description is strikingly similar to my own.

Many biblical scholars describe the prophetic experience with the term "ecstatic." In his classic book *The Prophets*, Abraham J. Heschel defines the ecstatic state of prophecy in this way:

> The Greeks, who coined the word "ecstasy" (ekstasis), understood by it quite literally [as] a state of trance in which the soul was no longer in its place, but had departed from the body, or a state in which the soul, escaping from the body, had entered into a relationship with invisible beings or became united with a deity.

In my own experience, my spirit or soul does not leave my body, but feels pushed to the back of my body, creating a spiritual opening for a messenger of the Holy to inspire my mind and put words on my lips. When the Spirit comes over me, I lose the ability to move my own body, and I feel a deep merging with the Holy in body, soul and mind. Heschel describes this type of prophetic experience as he continues his discussion of ecstasy:

> In order to make room for the entrance of the higher force, the person must forfeit the power over the self. He must abandon his mind in order to receive the spirit. Loss of consciousness, ecstasy, is a prerequisite.... Ecstasy is a state in which the soul is, as it were, freed from, or raised above, the body. It is a state in which breathing and circulation are depressed. Sometimes entrancement is so deep that there is complete anesthesia.

From Heschel and other biblical scholars, I began to identify my gift as ecstatic prophecy, and--to be honest--this is still the most accurate characterization of my experience.

Through biblical study, I also ran across what I will call the "Sophia tradition," which further helped me to understand the source of the wisdom which comes through me. In the Old Testament, Sophia is known as the Spirit of Wisdom, and her role is to be the messenger of wisdom to humanity. She appears in Proverbs, chapter 8 as God's companion at creation, and she is characterized as calling out to the people to teach them wisdom. In the Wisdom of Solomon, Sophia is characterized as "entering into" people to aid in prophecy: "The Spirit of Wisdom is but one, yet can do everything; herself unchanging. She makes all things new; age after age she enters into holy souls and makes them God's friends and prophets" (7: 27-28). I became thrilled to think that my messenger may be a manifestation of Sophia or an extension of the Sophia tradition.

While the Bible and biblical scholarship offered background on prophecy, it was my researching in the tradition of Kabbalah (the mystical branch of Judaism) where I found the most striking explanation of the prophetic trance. In *Meditation and Kabbalah*, Aryeh Kaplan translated portions of a book called *Shaar Ruach HaKodesh*, which means "The Gate of the Holy Spirit." In this book, a seventeenth-century rabbi wrote of a type of prophetic experience similar to mine. According to Rabbi Chaim Vital, a spiritual messenger (called a *maggid* in Hebrew) serves as a messenger from God, and the message itself must become "clothed in the prophet's own voice" while the prophet is raised into a mystical state of union with God's Spirit. Without the use of the prophet's own voice, the word of God could not be heard. Today, we would probably call such a maggid an angel, but the ancient perspective of Kabbalah provided a much more accurate description of my experience than any contemporary book on angel guides or channeling.

Despite the rich tradition of prophecy in the Judeo-Christian tradition, I found it difficult to name and practice my gift in the institutional church. First of all, I did not want to call myself a "prophet." That seemed like a name given to a person from the community of faith, not a role claimed by an individual. As a result, I was careful to call my gift "prophetic awareness."

It did not take long for me to realize that my gift needed to be shared, and I began to work with friends, most of whom were outside of the institutional church. I found that if I went into my trance state with a group of 10 to 12 people, an amazing pattern emerged. First, the Messenger of the Holy would provide a general wisdom lesson for the entire group. Then, each member of the group would receive specific guidance. The individual messages usually contained observations about each person's spiritual gifts, their spiritual growth and their relationships. Finally, there is often guidance for engaging and enhancing a person's spiritual purpose in life.

Because of my love of wisdom literature, the Sophia tradition and the history of the oracle, I began to call these "Wisdom Sessions" and later changed them to "Oracle Sessions." I have conducted more of these sessions than I can count. Through networks of other "spirit people," I scheduled sessions at holistic health centers and in people's homes. Through these Wisdom/Oracle Sessions, I met spiritually mature people from a variety of traditions, and I began to understand my role as much wider than the prophet or channel.

Finally, several experiences in which Christians accused me of being a false prophet or of being possessed by the devil made it painfully clear that the Christian tradition was not a stable, inviting or safe home for my spiritual gift. Though I still view Jesus as the mentor of my soul, I had to move beyond and outside of the Christian tradition.

The Oracle

Finally, I gravitated toward the term "oracle." In the Greco-Roman world, the oracle was one who went into a trance state and spoke for the "gods." It was yet another way to name and understand the intermediary experience. In his excellent book *The Seer in Ancient Greece*, Michael Attyah Flower describes the role of the seer and the oracle. The Greek word *mantis* can be translated as prophet, diviner, soothsayer or seer. Flower writes, "a *mantis* was originally a person who prophesied in an altered state of conscisousness." However, the *mantis* or seer of ancient Greece also took on the roles of the diviner who interpreted signs and the healer. The role of the *mantis*, who spoke for the gods, was adopted by the oracle, translated from the Latin verb *orare*, meaning "to speak." The famouse Oracle of Delphi was believed to sit over a fissure in the ground, out of which a gas emerged that caused an altered state of consciousness. However, the trance state of the oracle is well established without such mysterious gasses. Oracles are cross-cultural and are a part of Hinduism, Tibetan Buddhism and the Igbo culture of Nigeria, just to name a few. Of the Tibetan Oracle, whose name is Kuten La, his Holiness, the Dalai Lama has written:

> As I look back over the many occasions when I have asked questions of the oracle, on each one of them time has proved that his answer was correct. This is not to say that I rely solely on the oracle's advice. I do not. I seek his opinion in the same way as I seek the opinion of my Cabinet and just as I seek the opinion of my own conscience. I consider the gods to be my 'upper house'. The Kashag [Cabinet] constitutes my lower house. Like any other leader, I consult both before making a decision on affairs of state. And sometimes, in addition to Nechung's [the Tibetan State Oracle's] counsel, I also take into consideration certain prophecies.

The experience of Kuten La, the Tibetan Oracle, bears striking similarities to my own. In his autogiography, *Freedom From Exile*, the Dalai Lama describes that Kuten La will prepare for his oracular trance with a ceremony. As he goes into trance, Kuten La's "face transforms, becoming rather wild." Soon after this transformation, "his respiration stops" for a time until, as the Dalai Lama explaines, "the possession is now complete and the mortal frame of the medium expands visibly." After the interhange between the Dalai Lama and the oracle, the Daila Lama explains that the oracle "makes a final offering before collapsing, a rigid and lifeless form, signifying the end of the possession."

The transformation of the face, the change in breathing and the alteration of the body are all manifestations I know intimately. Although the rituals surrounding the oracular activity of Kuten La differ dramatically from my preparation, the similarities of the manifestions of body, mind and spirit help me to accept the universal patterns of the trance state, which include: the entrance and gentle possession of the spiritual guide, the physical transformations, the prophetic speech and the paralysis after the oracle session. Kuten La is one of the few contemporary examples I have found of the very ancient tradition of the oracle.

What appeals to me about the term "oracle" is that it accurately describes my intermediary experience without the cultural trappings of the terms "channel" and "prophet." The role of the oracle is mysterious and ancient, and it gained a rather "hip" presentation in *The Matrix* movies. Finally, the term "oracle" is a noun with three meanings: the person who receives the message, the message itself, or the place of inspiration—such as the

Oracle of Delphi. The only clumsy element to the term is that the adjective form is "oracular," which is a mouth full. To avoid this odd adjective, I have come to call my trance experience the "oracle state."

The Structure of this Book

As you will see in this book, it was a long journey to come to peace with the term "oracle." I first had to wade through books about channeling, research the roots of prophecy and practice Wisdom/Oracle Sessions with family and friends. In the meantime, life presented challenges in which my prophetic gift became an invaluable resource to guide me and my family through grief and transition.

I am a trained storyteller, and this book is my own personal story. The narrative arc of the book will take you through a journey of grief as my wife and I experienced the stillbirth of our second son, Jordan. The narrative finally ends in hope and promise as my family and I traveled to China to adopt our daughter, Lydia. In the midst of this story of loss, grief and hope, I have added transcripts from our "Prayer Sessions" which later became known as "Wisdom Sessions" and finally called "Oracle Sessions."

As a result, this book is a hybrid of several genres: memoir, research, and channeled material. My hope is that the story will engage you, the research will inform you, and the transcripts will inspire you.

There are four sections to this book: Section I, entitled "The Call of The Holy," chronicles my discovery of this prophetic gift and my struggle to understand the experience and its place within my Christian faith. Section II, entitled "Wisdom of The Holy," is focused on the remarkable wisdom teachings from the spiritual Messenger—astounding teachings, really, that are intended to deepen the spiritual lives of 21st-Century seekers. Section III, "Hope of the Holy," updates the story of my family's journey of faith and provides closure for the personal journey of Section I. Finally, there is an Epilogue, which provides an update from the end of the book's narrative in 2006 until 2016.

I offer my story to give courage and guidance to the spiritually gifted people among us, who are often lonely and without guidance in our current society. Many people with spiritual gifts choose not to share their gifts for many reasons, one of which is that our culture does not know how to accept the reality of spiritual gifts or how to encourage their development. According to Robert Wilson in *Prophecy and Society in Ancient Israel*, there are four social prerequisites for "intermediation," as Wilson labels prophecy and mysticism:

- A culture must believe in the reality of a supernatural power or powers.
- A culture must believe that these supernatural powers can influence earthly affairs.
- A culture must positively view or at least tolerate intermediary activities.
- A culture must experience the social conditions that require the services of an intermediary.

Wilson states, "When these crucial social features disappear after having been present, existing intermediaries must also disappear or be relegated to subgroups where the necessary conditions are still present."

Our culture is on the verge of regaining these social requirements for accepting the reality of spiritual gifts, such as prophecy, spiritual sight, healing, prophetic dreaming and spiritual discernment. The yearning for spiritual depth among the people is evident in our movies and books. Spirit people are being called together in book groups, meditation groups, holistic health centers, interspiritual organizations, as well as in traditional places of worship.

I invite you to join me on my journey through spiritual discovery in the midst of a personal story. It is a story of a skeptic who turns toward the Spirit, of a husband and father who loves his family deeply in times of pain and joy and of a transformative surrender to the Holy. As you read my story of discovery, I hope you will deepen your own spiritual life and open to the Holy, who comes to us in the moments of our very human days and nights, who casts sacred images in our minds and lends holy words to our lips.

Peace for your journey,
Michael Olin-Hitt

1
Call of The Holy

1
A Dark and Holy Time

On December 24, 1999, I stood by my wife, Jennifer, as she lay in a hospital bed giving birth to our second son, Jordan. Under normal conditions, this would have been a joyous time. A Christmas Eve baby. But Jordan's delivery was coming two days after we'd learned that he had died in utero. He was at thirty-six weeks of development. Full term.

In the delivery room, we rocked him in our arms and wept over him. The family gathered. My mother-in-law rocked Jordan, shifting him in her arms to make him look as natural as possible. Jennifer, a United Methodist minister, sat up in the hospital bed and asked for a bowl of water so she could baptize Jordan. I filled a Styrofoam bowl with tap water and set it on the tray by her bed. Jennifer reached for our son, and her mother laid Jordan's body in her arms. The family was quiet. The crying had eased. Jennifer was exhausted from the delivery. Her hair was mussed, her eyes weary. She sprinkled water over Jordan's head.

"Jordan Paul Olin-Hitt," she said. Her voice cracked. Her eyes filled with tears. "I baptize you in the name of the Father and of the Son and of the Holy Spirit."

Despite the grief that rose to my throat and burned my eyes, I could feel the presence of the Spirit.

It was a dark and holy time.

We had known that Jordan would need corrective surgery for his esophagus soon after birth, but we had not been prepared for his death.

Jennifer and I spent the next weeks in numbing sorrow. On New Year's Eve, 1999, when the rest of the world was celebrating the dawn of a new millennium and worried that their computers might forget how to tell time, Jennifer and I put our other son, two-year-old Samuel, to bed and prepared for prayer. It was the first time since Jordan's funeral that our family did not surround us. We needed to enter into prayer in private. We wanted answers directly from God.

For over a year, Jennifer and I had held discussions with a messenger of God. I mean this literally. Beginning in 1998, my prayer life took a dramatic turn when I began to sense the presence of spiritual messengers. Through guidance by these prayer messengers, I learned to surrender my body and mind to the Holy and become a vessel for inspired speech. Some would call this gift prophecy, others deep-trance channeling, others oracular speech. But when it first began in 1998, I just called it prayer. I learned to allow my prayer time to deepen until I went into a trance state I called prophetic awareness. During this trance state I learned to surrender my mind, body and spirit to the Holy, and a spiritual messenger enters me, and holy wisdom flows from my lips in poetic eloquence. The spiritual messenger who speaks through my voice—identified to me only as a "Spirit of the Holy"—uses my words, my cultural framework and my understanding to mold messages beyond my awareness. This spiritual messenger is a conduit for the wisdom of the Holy to be expressed in human language and understanding. I have come to call this speaker the Messenger of the Holy or, simply, the Messenger.

Because of this intermediary gift, Jennifer and I were able to enter into prayer expecting to receive answers to our questions. While in a deep, meditative state of prayer, I always lost the ability to move my body and speak for myself, but Jennifer had often asked the Messenger questions during these wisdom lessons, and she had received startling, faith-expanding replies. This time, we came to prayer with laments, hoping to discover some meaning and purpose in the death of our son, Jordan.

I set the tape recorder on the piano bench in our living room. Jennifer went to the bookshelf to get a Bible. She still moved slowly because of her recovery from Jordan's delivery. She wore sweat pants and a sweater. Her hair was neatly brushed, and she had applied some make-up. I saw a glimpse of the dynamic and vibrant woman I had known before our loss.

Jennifer read Psalm 13, a psalm of lament, which moves from a sense of loss to an attitude of hope. It expressed our desires. We wanted to feel God's hope and promise in addition to gaining some understanding of our grief.

Jennifer turned to another psalm, this time 28, and as she read it, I felt myself moving into a trance state. It began with a sensation of being drawn into myself. My eyes were clenched shut. My head lowered. My jaw muscles tightened. I felt a tingling come over my fingers.

Jennifer finished the psalm and prayed aloud. "God, we need you. We need you. We need you." She began to cry, but she continued to speak. "It's been so hard, God," she said. "I know you have been with us, but I miss our boy so much I can hardly breathe."

The Spirit came over me. My limbs trembled. My stomach muscles quaked in spasms. I had come to know these involuntary tremors as a result of spiritual energy, and I relaxed into them. My breathing deepened, and I surrendered my body. I felt pulled to the back of myself, as if my conscious mind and my own spirit were gathered along my spine, making room for the Messenger of the Holy to come into me as a gentle presence. My throat tensed and relaxed. My face contorted, and I heard the Spirit speaking through me.

I see you, my children. I bring what comfort I can. Temporality yields such suffering.

It is a rupture, a tearing. It shall not heal without a scar, and where shall the scar be hidden when it is your whole being? What shall you offer if not your pain?

Ironically enough, it was a great comfort to hear the Messenger acknowledge our pain. Despite this needed recognition of our sorrow, I was ready for more than compassion. I was ready for answers.

As usual, while I was in the deep state of prophetic awareness, I could not move my body, and my eyes were closed tightly. But my focus on the message was intense, and I could hear my own voice. I, myself, could not speak, but Jennifer—in the meditative, gentle voice of prayer—asked what was on both our minds, "We seek answers, O God. I don't mean to be demanding or harsh, but we need answers. But first, I need to know about our boy, our little Jordan. I pray for his spirit."

What cannot be born of flesh shall be born of spirit. What cannot be seen with eyes shall be sensed in heart. What cannot be felt in touch shall be known in soul. What cannot be tasted in mouth shall be treasured in breath. What cannot be held in your arms, shall be known in your spirit. Beyond the physical, my daughter, beyond the moments of your pain, beyond the emptiness you see, is a spirit born and living; the spirit of your son. What could not be corrected in the body is perfected beyond the body.

My daughter, do not be ashamed of your grief. You have borne much. The Spirit dwells within you, and a spark of the Holy grew within you, lived within you. That was not taken from you; it was delivered to you. But you cannot see this now. For now, know that the Spirit of God is with you. In and through the pain, the Holy is with you.

The process of inspired speech had become routine to me. My awareness deepened and expanded to include several levels. My own mind was free to question and react, but there was also an awareness of peace and a sense of endlessness that came from beyond me. On this night, my own mind was not satisfied with what the Messenger had said. I needed more than promises of things beyond my awareness and the assurance of God's presence. At other times in my life, such answers were more than enough to sustain me and support my faith, but on this night the words seemed empty. I wanted some knowledge beyond the comforting presence of God. I wanted to know why we suffered the death of our baby.

The Messenger of the Holy must have read my heart and mind because words began to pour forth that addressed my disappointment:

What can be offered but assurances? What can be brought but presence? I regret it is not enough for you now. The nows shall become the promises. The nows shall reveal the unfolding. The nows shall stretch out. The nows shall bring you the presence of the Holy, again and again. The nows will bring you to joy. The nows will see you holding an infant. The nows will unfold.

Know this: a spiritual presence was within the physical that you knew, and while the physical had malformations, the spiritual did not and does not. There could not have been that spiritual presence without the physical development, and yet when the physical showed it could not sustain the spiritual, separation occurred, and transformation took place.

At a later date, Jennifer and I would return to the transcript of this prayer and see the promises of a future child in what the Messenger had said. We would also take great comfort in the message that Jordan's spirit was with God. Now, however, we were both focused on our loss, and Jennifer's next question went straight to our central concern:

"Thank you, O God, for your care in our lives, for caring for those things we understand, and for caring for those things beyond our awareness. I am thankful for your presence tonight, and so thankful for your messenger that comes through Michael. But God, I have to admit, I am confused. We prayed for Jordan. We prayed for healing. And there are so many examples in our Bible of healing. I guess...I guess my question is basic. Why wasn't he healed? People ask me this question all the time when I deal with a family in grief, and I never know what to say."

There is healing and then there is miraculous healing. Miraculous healing is a sign of divine presence. The intensity of the presence is so great that the physical yields and is altered. Such intense manifestation, my daughter, comes only with the highly developed in spirit. While miracle is a divine sign, healing is cooperation of physical and spiritual.

"We have had many divine signs," said Jennifer.

The question is why was not the presence of Christ so concentrated that your son was miraculously healed? That is the heart of the question, is it not?

"Yes."

For if such a divine, miraculous presence is possible, why was it denied? That is the heart of the question. Was it a failure on your part to bring Christ's presence so strongly? No. For the presence of Christ and the Holy Spirit were with you. Christ's miracles were possible while he was on earth because he contained such a strong presence of the Spirit. He was made of light. He brought the presence of the Holy with such concentrated energy that the physical would break down and reconstruct. The physical would become spiritual and then would become physical again. This transformation is known only in part when the physical becomes spiritual at death. Becoming physical again, after the dissemination of death, is the step that the Christ could make. He made it not only for himself, but made it possible for others. I am not speaking here of the passing into the spiritual at death, for that transformation has always been possible for others. I am speaking of the passing into the spiritual and BACK into the physical. Sections of bodies: legs, eyes, arms, becoming spiritual and then physical again. The Spirit of Christ has made such miraculous healings possible before the incarnation, during the incarnation, and since that time.

Are there people on this Earth capable of such a transformation? Certainly healings take place. Certainly people can bring the holy presence. But such a healing as I have spoken of does not happen often, and only in a concentrated power of the Holy such as Christ can bring. A rare convergence of the Spirit of God within the physical world must take place for such a healing.

"Thank you, God. Thank you," said Jennifer. "But there seems to be such randomness to everything, like a circumstance of just the right elements have to be present for a miracle. I don't like this randomness."

There are dependencies between the spiritual and the physical in your lives. The Spirit resides in the physical and relies on the physical in your existence. These dependencies within the limitations of the physical must be accepted. Even the Holy must accept them. There are limitations. The Spirit moves and responds in cooperation with the physical. The limitations of the physical create limitations for the Spirit. The secret of the sacred life is to find spiritual possibility in the limitations.

"I don't understand."

The spirit of the Holy sweeps over the Earth, saying, "I shall not fix it; I shall BE IN IT." Do you see? "I shall not reconstruct it; I shall be in it. I shall come. I shall be broken. I shall weep. I shall be in it."

And the Wisdom of the Holy said, "I shall bring myself forth in the physical wherever the opening is made. I shall lead them out of the physical into the spiritual. Moment by moment, I shall be there. And they shall know me, and I shall know them."

How can the Holy acknowledge inadequacies and through these reveal wisdom? If the Holy can find the power and glory of creation within the inadequacies of the physical, shall you not look within your own inadequacies to find God's love, your own brokenness to find God's wholeness, your own pain to find God's comfort?

The image of God's Spirit sweeping over creation, seeking to enter into our broken lives was a great comfort to me. By this time in the prayer, I had reached the deepest state of prophetic awareness, and my own mind stopped questioning but marveled at the message as it came forth through my voice.

The lesson from the Messenger of the Holy lasted over fifty minutes, and after more explanation about the limitations of the physical world, the Messenger returned to the topic of healing:

And even if the the Holy fixes the brokenness, even if the power of creation is concentrated and there is healing, in the physical it is only temporary, is it not? The individual moment of healing does not last in the physical. So the Spirit of God says, "I shall make the ultimate correction in the realm of the spiritual." THAT is the wisdom of God, the power and the glory of the Holy. The correction shall be made where the Holy can make it. It shall be made beyond the physical.

This time, I heard the comfort that the Holy intended. Despite my own sorrow, I understood that Jordan's body could not support his spirit. In this life, the Holy works within our physical bodies, despite the limitations we present. What is more, I was beginning to see that the limitations themselves were avenues for the Holy to be made manifest in our lives.

The Messenger then turned from our sorrow to the suffering of Jesus. When this new topic began, I thought, "Of course. This understanding of God's presence in the midst of suffering explains why Christ was crucified," but I had not seen this turn of the message coming:

Give the pain to the Spirit of Christ, and the Spirit who knows the pain shall transform it; not erase it; not take it away, but shall transform it. This is the fundamental truth, is it not? The purpose of the crucifixion is to take the pain and transform it. Does that mean the pain did not exist? Does that mean the brokenness did not occur? Does that mean the blood was not shed? Does that mean the tears did not flow? Does that mean the darkness did not come? Does that mean the heart did not burst? See the wisdom of it. This is the only wisdom that can be constructed from the present, from the way the fabric is constructed. Do you see? The fabric was already constructed. The dependencies of the physical and the spiritual were already made, and the wisdom came out of it, through it. Through the dependencies themselves did the wisdom come. The only wisdom possible is within the limitations. See the possibilities of the limitations. Grab fast to those limitations for they shall reveal to you the transformations. The Holy works within the limitations. The ruptures become openings for the Spirit and the physical to intermingle.

In the final moments of the prayer, the Messenger of the Holy added a confirmation that I needed. Since I had first learned of Jordan's death, a nagging question had brought confusion and anger: Had God intended this death to happen in order to teach us something? Many who have suffered the death of a loved one or the news of a terrible illness have asked the same question, and, unfortunately, there are well-wishers in our communities of faith who think God gives us hardships for a purpose. Such phrases as, "Don't worry, God has a plan for everything," are often spoken from the lips of the pious. So, I was relieved by what the Messenger told us next:

The pain was not created to teach a lesson. The lesson was created to give meaning to the pain. The possibility came when the Spirit sought wisdom in the limitations, which had caused such pain and anguish. Do you think the Spirit does not feel it also so acutely? So the Spirit said, "I shall take this brokenness; I shall take this interdependence, and I shall make of it something beautiful. I shall reveal myself in it."

In these words I found the hope that if we gave our grief to the Holy, we would find the workings of the Holy in the midst of our loss.

As the Messenger was leaving me, Jennifer prayed for intercessions. She prayed that God would be with our first son, Samuel, who was sleeping upstairs. She also prayed that we would have the resources to help Samuel through his grief at losing a little brother. She wanted God's help to be good parents for Sam even while we were in such sorrow.

Then there was silence. I heard Jennifer turn off the tape recorder. I heard the ticking of a clock. I was not able to move my body. I was in a state of deep relaxation and peace. At last, when I could open my eyes and move my head, I looked toward Jennifer.

She smiled. She rose from her chair and sat next to me on the couch.

"That was something," she said. "God is so present. And God wants us to understand why suffering happens."

I swallowed hard. My mouth was dry. I wanted to get control of the rest of my body so I could talk with Jennifer. My mind was buzzing with more questions. But I also did not want to disturb the peace I felt.

Jennifer put her head on my shoulder, and I relaxed. I knew she felt the comfort of God, who did not dismiss our pain, but was present in the midst of it.

Jennifer and I went to bed before midnight. The coming of the new year had no significance to us that night. We talked about the prayer as we lay in the dark. We cried. And we both expressed the amazing blessing of this prophetic gift. Then we went to sleep with the hope that the "nows" would indeed unfold and reveal wholeness.

I DO NOT KNOW why this prophetic gift comes to me. I don't think I was chosen for the gift. Rather, I feel I was invited. Some combination of physical and spiritual inheritance in me produced this possibility for intermediary, oracular experience. The prophetic gift runs in my family. Through prayer I was invited to open this gift to the Holy. I am quite sure there are many more people who cary spiritual gifts and abilities for the Holy, but sadly, many people with spiritual sensitivities never hear the invitation to give these gifts to the Spirit.

I am one of the lucky ones. When I was thirty-four years old—more than a year before Jordan's stillbirth—I began a serious prayer routine in the Christian tradition, and the Holy revealed to me the possibility for prophetic awareness and speech. But, as I look back, I see that there was evidence of this ability from my earliest memories. The unfolding of this gift in the context of my very human struggles and fears is the story I want to share with you.

2
The Awakening

As a child, I called them "the watchers." I would often receive a sudden, distinct awareness of not being alone. First there would be a sensation in my chest—a hollowness that would startle me—then a tingling along the back of my neck. I could usually sense the part of the room that was occupied; I would *feel* the presence.

This experience began very early. My parents tell me that as a three-year-old, I would casually mention that an old man in a suit sat in the corner of the living room and smiled at me.

The sensation of "watchers" became intense during several periods of my life, but never with the intrigue or sensationalism of a ghost story. Not until I was thirty-four did I come to realize that these sensations were an indication of a spiritual gift. This gift has now become a doorway to a powerful awareness of the Holy. Learning to cultivate this spiritual gift and to allow the Holy to work with and through the gift is the journey I will share in this chapter. I am no longer troubled by "watchers"; instead I sense the presence of the Holy Spirit at any moment that I open myself in prayer.

There are many popular books in the New Age or Metaphysics sections of bookstores that could have provided a framework to understand my sacred experiences. However—as I mentioned in the introduction—I first found guidance to come from the Bible and biblical studies, where I discovered a grounding to understand my experiences and ways to test and share the revelations. I encourage people to find personal grounding of spiritual experience in one of the many ancient traditions of our world faiths. Such a foundation--whether in Christianity, Judaism, Buddhism,

Hinduism, Islam, indiginous ceremonies, or any other faith tradition, provides the perspective and wisdom of centuries of practitioners.

In order to give my spiritual gift to the Holy and see the Bible as a guidebook for sacred experience, I had to do two things: trust my spiritual intuition over my intellect and surrender to the Holy. Both were difficult, partly because of my academic training and partly due to simple human nature.

My wife, Jennifer, went to seminary just after we were married and became an United Methodist minister. I was active in her churches and taught adult Bible studies; however, I was very much an intellectual Christian, living my faith through my mind instead of through my spirit.

In 1995, Jennifer took a position as the associate pastor at Church of the Savior, United Methodist in Canton, Ohio. It was President McKinley's home church, and his funeral was held in the building after his 1901 assassination. I felt many "watchers" in the building, which caused me no shock or particular concern. It was an old, stately church with a labyrinth of hallways, and I was accustomed to feeling various presences in old churches. At times, I knew the presence to be holy. At other times, I could feel the isolation of the spiritual shadow.

The senior pastor was a mid-career minister named Daniel. One day, as I sat in the hallway reading a book, I overheard the Christian Education Director, Sheryl, talking to Daniel in the church office. Sheryl said something about a parishioner's comment about an oppressive presence in one of the Sunday school rooms.

"Is it a dark presence?" asked Daniel.

I lifted my eyes from the book and tilted my head toward the door.

"I'm not sure," Sheryl said. "She just said 'oppressive.'"

I knew the presence Sheryl had been told about. In the room at the end of the hall in the education wing, I had felt and "seen" with my mind's eye a dark presence, heavy with sadness. I wondered if I should say something.

"I mean, is it an evil presence?" Daniel asked. "Do we need to be concerned for the children?"

"I don't *know*, Daniel. I'm just telling you what Linda said."

Finally, I couldn't help myself. "If it's the room at the end of the hall," I said, "it's not an evil or mean presence. Just sad."

Daniel stepped into the doorway of the office. He stared at me for a moment. I shrugged, then gazed down the hallway toward the room where Jennifer was counseling a young married couple. When I glanced back at the office door, Daniel was gone.

Two days later, Jennifer said to me, "Daniel is forming a prayer group, and he asked if you want to join."

"Me?" I asked.

"He says you have a spiritual gift," Jennifer said. "I'm joining them for prayer tonight."

To me, prayer had always seemed a very crafted presentation by a pastor to focus the congregation on a spiritual agenda. I had never seen the purpose for prayer, or, for that matter, most of the liturgical requirements of traditional worship. Jennifer had always been the reason I had remained connected to the Christian tradition. Her passion for the Bible helped me see the integrity of the scriptures, and she was a wonder to watch in the pulpit. She wore a white alb with a rope belt that hugged her waist. She preached with confidence, and as she did, her wire-framed glasses glinted, her earrings dangled and shook. If it had not been for Jennifer, I would have strayed from Christianity like many people with spiritual gifts who don't see how they fit into the established order.

But here was a pastor named Daniel asking me to be in a prayer group *because of* my spiritual perceptions. The invitation was so unexpected, I didn't hesitate.

"I'm in," I said.

So, Jennifer and I went to the pastor's study that evening, and we were greeted by a small group of six church members. It was in this group that my spiritual gift for prophecy began to fill my body with holy energy, send my hands quaking, place images in my mind and words on my lips. In short, I quickly moved from an intellectual, skeptical Christian to a man of the Spirit.

The Holy has a way of turning doubters into disciples and skeptics into prophets.

THE PRAYER GROUP included Rose, a gifted and experienced woman of prayer with red hair and clear, blue eyes; Deborah, a solid woman of prayer with dark hair and a gentle presence; Daniel, a passionate minister with an interest in spiritual gifts; and Roger and Alice, an older couple with a history of prayer and service to the church.

On the first evening Jennifer and I joined the group, Daniel wanted to pray in the room known as the parlor. It was a room with a brass chandelier, lace curtains and formal furniture. Jennifer's interview for the church had occurred in this room, as well as several Bible studies and a few administrative committee meetings of the church. We settled onto the sofas and chairs and bowed our heads in prayer. Daniel and Roger prayed for the presence of Jesus, then we prayed in silence, and I felt impressions come to me, then phrases came to my mind. At first, I ignored the phrases, but the sensation came so strongly I felt compelled to say, "This room is the heart."

"Yes," Rose said. "I'm sensing the same thing."

I was amazed that Rose confirmed my impression. Another impression came to me, and I voiced it: "The heart needs to be cleansed."

Roger began praying for cleansing, and others joined in.

In the next pause of silence, another impression came to me: "The mind is down the hall," I said.

"The choir room," Rose said. "The choir room is the mind."

"Yes," I said. "That's it."

"And the congregation must follow the heart," Rose said, "must learn to listen to the heart."

"And put the mind at rest," I said. "The heart can inspire and direct the mind."

Soon Deborah received impressions and added her insights from the Spirit, and I felt a deep connection to everyone in the room.

In this way, my training from the Holy Spirit began.

Each person in the prayer group had a unique spiritual gift, and when we prayed together, these gifts combined into a unit. It was my first experience of the Body of Christ. Rose received impressions from the Spirit, but she also had a gift for healing. Her hands would become hot in prayer, and I once felt the heat of her hands penetrate a sweater and a shirt as she laid her hands upon my shoulders. Deborah saw images in prayer. Jennifer had discernment, a deep sense of knowing. Daniel intuitively knew how to guide the prayer. And my gift blossomed week by week.

Roger and Alice were disappointed they didn't have flashy gifts like the rest of us. I can recall a conversation before prayer when Roger said, "I don't know what my gift is." We all stared at him for a moment.

Deborah said, "But you're the one who can focus us," she said. "You always know how to pinpoint the issue."

Everyone agreed. Without Roger, the group would flounder.

"And Alice," Deborah said. "You're our rock. You keep us in place, grounded in Christ."

It was true. The group needed every member, and we all knew it to be so. Some of us had flashy gifts, but all of us were essential. The Holy Spirit worked through each of us, just as the Apostle Paul explained in I Corinthians chapter 12:

> In each of us the Spirit manifested in one particular way, for some useful purpose. One, through the Spirit, has the gift of wise speech, while another, by the power of the same Spirit, can put the deepest knowledge into words. Another, by the same Spirit, is granted faith; another, by the one Spirit, gifts of healing, and another miraculous powers; another has the gift of prophecy, and another the ability to distinguish true spirits from false; yet another has the gift of ecstatic utterance of different kinds, and another the ability to interpret it. But all these gifts are the work of one and the same Spirit, distributing them separately to each individual at will. For Christ is like a single body with its many limbs and organs, which, many as they are, together make up one body. (I Cor. 12:7–13)

Over the period of several months, we prayed from room to room, and this gave me a deep, spiritual connection with the building and the ministry in it.

THE PRAYER GROUP at the church opened me to the power of prayer, but the major lessons from the Holy Spirit about my own gift for prayer took place at home. In the midst of the spiritual renewal that was taking place at church, Jennifer and I had our first son. We named him Samuel Riley. We chose Samuel—which means "God hears"–because we wanted him to know the voice of God. We chose Riley—which means "strength"—because anyone who hears God will need to be strong.

At 13 months, Sam had a troubling history of ear infections. It seemed that every month Jennifer and I were forcing another type of antibiotic into his mouth. On an October Monday in 1998, I sat with Sam in his nursery. His ear hurt because of another infection. He cried in my arms, and I soothed him by rocking and singing. Finally, he fell to sleep in my lap.

Sam's limbs were relaxed. His head was heavy against my chest. He took a deep breath that shuddered with the aftershocks of his crying. I rubbed my fingers over his little hands and his dimpled knuckles. I put my lips to his head, kissed him and took in the scent of baby shampoo in his hair. My chest seemed to open gently with a deep love and peace.

Prayer had become a source of strength over the last few months, so I began to pray for my little boy. I prayed that Jesus would touch him and heal his ear infection. I prayed that Jesus would stay close to him and guide him. I prayed that our family would know the presence of Christ in a deep way. And while I was at it, I prayed for Jesus to come into my own heart.

A warmth came over me. The space below my heart filled, and I felt lighter, as if the gravity of the earth had been subsided slightly. The fingers on my right hand extended, but I was not willing them to do so. Then my hand began to rise before my eyes.

I sat with Sam asleep in my left arm and watched as my right arm lifted, then turned. My mind was not willing my hand to rise. This I knew to be true. I had no idea where my hand and arm were moving, but before long, my arm was fully extended up, above my head and my hand was open upward. The extension of my arm became extreme, but not painful. My fingers were stretched open so completely my skin felt tight around my knuckles. My right arm began swinging around my head in a graceful manner. Then it reached back behind me, then swung around in circles. A phrase came to my mind: "I am all around you."

I remained calm because of the peace that swept into me. Had I not felt the peace, I may have panicked. I knew I was on the verge of something tremendous. I did not feel threatened, but I sensed that something was coming to me that was beyond my expectation.

I took control of my arm, and I put Sam into his crib. He relaxed with the calm breathing of toddler sleep. I placed my hand on Sam and began to pray for Jesus to touch his ears. However, my knees buckled and my stomach went into spasms. I knew I was meant to go down on my knees. I went down to the floor, thinking that I was not allowed to pray for Sam at this time. There was a message from the Spirit coming that had to do with me. This conviction was very clear. There was a message for me. I felt surrounded by the Holy Spirit, and the phrase that came to me was, "Be still and surrender."

I got up from the floor. I found Jennifer folding laundry in our bedroom, and I said, "Something is happening."

She set one of Sam's sleepers onto a pile of folded baby clothes on our bed.

My stomach muscles tensed. I folded over. I could hardly stand straight.

"What's wrong?" Jennifer asked.

"You have to pray with me," I said. "Right now."

I needed Jennifer to share this. I needed her to tell me what was happening. And I needed her to be a part of what was to come.

SOME WOULD CALL IT being born again, some would call it sanctification, others may call it a spiritual emergency or awakening; all I am sure of is the date: October 12, 1998.

I led Jennifer downstairs, and as I walked, I felt like I was passing through static electricity. My limbs felt charged; they tingled. The air was thick. My stomach muscles twitched and quaked. I went to the living room and sat on a chair.

"Are you okay?" Jennifer asked.

"I don't know," I said. "Something is happening. Something from God."

Jennifer sat in a chair next to me. It was just past eleven o'clock in the morning. Our windows were open, and the autumn breeze carried the scent of crisp, fallen leaves.

I told Jennifer what had happened while I tried to pray for Sam.

She squinted and leaned toward me.

"We have to pray," I said. "We have to pray right now."

"All right," Jennifer said.

I closed my eyes and settled into my chair. There was silence.

"Lord Jesus," Jennifer prayed. "Lord, we seek your presence and your guidance."

That is all I remember of Jennifer's prayer. I think she kept speaking for a short time longer.

Energy swept into me. Once again, it filled the hollow beneath my heart, not with air but with spirit. It was gentle at first, then I was seized with a tremendous power. My entire body tensed, as if electricity were coming through me. I curled over and fell to the floor.

I could feel that my face was contorted and my hands were bent stiffly like claws. Tremors began in my belly, and in an instant my entire body shook.

Jennifer knelt beside me and put her hand on my arm. Later she told me she didn't know what to do: call 911 or keep praying—or both. She was afraid I was having a seizure.

The shaking of my body became intense. My head, feet and knees thudded on the floor.

I was in the grips of something beyond me, and I fought for control of my body. It was frightening, but somehow I knew it was holy. And I knew there was a message in it.

"What's wrong? What's happening?" Jennifer asked.

"I don't know," I squeaked out. By this time, I was in a seizure. But my mind was alert. I could speak. The shaking wasn't from me, it was beyond me. I was *being* shaken. The tremors came from within me, yes, but they were not *of* me. "It's something I need to release," I said. "Something I need to let go of."

"You just need to surrender," Jennifer said. "Just let go to the Spirit."

Jennifer had known my stubbornness toward God, and I knew that her discernment was right. The Spirit of the Holy had given me a shake down. And now, I was in the grips of seizure-like contortions on my living room floor, with the Spirit holding me down until I surrendered.

"I don't know how," I said. I began to cry. I wanted to release myself to the Spirit so badly the desire welled in my stomach and burst into my mouth with weeping, and as my weeping increased, the tightness of my limbs and the seizure-like spasms subsided.

I lay on the floor in a fetal position. My crying eased. My cheek rested on the carpet. Jennifer stroked my arm. I told Jennifer I realized that I needed Christ to help me surrender to the Holy Spirit.

"Just ask for it," Jennifer said.

I sat up and closed my eyes to pray, but before I spoke a word, I was suddenly seized once again, but this time with a gentle sweep of energy. There was a lightness in my limbs. My breathing became deep and steady. Then my lungs filled and filled and filled with breath, and I realized I was not causing the inhalation. My lungs were expanding with air, but I had no control.

My hands rose. My arms extended. I was not willing these movements. I knew I could take control of my arms if I wanted, but the movements were so gentle and the peace in my body so complete, I relaxed my will and surrendered to the presence of the Holy.

My hands began to dance. They extended and twisted and twirled, like the Hindu images of the dancing Shiva. I opened my eyes and watched my hands move with grace. The tears on my cheeks dried.

"It's beautiful," I said. "Look."

I was filled with a sense of warmth and liberation I had never known. I was entirely relaxed, despite the fact that my arms and hands were dancing in front of me.

The movements slowed. My hands lowered to my side, and the Spirit left me.

I looked at Jennifer, my eyes still wet. She was stunned and quiet.

"It's a promise," I said. "A promise from God. If I surrender and seek cleansing, I'll dance in the Spirit."

I don't know how I knew this, but I knew it with certainty. The Holy Spirit had swept into me, and had left a message: "Welcome. But before you can pray for Sam or anyone, you have to prepare yourself."

For almost two weeks, I felt the energy of the Spirit continually. There was a warm energy in my chest. I told Jennifer it felt like a door had been opened in me, and there was no shutting it. When I drove to work, my hands would begin moving in the Spirit. I could drive with my left hand and let my right hand twirl around. When typing e-mails or assignments for my students, my hands would suddenly extend, then lift from the keyboard. The Spirit was so close to me, I could catch its motions at any moment.

I was suddenly thrust into an understanding of the phrase, "pray without ceasing." I was living in a constant awareness of the Holy. I taught my literature classes at The University of Mount Union with a humming and fluttering in my chest, and even washing dishes became a holy ritual. I ate and washed in the presence of spiritual energy. At church while Jennifer led the congregational prayer, my hands started to flutter. I was the drummer for the contemporary worship service Jennifer founded, and I leaned over and hid behind my drum set when the Spirit began to send me into the quakes. I could not pray in groups because the twitching in my stomach and the shaking of my hands would quickly become extreme and very difficult to explain. I was often awakened in the middle of the night with warm tremors coursing through my body. Several times, I woke up with my hands moving gracefully before my face. It was wonderful, exhilarating and—to be honest—exhausting. But I was afraid to ask the Holy for a break, afraid the gift would fade and leave me altogether. I wanted the feelings to stay; I wanted to stay in the presence of the Holy Spirit every second of the day and night. I didn't miss the sleep I was losing. I was like a desert walker, swimming in a pool of pure water. And in sleep, when I was not consciously drinking, my body was soaking in the spiritual water.

At any moment that I quieted to pray and put my mind and heart on

God, my arms and hands would dance. My fingers would extend, as if catching a wave of energy; my hands and arms soon followed. Led by my hands, my arms glided in graceful movements. It was as if my hands spun, dove and turned on currents of wind and my arms followed like streamers attached to kites.

THE MOVEMENTS BEGAN to take on meanings.

The first time I realized there was a message in the hand movements, Jennifer and I sat in prayer in our living room. My hands rose to my face, not in my control. My fingers tapped along and around my face, as if to signify bathing in the presence of Holiness.

I opened my eyes and saw that Jennifer's eyes were closed in meditation. The presence of spiritual energy surrounded me and entered me.

With the energy and direction of the Spirit, my forefingers tapped upon my lips. I thought this meant I should speak. My hand then went outward, toward the wall gracefully, with my fingers sending forth something. I thought I should talk to Jen. Then the hand came back to my lips. The pattern was repeated again and again.

"There's a message in it," I said aloud.

Jennifer opened her eyes and watched my hands moving in the Spirit.

My fingers went to my lips. "Maybe it's my writing. Like my fingers typing on the computer keyboard," I said.

My hand slapped my cheek repeatedly, as if to say, "No, no, no, no."

I didn't particularly like being reprimanded by my own hand, and I was ready to quit praying.

"What's this," Jennifer said, "spiritual charades?" She chuckled.

Her humor put me at ease. I knew there was a message in the movements, but I could not understand it. I stayed open to the Spirit and watched my fingers and hands repeat the pattern. My fingers rose to my lips; my arm extended; my fingers threw something forth.

Jennifer gave me a look I'd seen many times. A combination of wonder and confusion. A wry smile came to her lips. It was a look that said nothing could surprise her anymore.

"A song," Jennifer said. "It's a song?"

My fingers turned away from my lips, my arm extended toward the ceiling this time, and my hands opened upward. Then my fingers went back to my lips.

Jennifer laughed. "It's like holy sign language."

I laughed, but the motions continued. The pattern repeated.

"It looks like prayer," Jennifer said. "It means prayer."

"Prayer," I said. Joy washed over me and through me. My eyes filled with tears. The motion stopped, and I knew we had the meaning of the movements.

"It means prayer," I said. I felt at complete peace. I cried with a relief that was both in me and beyond me. "It means prayer."

3
Through the Darkness

I CALLED MY MOTHER to tell her what was happening. When I explained the lesson in spiritual sign language, the slapping on the face, the flood of joy when the meaning was realized, she said the most surprising thing to me:

"Michael. It's an entity."

My mother had left the conservative Christianity of her childhood and was attending a Unity Church. I had always respected her approach to spirituality, even though I gravitated toward mainline Christianity and had married a United Methodist minister. Despite a different religious terminology, my mother and I had always found common ground when talking about spirituality. But the word "entity" did not sound like anything from her Unity background.

"What do you mean an *entity*?" I said. I stood in the kitchen, leaning against the counter. "I think it's some part of the Holy Spirit that's coming into me."

"I need to send you a book," she said. "You could be in danger."

In my mother's voice, there was both authority and fear. This was not the response I had expected. I had expected disbelief or questions, not a warning. "Danger?"

"Michael, you don't know what's happening," she said. "You're like an open door right now. You're an open channel."

"What are you talking about?"

"Oh, Lord," my mother said. "There's no simple way to tell you." There was a long pause. "Michael, I used to channel an entity. She was a spiritual guide who spoke through me."

"Channel?" I said. The only things I knew about channeling were that it was associated with Shirley McClain and it caused most Christians to shudder.

"That's what it's called when you go into a trance-like state and let a spiritual guide speak through you."

I began to walk through the house with the cordless phone to my ear. "You've done this?"

"Only a few close friends know," she said. "This was years ago. In the early 1980s. There was a lot of interest in channeling back then. I was in a study group, and we tried to channel. It hit me pretty quickly. For several years, we'd get together weekly to receive wisdom and guidance. But we stopped meeting years ago, and I don't do it anymore. I'm not even sure I still can."

My mind was filled with questions about this unknown part of my mother's life, but I also felt incredible relief. "So, you know what's happening to me?"

"I think I do."

"Did you ever have tremors in your hands?" I asked. I sat in a chair in the living room. "Have you ever been pulled inside yourself so deep you lose a sense of everything."

"That's a trance," she said. "Oh, Lord. You're farther along than I thought. Do you hear anything? Do you speak anything?"

"Sometimes," I said. "If it weren't for a few good friends who pray with me, I'd think I was going crazy."

"You're not crazy," my mother said. "Just gifted. I think it can run in a family, and I should have told you about all of this before now."

There was a long pause. I glanced around the living room. Pictures of my two-year-old son lined the top of the piano, and I had a sudden fear about the spiritual heritage of my family and what I could have handed down to Samuel. I had no idea what I was getting into.

"I'm sending you a book," my mother said. "You need to read it. There's an intelligence coming into you, and you need to be careful. You need to protect yourself."

"Protection?" I said.

"And don't tell anyone," she continued. "They'll think you're crazy. Or they'll think you can read their minds. People don't understand this, and they'll treat you differently."

I chuckled.

"I'm serious," my mother said. "Read the book I'm sending you. It's short. Read it."

My mother was a combination of wisdom and caution. My brother and sister knew this, also. We all sought her advice. She was the first person to hear our problems. She was the calm voice in the midst of turmoil. At the same time, she was the caution my brother, sister and I always ignored. My mother was the type to tell us not to drive if there was a dusting of snow. She kept a coffee can in the car in case somebody needed an emergency pee stop. Of course, nobody ever needed the can, but—in my mother's eyes—it was good to be prepared. My brother, sister and I treasured our mother's wisdom and ignored her caution. As a result, all three of us turned out a little reckless. Wise, but reckless.

This time, I would learn that my mother's caution was a part of her wisdom, and like a foolish little boy, I had to learn it the hard way.

AT CHURCH, the prayer group gathered to help a church member—I will call him Joel—who wanted to be free of feelings of vindictiveness and anger. We gathered around this person for prayer in Daniel's office. The office was in the oldest part of the building. It had a high ceiling and a marble fireplace. Built-in bookcases with glass doors lined the walls. The furniture was old but comfortable. The desk was large. We put Joel in a chair in the middle of the room, and we stood around him and laid our hands on him for prayer.

The prayer lasted for more than an hour, and during the course of the prayer, my hands, arms and—at times—my entire body were seized with messages from the Spirit. At one point, I found myself on the floor in the position of a crucifix. Deborah opened her eyes and saw me. She said, "Oh, Lord. I just saw that image in my mind. I saw Joel on a cross, and the message was, 'Come down off the cross. The cross is for Jesus, not for you.'"

I was released from the position on the floor. The pattern was repeated: Messages came to my body, and when the message was understood, I was released from the movement.

The praying became intense. Joel began to cry. Through combined gifts of the group, we began to focus on old pains and hurts in Joel's life, things he needed to release and surrender to God.

Then all at once, I felt chilled. There was no breeze in the office, but I felt a cold wind blow by me. My backbone tingled. It was the impression of a "watcher," but stronger than I had ever felt before.

"Does anyone else feel chilled?" Jennifer asked.

We all looked up and shared glances.

"I feel it," Daniel said.

"That's a spiritual chill," Rose said. Her eyes narrowed. Mine widened.

"Oh, Lord," Deborah said.

I glanced around the office: the mahogany desk, the bookshelves lined with Bible commentaries, the molding around the ceiling. The windows and the door were closed. There was no source for a breeze.

I settled back into prayer. My right hand became a claw, and it went towards Joel's head. My hand motioned as if it were trying to claw into Joel's skull, but it appeared to be held back. My hand was clawing the air around Joel's head, so close to him, strands of his hair moved.

"It can't get to him," Daniel said. "He's protected by Jesus. Whatever it is, it can't get to him."

All at once, I was overcome by a force. I spun around and was thrown against the wall. I could not control my own body. I writhed. My face contorted. I heard my voice growling. My limbs twisted. My face wrinkled into a snarl that matched my voice.

I was trapped against the wall and also trapped in the shape and snarl of something very dark. I looked at Jennifer. I saw terror and surprise in her face. I became frightened, also. I wanted released.

For a moment, everyone was stunned. I saw them all stare at me, but I could not get free. I could not speak. I remained against the wall, growling like a trapped animal.

"In the name of Jesus," Daniel said, "I command you to release Michael and go from this place."

There was no fear in his voice. The others began to pray in the power and name of Jesus. Their prayers became strong.

I was released and fell to the floor.

I stood up and got back into my chair. I said I was fine. And we continued to pray for Joel, who shook his head and cried. "Thank you, Jesus," he said between his sobs. "Thank you, Jesus."

"You've carried that long enough," Daniel said. "Now, accept the grace of Christ, Joel. Take it in."

I had a hard time concentrating on the praying. I was stunned and shaken by the darkness that had passed through me.

Although I had grown up sensing the presence of spiritual visitors, which had always made me receptive to the idea of spirits, I had never thought of the biblical stories of possession as anything but ancient ways to explain mental illness. Suddenly, however, all of that changed. I had *been* possessed, if only for a moment. I had felt the invasion and control of something dark. I had felt the panic of not being able to stop this dark force from entering me, and the growls from my own throat and the snarls of my face had brought with them emotions of anger and desperation.

I did not *want* to believe in evil spirits, but I could not deny what I had experienced.

AFTER THE PRAYER, I stood in the parking lot with Rose, who was waiting for her husband to pick her up. Jennifer and the others were still in the church, working with Joel.

"You're a channel," Rose said. She caught my eyes with hers. "You need to be careful."

I wanted to say, "So I hear," but I didn't. "How do you know?" I asked.

It was a warm evening, and the security light on the church cast shadows around us. There was very little traffic in downtown Canton. Only a few cars breezed by the building on Tuscarawas Avenue.

"I've suspected it, but now I know. That demon channeled through you." She pursed her lips. "That's not good," she said, her eyes squinted. "You don't want that kind of thing to happen."

"No kidding," I said. "What do I do?"

"Pray," she said. "Pray for guidance and protection."

I realized at that moment that Rose and my mother had a lot in common. I had sensed it all along but had never recognized the source of my comfort with Rose. It wasn't just that Rose was a redhead like my mother and about my mother's age. She was spiritually wise. "Did you ever channel?" I asked.

"I used to," she said. She glanced down the street, as if it were nothing significant she was telling me. "It doesn't happen to me anymore. I used to call it going on automatic."

"Did you speak?" I asked Rose.

"That's usually how it happens," Rose said. "But the message was always for the other person. Never for me. That's how it works."

I looked at the night sky for a moment. It seemed full of possibility.

Despite the confrontation with a dark spiritual presence, I felt charged with holy energy. "Do you think it will come to my voice?"

Her husband's car pulled up to us. "It will come only when you are ready," Rose said. She moved toward the car and opened the passenger door. "I'll be praying for you," she said. She gave me a nod, then got into the car. I watched the tail lights trail off around a corner, my mind swarming with thoughts.

Jennifer came out of the church, and we walked to our Honda Civic. "Now *that* was wild," she said.

"It was a demon, wasn't it?" I said. "An actual demon."

"I don't know what else to call it," Jennifer said. She took the driver's side, and got into the car. "And those chills," she said after I got in the passenger seat. "Those chills were real."

Jennifer began to drive home. We had already stayed out later than our babysitter had expected.

"Daniel called it a spirit of depression and anger," Jennifer said. "I'm not sure about all this, but I think demons can take advantage of our psychological weaknesses. This thing was feeding on Joel."

"I felt the shape of it," I said. "That demon. It was desperate and clingy."

Jennifer took her foot off the gas pedal. The car slowed. "We have to pray for protection," she said. " I don't want that thing following us home." She pulled the car over. "We have to pray. Right here. Right now."

And that was what we did on the roadside of Cleveland Avenue, with the light of a streetlamp shining into the windshield and the sounds of traffic around us. We prayed to God for protection.

THERE WAS A LOT to take in. First there was an encounter with what seemed to be a demon, then there was the whole issue of a spiritual presence passing through me. I didn't understand what was happening. This was a world that my background and academic training did not prepare me to accept quickly. My rational mind rejected these spiritual experiences as superstition.

My mother and Rose both called it channeling. If they understood the experiences, perhaps others did as well.

I went to a bookstore and found myself in the New Age section. I did not know at the time that my best guidance would come from the Bible and the Holy Spirit. At the time, I didn't know Christianity could help me understand the experiences I had in prayer.

I picked up a copy of *Conversations with God*. I'd seen the title before, but shrugged it off as New Age, fluffy material. I stood in the bookstore and skimmed the introduction. It appeared that Neale Donald Walsch used a form of inspired or automatic handwriting to speak with God.

The thought hit me quickly. If my hand moves in prayer, why not give it a pencil? I set the book back on the shelf with a plan forming in my mind.

In my office at The University of Mount Union the next day, I closed the door, sat at my desk with paper in front of me, picked up a pencil, and said, "Okay. Got anything for me?"

My hand twisted and tensed. My arm writhed a bit. It was not a comfortable sensation, but it worked. My hand began to write.

"I can help you" scrawled out, like a child's handwriting.

"Help me what?" I asked out loud.

"With your writing," came spelling out, letter by letter, this time quicker.

Since childhood, I had yearned to be a writer. It was the first thing I remember wanting to be. I wrote my first storybook called "The Haunted Castle" when I was five, and my father bound it with a cardboard cover. In college, I majored in English with a concentration in fiction writing. In graduate school, I used my tuition waiver to take as many fiction writing courses as I could, and while I worked on my dissertation, fiction writing helped me keep my sanity. Now that I had a full-time job at Mount Union and after publishing a few scholarly articles, I turned my attention to my first love: short story writing. In the past year, I had gotten three short stories published in literary journals, but I felt like a beginner. It was a lonely task to write a short story, and I had longed for a mentor.

"How can you help me?" I asked.

"With your project," came spelled out.

I had been working on some stories based on my great-grandmother, who had been a prayer healer in a Southern Ohio town in the 1920s, 30s and 40s. The project would finally become my first novel, entitled *The Homegoing*, published in 2013. But at the time, I was finding that the time period and the language of Appalachia Ohio were not mine. The project had a spiritual purpose and power, but I wasn't sure I could pull it off.

"I can help," came written from my own hand.

"How?" I asked again.

"I lived it."

"Lived what?" I asked.

"I died in 1952."

I was speaking with the dead. I trembled. "No," I said. "I don't think so."

"Let me stay," my hand wrote.

At this point I was apprehensive, but also very curious. To be honest, I really *did* want help with my writing project. I wanted to be a writer with all the passion I had.

"I can live through you," my hand wrote. "You need me. I need you."

My curiosity was increased, and I felt that I was in no danger. The writing was not comfortable, but it was getting quicker. "Who are you?" I asked.

"I'm your great-grandma."

This was a downright lie. My great grandmother died when I was in the sixth grade. In 1974. My curiosity was now replaced with apprehension.

"Let me stay. Please," my hand wrote.

I felt desperation running through me, and it was not mine. I remembered the desperation and clingy feeling of the darkness that had pinned me against the wall in Daniel's office.

I stood quickly and backed away from my desk. The writing was before me. "Let me stay. Please." It was a shaky handwriting that had come from my own hand, twisted by tensed muscles.

This was not holy. It was not right.

I left my office and wandered the hallway of Chapman Hall. Students were milling about, looking for professors. My colleagues were talking in the mailroom. They were all secure in their everyday, rational world. I went down the stairs in a daze. I wandered without direction, out of Chapman Hall and into the quad. It was a chilly November day. Students wore jackets, backpacks slung over their shoulders. I stopped at the bell tower and sat.

What had just happened? The presence was not a comfortable fit. It was clingy and desperate, and it lied. I was not entirely comfortable with the world I was entering. I did not want to believe in these dark spiritual forces, but I could not deny what I had experienced. I wanted the presence of God and the grace of Jesus Christ, not "demons" and lost souls.

I gazed up at the clock tower on Chapman Hall. It was a stately, brick building, erected in 1865. It seemed solid and sure of its place in the universe. But I was suddenly not sure of anything.

I HAD TO TRY AGAIN. My mother and Rose both said I needed protection. I decided to do it again, but this time I would pray for Jesus to be my guide and protection. I had learned to trust the presence and power of Christ in my prayer life. And for some reason, I had to try the automatic handwriting again. If my handwriting was an avenue to the spirit world, I needed somehow to get beyond the dead and the dark. I sensed that it was possible to reach Holiness, and that was what I was determined to do. I could not deny my yearning for God, and I didn't want fear of lost souls to keep me from the Holy Spirit. Perhaps I was crazy, but I was also determined.

I went back to my office and closed the door. I folded the previous paper on my desk and stuffed it in a drawer. Laid out before me was clean paper.

I picked up the pencil, bowed my head and prayed:

"Lord Jesus. Sweet, Lord Jesus. Be my protection and my guide. Be my all. And thank you for the gifts of the Spirit I have received. And now, Lord. Teach me. Guide me. Help me be what you want me to be."

My fingers began to extend. It was a motion I had known in the past weeks as the presence of peace and Holiness.

"Speak to me, Lord," I said. "I am yours, Lord Jesus. I am yours."

My arm and hand began to move with a fluent, comfortable motion, and the writing began:

Only in the center of peace can the Spirit flow.
The center is an awareness of the Holy.
Don't try to anticipate.
You hear as you write.
Write what you hear.
Let it flow quickly. You are on your way.
I will direct you in general principles only.
I am Light. You know me as Holy Spirit.
I am tutoring you into awareness.
Awareness is a state of existing
through humility, self-awareness and
openness to the Holy Spirit.
Empty yourself,
and the Holy will enter you.
Let the words flow without stopping them.

You have not yet reached the point that
allows more complete communication.
You will be lead toward opening and surrender.
Oral communication is more efficient.
Relax. Do not strive so.
Be present in the moment.
Know my peace.

I felt the peaceful presence leaving me. My hand and arm became under my own control once again. I leaned back into my chair.

Now, that was more like it.

But how much could I trust? Was this another trick? It felt peaceful and holy, but I had to wonder. And perhaps it was all just coming from my own mind.

It was now time to leave my office. It was my day to pick up our son, and I drove to Canton with questions swirling through my mind. At Sam's preschool, I walked under the construction paper leaves hung by fishing wire in the hallway, got the note from his teacher about the number of times he pottied, his nap time, how much he ate. I picked up the little guy, kissed his sweet head, and took him home.

In the mailbox was the book from my mother. It was called *A Guide to Channeling and Channeled Material*, and she had highlighted passages, knowing that I might ignore her caution.

I got Sam settled playing with Mega Blocks, and I flipped through the book.

It was channeled material. The scholar and writer side of me wondered how one would cite such a source. Was there such a thing as spiritual plagiarism? I was clearly entering a different world than what I had known.

I found several passages that described my recent experiences. It was a book of guidance for beginning to channel. The book explained a spirit world in which there are "lower astral beings" and "higher astral beings." It explained that a new channel may have many spirits vying for her attention, and the goal of channeling is to contact a higher astral being to become a teacher or guide. One passage highlighted by my mother was this: "The presence of a Ouija board is a signal to those on the lower astral plane that someone wants to talk, and those willing to oblige come rushing forward, leaving no room for the person's guide, who will not usually assert his presence among the rest."

This rang true with my experience. In my preparation for automatic handwriting, I had sent up a signal that I wanted to contact a spirit, and that was what happened. Was the problem that I did not specify what type of spirit?

The book also indicated that "protection will not be given until the individual is able to discriminate between information given from a lower being and a higher one, and until the person is able to know intuitively what is in his own highest good."

I had to wonder if I had just been through this journey of being able to discern between spirits of God and spirits not of God.

The book used an unfamiliar framework to describe spiritual experiences, but the experiences of being a "medium" hit me with a truth. Instead of spirits, the book spoke of "astral beings." I had experienced three different spirits: that of a dead person, what seemed to be a demon and what felt like Holiness. The book explained all of these experiences with a New Age terminology. In this book, the dead person was a spirit on a lower plane, the demon was a childish spirit on this lower plane, and the feeling of Holiness was a guide on a higher plane.

Later, I would learn to place all of this in the Christian framework, but for now, I was grasping for a way to conceptualize and understand what was happening to me.

Another passage highlighted by my mother was about becoming a "medium" or channel, and it described early experiences of the medium, before the medium has connected with a "high level" teacher or guide:

> The worst thing that can happen is that you allow a lower astral being to speak through you rather than a higher one. This is no disaster; most mediums have experienced this. The beings who speak through you cannot hurt you or cause you to hurt yourself or others—not even when you are unconscious—because they do not have the strength to do so.... Because possession cannot be maintained for long periods of time and because lower astral beings can manipulate the body very little, these incidents, when they occur, are short-lived and relatively harmless. Furthermore, most beings on the astral plane, although they may be unevolved and childish, rarely seek to cause substantial harm.

This explanation was helpful. Though I would not use the same terminology, it gave me a sense of comfort to know that people have had experiences like mine on the way to a more productive communication with a "guide" among what I would call the heavenly hosts.

Sam was down for a nap when Jennifer came home from work. I heard the rattle of her keys and her heels clicking on the kitchen tile. She came into the living room where I sat. She smiled and took off her long coat. She wore a skirt and blouse, her lips painted with lipstick, her eyes tired from a day of visiting people in the hospital.

I wanted to share with Jennifer what had happened to me. I got out the sheets of paper from my office.

"I did some automatic handwriting," I said to Jennifer.

"You're kidding," she said. She hung her coat in the closet and spun to look at me. Based on the disapproval on her face, I flipped past the first writing from the clingy ghost who claimed to be my great-grandmother.

"Listen to this," I said. And I read her the message from holiness. She kicked her shoes off and walked to me in her hose-covered feet. She leaned over me. The cross she wore dangled and touched my head. She saw the scrawled, large handwriting.

"I need to sit down," she said.

She sat on the couch, and I shared with her the first message as well. I needed her guidance and support.

"Michael," she said, sitting up straight. "That's not right. This isn't right."

"No kidding," I said. "And take a look at this." I showed her the book from my mother, and read her a few passages. I stopped when I heard Sam crying upstairs in his crib.

Jennifer stood. She leaned her head to one side and unhooked an earring. "You stay away from automatic handwriting," she said. She unhooked the other earring and started toward the stairs to get Sam. "I can't believe you're messing around with this stuff." She stopped, spun and went to the bookshelf. "There's nothing in the Bible about automatic handwriting," she said. She flipped through the Bible. "You read I John," she said. "It's about wisdom and how to test it."

She plopped the Bible into my lap. Sam was crying louder.

"And Paul writes about prophecy in either first or second Corinthians. Read them both. Read the whole thing." She walked toward the stairs.

"I can't believe you're messing around with automatic handwriting. Who knows what's following you around." With that, she went upstairs. "And don't you dare pray to anything but Jesus. You hear me?"

DESPITE JENNIFER'S WARNING, I tried the automatic handwriting again the next day in my office. I had felt a holy presence and had received beautiful wisdom, and I had to try it again. I knew deep inside that something holy was happening to me, and I wanted to see it through. I began with reading scripture, then prayed through Jesus Christ, and once again, a peace came over me, and my hand began to write:

You are opening to holiness.
You will know holiness by the peace.
The lost and errant will not come with peace.
They reject the peace of the Holy.
Do not follow their lead.
Allow the Holy to cleanse you.

It seemed good spiritual advice, and a warm energy surrounded and penetrated me. Still, part of me was skeptical. Was this simply a part of my own subconscious writing? "What is the source of this wisdom?" I asked.

The source is the Source.
God is the source of many sources.
The hand of God is upon you
For a holy task.
In time, you will know it to be so.

The presence left me, and—though I felt a peace—I also felt confusion. I wasn't quite willing to trust the experience.

ON THE WAY HOME from work that day, I was seized by a dark presence. I felt it come into me, but instead of taking my hand, it took my throat and face. It was a powerful and troubled presence. My neck muscles tensed. My breathing deepened. My face contorted.

Something wanted to speak. Something was taking my vocal chords. I felt as if this thing had me by the throat, but from the inside.

I drove home in a sense of panic. Tears filled my eyes. I struggled to keep this negative force at bay. It was not holy, and it would not leave me. I could control my body perfectly, but my face and neck were leaving my control. I felt I was being pulled away from myself, and it took great concentration and will to drive.

I looked at the world around me. The signs of businesses, the other cars, the stop lights. It was all familiar, but I was feeling suddenly very foreign. I couldn't stop my face from twisting and contorting, and I was hoping nobody would look at me. At stoplights when other cars pulled next to me, I kept my eyes straight to avoid the glance of other drivers. I drove, short of breath. I gripped the steering wheel and hoped I would make it home. More than that, I hoped Jennifer would be there.

Jennifer's car was in the garage. I came into the house quickly. Jennifer was on the phone. She saw in my face that something was wrong. I must have looked like I was holding back from throwing up.

"I'll call you back," she said and hung up.

She was in a black pantsuit. Her purse was on the counter. Her shoes were in the middle of the kitchen floor, which told me she had just gotten home.

"Something has me," I was able to say. "My throat."

"Sit down," Jennifer said. She picked up the phone and called Daniel. Within minutes he was at our house, his leather-bound Bible in his hand.

"Something is coming into him," Jennifer said.

I looked up at Daniel from the chair in the dining room. Tears welled in my eyes. I could not speak. When I tried, my voice merely moaned. My face contorted.

"We won't let it speak," Daniel said. He took off his coat and threw it on the sofa. He loosened his tie. "Whatever we do, we don't let it speak. We don't entertain it in any way." He looked at Jennifer. "Are you ready?"

Jennifer nodded.

Daniel began to pray, but without bowing his head and closing his eyes. He looked straight at me. His eyes were intense. He put his hand on my head. "We praise you, Lord Jesus. We praise your holy name."

"Yes, Lord Jesus," Jennifer said.

Jennifer also put her hands on me. The warmth of their hands was a comfort. The power of their voices calmed me.

"We ask for your holy presence among us," Daniel said.

"Yes, come, Lord Jesus."

I began to squirm. It was a terrible feeling of being invaded and controlled.

Daniel kept praying. "We pray, Lord Jesus, that you come to Michael. Come to Michael and cleanse him of this unclean spirit."

My neck tensed, and I began to speak. Daniel put his hand on my mouth.

"In the name of Jesus Christ I bind you, silence you and rebuke you," Daniel said.

I could hear in my mind what the spirit wanted to say. It wanted to say, "You think you know whom you are dealing with."

Jennifer and Daniel continued to pray with force and authority in the name of Jesus Christ. They rebuked the spirit and cast it out. It was something right out of the movies, but it was real. All too real.

I was afraid. For the first time in my life, I was truly terrified of a spiritual presence, and there was no ignoring this one. This wasn't just a watcher, it was an invader, and I did not consciously invite this invasion.

The praying continued. Eventually, the dark presence left me, and I was able to relax.

Daniel stayed for almost an hour. We all prayed. When Daniel left, Jennifer turned to me, her eyes in a narrow squint.

"You stop messing around with this channeling stuff," she said. "This is nothing to play with."

I nodded. "I know," I said. "I'm sorry."

"I'm glad you're open to the presence of God and that you're a praying man now, but why can't you pray like normal people?" she said. There was no humor in her voice. She left the room. I heard her grab her keys, then heard her heels clicking in the kitchen, which meant she had slipped on her shoes. I knew she was off to pick up Sam from day care.

But instead of heading out the door, she came back into the living room. With her coat over her arm and keys in her hand, she said, "Stop reading books about channeling, and pray like a Christian." Then she left the house.

4
Voice of The Holy

JENNIFER HAD HAD ENOUGH. A husband with dancing hands. A mother-in-law who used to channel. Automatic handwriting. And a demon possession.

I had to admit, it was a lot to deal with. Jennifer had been a solid companion through a great deal of change, but the spirit who seized my throat was a bit much to handle. For both of us.

Jennifer was right. And so was my mother. I took a much more cautious approach. I wasn't sure how to explain the dark presences I had experienced, but they had brought with them feelings of desperation. They were grasping at me, and I sensed they wanted to feed upon me and survive through attaching to me. Were they simply "lower astral level" spirits? Were they evil? Were they demons? Were they lost souls? Were they simply elements of myself, parts of my subconscious taking on physical manifestations?

I decided I had to commit to a framework, and Christianity was my heritage. I had experienced the presence of Jesus. I knew there was integrity to the Christian tradition, and I decided to dive deeply into the scriptural and mystical depths of my faith heritage. I stopped experimenting with automatic handwriting and channeling. I decided the Holy Spirit would reveal what was to be known. I put aside the New Age books and decided to let the Holy Spirit instruct me. And I buried my nose in the Bible.

I had read much of the Bible before, especially the Gospels and the Epistles. But this time, I saw much more in the Bible than I had ever seen before. My spiritual awareness was magnified. I read with my heart and spirit. I released my critical, scholarly mind enough to absorb the truths I felt confirmed in my spirit. I no longer saw the demon possessions in the

Gospels as first-century understandings of mental illness. They were real. I did not want to believe in spiritual warfare; it countered every rational thought in my mind and defied my intellectual background. However, I could not deny the experiences of dark spirits, and I was coming to a deeper understanding of the spiritual forces that constantly surround us. I was also finding that there were consequences from this spiritual realm. I had to take the presence of unclean spirits or "demons" seriously; my safety depended on it. I also had to pray to Jesus for guidance and protection. I was in over my head, and I needed Jesus to show me the way.

During this period of my spiritual journey, I prayed often. I would begin with a psalm, then enter into prayer through Jesus. The hand movements began to lessen until they were all but gone, and I thought the gift was leaving me. In many ways, I was glad to see it go, but I also felt like a person missing an organ of perception. It was as if I'd "seen" into the Holy, and now I was losing my sight.

I was thankful for the blessing the Holy had shown me, and I figured I was going back to a more "normative" experience of prayer.

But the more I prayed, the more I noticed the presence of the Holy around me, and I began to feel spiritual energy enter me. It would seep into my chest, then swell into my lungs. And on more than one occasion, my neck would tighten, and I would have a quick vocalization, such as an explosive, "Ha."

Jennifer called my little outbursts in prayer "spiritual Tourettes." I called them holy hiccups.

Over the course of several months, Jennifer and I prayed almost daily, and our prayers lasted at least an hour. After Sam was asleep for the night, we would sit together, read scripture, then pray. In this context, my oracle gift began to develop. The depth of my meditative state increased. I felt my mind going into my own spirit, and from there I found a pathway that opened to the Spirit beyond myself. One evening, the motions came back to my hands. I felt a surge of spiritual energy come through the hollow of my chest, in the space just below my heart. This time, my mind did not will myself into meditative prayer. I felt drawn into the center of myself, as if my human spirit were water and a plug had been pulled at my core. My human spirit or soul rushed to this central portal, but instead of feeling drained of my own spirit, there came a rushing inward of more Spirit than I could withstand. My lungs filled with breath. My neck tightened. My arms were forced out, my chest rose toward the ceiling, as if a chord had been attached from my chest to the sky and I was being raised up. Then, the Spirit gently took control of my voice, and I hummed. My mind was disconnected from my body, and I could not move. My intellect was locked deeply inside of me, and my spirit became merged with the Eternal. Although my body was in an awkward position, I felt completely relaxed and completely open, and I felt words come into my throat, then flow out of my mouth:

Holiness. Holiness. Holiness.

I heard this spoken from my own voice, but the sound was muffled to me, and a level of understanding beyond the words came to my mind. The intention of the message was that holiness surrounded me. This knowledge of a deeper meaning behind the words was intense and certain, as if I had access to the mind that was forming the words. Then the speaking continued:

Be calm and center in. The Holy is upon you.

Jennifer prayed, "We are here, O God. We are open to your presence." Hearing Jennifer pray these words allowed me to relax further. I felt as if I were sinking into my own body, and from there, I could sense an opening to the universe, where what I understood as "self" merged with the infinite. It was like looking up at the night sky and feeling completely open and in unison with the expanse of the universe until the self *became* the universe. A peace sank into my bones and opened me to the heavens at the same moment, but instead of being a dual sensibility of "me" and "other," it was a unifying blend in which my sense of self was widened beyond any possible recognition of identity. And from this state of awareness, words came to my lips from a source beyond my human consciousness.

The vocalizations from the Spirit were short at first. Phrases came, with long pauses of quiet prayer time in between. And for a period of several weeks, Jennifer and I became comfortable with the process of prophetic speech. I experienced tremors while going into a deep state of prayer, and my face contorted before the Spirit spoke through my voice, but these strange ticks and twists of my body came to seem normal.

During this time of prayer expansion, Jennifer would tell me she enjoyed "basking in the Spirit" during our prayers. While in prayer she could feel spiritual energy she described as a humming in her chest.

It was humbling and wonderful to see Jennifer's spiritual journey deepen through our prayer life. I could hardly believe that God was using *me*, of all people, to assist Jennifer in her spiritual journey. The love of our marriage increased and took on multiple layers. Prayer became a form of intimacy and union. At times, the energy of the Spirit would course through us, and we would be swept with a joy from beyond ourselves. One evening, I felt the force of the Spirit come into me, and my hands went out toward Jennifer. She immediately burst into tongues, something she had never done before.

From all spiritual signs, our prayer life was bearing positive fruits in our lives, and the short, prophetic utterances became a normal part of this prayer life.

Then, the messages began to increase in length, and I recognized a consistent spiritual presence that would enter me. Because the messages were longer than we could remember and because of their poetic use of language, Jennifer and I decided we should tape record our prayers. Here is the first message from the Spirit that we taped:

December 15, 1998

There is energy and there is the Spirit.
The Spirit uses the energy and the Spirit is the energy.
Yet the Spirit is more than the energy.

There is Spirit and there is Light.
The Light is in the Spirit and the Light is the Spirit,
but the Spirit is more than the Light.
There is the individual and there is the unity.
The individual is in the unity and
the unity is in the individual,
but the unity is greater than the individual.
There are no divisions, yet there is the individual,
and there is the unity.

To see only in part is the human experience.
The part and the Whole are one.
The part can bring you to an awareness of the Whole,
the Holy Whole.

There are moments when you see the Kingdom of God;
these moments reveal the Whole.

We are in the Light.
The Light is the Light of Christ.
We are in the Light and of the Light,
but the Light is greater.
We are not Christ.
To say we are Christ would be deceiving.
We will not deceive.
To say we are connected to Christ is accurate.
We abide in the Holy Whole.
We are of the Holy.

Do not pray to us.
We are members of the Holy and servants of the Light.
It is a privilege we do not take lightly.
We are an avenue, a conduit for the Light.
From the Holy, we can bring the Light to you.
But you do not need us to access the Light.
When you pray to God, we can step out of the way
or we can act as connections,
intercessors, if you will.

Prayer is the great connector.
It allows the Spirit to reveal the unity.

Some, like Michael, are amplifiers.
Such people are conduits among the human
to bring others to awareness and action, to reveal the unity.

IN THIS PRAYER, the intercessors who spoke through my voice were identifying themselves. I began to call them holy Messengers, and I understood them as part of the heavenly hosts. I would later learn that receiving wisdom through an intercessor is customary for prophecy, hence the presence of angels, seraphim and cherubim in the Bible.

The holy Messenger (or Messengers) who contacted me made it clear I was not to pray to them, but I was to pray directly to God. They mentioned that they were servants of the Light. Later, I would find that the angel who spoke to John in Revelation made a similar point when John asked who the angel was:

> I, John, am the one who heard and saw these things. And when I heard and saw them, I fell down to worship at the feet of the angel who showed them to me; but he said to me, "You must not do that! I am a fellow servant with you and your comrades the prophets, and with those who keep the words of this book. Worship God!" (Rev. 22:8–9).

Many times, the Messenger who came to me would tell me to pray only to God (or the Holy), and I never received a name for this "fellow servant." It was the first of many parallels between my experience and biblical teachings.

In this prayer I was also being told that the Holy Spirit is an energy upon which heavenly messengers travel. In addition, a new terminolog for the heavenly realm were being introduced. The Holy seemed to be synonymous with the Light of God, and heaven was described as the Holy Whole, a concept that would be expanded in later prayers.

Through the coming weeks, two sentences became prominent in the way the heavenly messengers spoke about themselves: "We are a part of the Holy," and "We abide in the Holy Whole." Because of these repeated references, Jennifer and I began to refer to the voice as "the Holy." And though the Holy used the plural pronoun to speak of itself, I sensed that there was only one Messenger of the Holy who contacted me. I simply accepted that my intercessor felt to me like a singular presence but often used plural pronouns for self-reference.

In the wisdom books of the Old Testament (i.e., Proverbs, Ecclesiastes, Job, The Wisdom of Solomon and the Wisdom of Ben Sirach), the messenger of God's wisdom is the Spirit of Wisdom, who is personified as a woman. In Hebrew she is known as *hokmah*, but in Greek translations of the Bible, she is known as *Sophia*, which is also a woman's name.

In Proverbs, Sophia is the presence of God among the people, and she says, "I will pour out my thoughts to you; I will make my words known to you" (Prov. 1:23). In Proverbs 8, Sophia speaks to the people, establishing her role as the teacher in the ways of God:

> "And now, my children, listen to me: happy are those who keep my ways. Hear my instruction and be wise, and do not neglect it. Happy is the one who listens to me, watching daily at my gates, waiting beside

my doors. For whoever finds me finds life and obtains favor from the Lord." (Prov. 8:32–35)

In the Old Testament, then, the Spirit of Wisdom (Sophia) is a spiritual messenger, teaching God's Holy Ways.

But for me the most striking passage about the Spirit of Wisdom is found in *The Wisdom of Solomon*, a book in the Catholic Bible, which was shifted to the "Apocrypha" in the Protestant Bible at the time of the Reformation. In this book, the writer provides an eloquent and fascinating description of the Spirit of Wisdom. We discover in the Wisdom of Solomon that, although the Spirit of Wisdom has many parts, she is yet unified as one: "She is but one, yet can do everything; herself unchanging, she makes all things new" (Wisdom of Solomon 7:27). The writer of this passage helped me to accept the apparent paradox of the singular presence I felt in my messenger and the occasional use of the plural pronoun.

Finally, this description of the Spirit of Wisdom ends with the most striking parallel to my own experience. The writer of The Wisdom of Solomon describes the Spirit of Wisdom "entering" the souls of the living: "Age after age she enters into holy souls, and makes them God's friends and prophets, for nothing is acceptable to God but the man who makes his home with wisdom" (Wisdom of Solomon 7:27–28). When I first read this passage, I shuddered and nearly wept. My own experience had been that this spirit of wisdom whom I called "the Messenger of the Holy" entered into me and merged with my soul. And indeed, I was being drawn closer and closer to God in the process, becoming a "friend of God."

Was my messenger the Spirit of Wisdom? Was she indeed Sophia? The parallel to the spiritual experience described in The Wisdom of Solomon confirmed that my spiritual journey was indeed biblical. And though I saw similarities to the Old Testament presentation of Sophia with my experience, I continued to refer to my messenger as "the Messenger of the Holy," for that was the way the spirit described itself.

The discovery of the Sophia tradition was like many other biblical references to experiences like mine. My prayer messages paralleled many biblical teachings and biblical representations of prophecy, but in my prophetic prayers a contemporary terminology was coming forth. I came to realize that my mind and my understanding of the world and universe were tools the Messenger of the Holy was using to construct a fresh and contemporary perspective of the Kingdom of Heaven. However, traditional language was also utilized, so the prayers were laced with phrases such as "the Spirit of God" and "the Spirit of Christ." As time passed, these traditionaly Christian terms became rare, and the Messenger used the language of the Holy to describe the spiritual realm. At the time, I realized my traditional background and my contemporary mind were both providing spiritual material for the Messenger of the Holy.

IT DID NOT TAKE LONG for us to discover that Jennifer could raise questions to the Messenger and have them answered. The first prayer that became a dialogue between Jennifer and the Messenger centered on issues surrounding Jennifer's ministry at Church of the Savior, and the message will not have a wide appeal beyond Jennifer and myself. However, I will share the end of this prayer because it provides an example of the type of messages we were receiving at this time in our journey.

January 21, 1999

You are learning the power of spiritual presence. You are a vehicle of the Spirit. Your physical presence can become a fountain of living water when you open yourself. The Spirit surrounds all, constantly, but through people the Spirit can become amplified, touching one another, opening one another. Walk with the Spirit, and behold, you will see transformation. For the work of the Spirit brings new life.

Jennifer prayed, "Lord, I am thankful for the time I spent in ministry in [my first parish]. I baptized many before I fully knew what I was doing. Bless them. Bless them, Lord."

Awareness is felt and not understood; you were aware of what you were doing. Awareness is in the heart, not the mind. Your prayers have been lifted.

"Bless Michael, Lord. Keep him close to you, and continue to reveal to him your Holy Ways."

He does not feel entirely worthy, yet his actions are those of a child of the Light. There is still a journey to take place. The Spirit came as a rushing wind upon him, and he is obedient.

It has been a privilege to work through you today, Michael, but I sense that it is time for us to make a separation from this direct contact. We will return to where we exist, but, Michael, it is not far from you. In fact, it is so close that we pass through each other continually.

In the early months of 1999, the prophetic experience continued to develop. The mystical state I entered during prayer became deeper, and the messages became longer and more focused. Often, there was a rhetorical structure to a message. At the opening of the prophetic prayer, I would feel the message enter me, whole and complete, like a ball of string. During the prayer lesson, the message would slowly unroll in language. For this type of lesson, the Messenger of the Holy would begin with a word, then deliver a message around the meaning of the word, and finally the message would end with the same word, but by the end of the message, the word had multiple meanings with spiritual resonance. One such prayer occurred on the evening of March 26, 1999. By this time, I began to place titles on the prayers after I transcribed them from tape to paper, and this one is titled "The Voice of the Holy."

The Voice of the Holy

March 26, 1999

Jennifer and I prepared for prayer by gathering a Bible, a Christ Candle, and the tape recorder. I lit the Christ Candle, inviting the Spirit of Christ to be among us; while doing so, the tremors began in my belly. Jennifer opened to the Psalms and randomly picked Psalm 29 to read. It is a psalm which describes the voice of the Lord:

Psalm 29

Ascribe to the Lord, O heavenly beings,
Ascribe to the Lord glory and strength.
Ascribe to the Lord the glory of his name;
Worship the Lord in holy splendor.

The voice of the Lord is over the waters;
The God of glory thunders,
The Lord, over mighty waters.

The voice of the Lord is powerful;
the voice of the Lord is full of majesty.

The voice of the Lord breaks the cedars;
the Lord breaks the cedars of Lebanon.
He makes Lebanon skip like a calf
And Sirion like a young wild ox.

The voice of the Lord flashes
forth flames of fire.
The voice of the Lord shakes
the wilderness;
The Lord shakes the
wilderness of Kadesh.

The voice of the Lord causes the
Oaks to whirl,
and strips the forest bare;
and in his temple all say,
"Glory!"

The Lord sits enthroned over
the flood;
the Lord sits enthroned as
king forever.
May the Lord give strength to
his people!
May the Lord bless his people
with peace!

Jennifer's reading of scripture had become a "trigger" for me to enter into prophetic awareness. It brought tremors through my body, which was the first indication that the Holy was coming over me. I learned that I could stop the process at this point, but if I surrendered, I would become "pulled into" prophetic awareness.

On this night, I surrendered to the Holy. While Jennifer read Psalm 29, the process began: My belly quaked with spasms, I vocalized, my arms stretched downward, between my legs. My breathing became deep and involuntary. I felt the Spirit of the Holy come into me. My limbs trembled. I sat up. My neck muscles tightened as the Spirit took control of my vocal chords. Then a peace came over me, as if the transition into prophetic prayer had been completed. After Jennifer finished the psalm, I sat straight up, with the voice of the Messenger in my throat.

In general, the topics of the prayer lessons from the Messenger often came from the concerns that we voiced before we began to pray. But if we came to prayer without heavy concerns, the Messenger would take a theme, image or issue from scripture. On this occasion, the Messenger provided a lesson on the "Voice of the Holy," a variation of the major theme of Psalm 29.

While I was in the trance state, I could not speak. Jennifer began the prayer by inviting God's presence:

JENNIFER PRAYED, "Come, O Lord. Hear our prayers. Speak your voice. We love you. We worship you. We lift your name. We give thanks, O God, for all the ways that you bless us. Help us to see your goodness."

The Voice of the Holy. The Word of the Holy. The Will of the Holy. Shall I tell you of the Voice, the Word and the Will? Prophecy is revealing the Will and the Word through the Voice.

As the lesson began, I felt the whole of the message enter my mind. I could sense that there was a long lesson coming, and I knew the lesson would center around the three elements of "the Voice of Holy, the Word of Holy and the Will of Holy." I relaxed into the prayer, ready to hear the message unravel.

Let us begin, then, with prophecy. The Voice of God is the power of creation. The subject of prophecy is the wisdom of living in harmony with the power of creation. The voice of prophecy is speaking from the voice of no sound. The Word of God is a word of no language. Language is embodiment as life is embodiment, so let us embody, let us live, let us give voice to the Word of no sound and hear the Voice of the Holy.

The power of creation is present, is now, is churning, is blowing, is swelling, is moving, is uniting. The power of creation surrounds you. It is the Voice of

God. It is the Word of no sound. The Voice of God still carries over the deep. This place has no end, and from this place the Holy calls into being all that you know, all that you see.

And how shall you know the Voice of God? Only through intermediaries, the messengers working within the limitations of your perceptions. Through intercession, the Voice of the Holy shall come to you in your hearts, in your prayers, in your imaginations, in your dreams and in your very vocal chords. Yes.

"Are you an intercessor?" Jennifer asked. "Is that what you call yourself?"

Yes. It is my purpose. Here I am in the Holy seeing the Voice of God in its splendor carry forth through and beyond this moment. And here I am coming to you now through your body, through your mind, in your words to give flesh, to give embodiment to the Voice I see, to the splendor I know. I see the tongue of God shooting through the spheres of time as lightning, and I see that the tongue of God is upon you. I come to aid and interpret, to bring the Voice of no sound to you, embodied in language.

As I heard these words coming through my mouth, I suddenly understood how the Messenger of the Holy was molding messages through me. Perceptions beyond my awareness were coming through my own words. Several years later, I would find the book, *Meditation and the Bible*, in which Aryeh Kaplan translated the writings of a rabbi who explained this process in this way:

> The prophetic experience must come about through intermediaries. A human being cannot directly attach himself to God's glory, perceiving it as one sees a man standing in front of him. The perception of God involved in true prophecy must therefore come about through God's servants, whose task it is to provide such a vision.
>
> When God reveals Himself and bestows His influence, the prophet is greatly overwhelmed. His body and all his limbs immediately begin to tremble, and he feels as if he is being turned inside out.
>
> This, however, is due to the nature of the physical. It cannot tolerate the revelation of the spiritual, and this is particularly true when this consists of the revelation of God's own Glory. The prophet's senses

cease to operate, and his mental faculties can no longer function independently. They have all become dependent on God and on the influx that is being bestowed.

From the experience of a messenger, to the physical trembling and paralysis, this rabbi from the Kabbalist tradition verified what I had experienced in prophecy. As the prayer lesson continued, Jennifer began to question the Messenger's lesson:

"I don't quite understand how the message comes. Does the Lord speak? Are these messages coming directly from God?"

The message is always the same, but in the here and now it is lived in your moments, expressed in unfolding variety. The message is the Word. So, then, let me speak of the Word of God.

The Word of God is vast and encompassing. It unifies all. It is a Word beyond language. The Word of God is the Holy Way. Therefore, make of your lives a Holy Way, and your lives shall reveal the Word of God. Do you see it? The Word is the vast design. The voice of prophecy, then, brings forth the Word, which is the design and the grand message.

And the Will of God is in the living Word. Living the Word fulfills the Will. The Will of God is completed when the Word of God is embraced and lived out. Such is the Will of God. The Will of God shall be completed, for the Way of God is completeness out of brokenness, unity out of division, community out of isolation. The Holy calls into wholeness and fulfillment. It is the Will of God that all shall know the holiness of completeness, all shall be embraced into the Holy Whole. Yes, this is the Will, the mighty Will, the great Will of God. Spoken in the Word is the Will.

And you, my children, must place yourselves in the Will of God. Through the Voice, through the Word, know the Will. Through the Voice, through the Word, know the Will. Yes. Yes. Yes. Yes.

It is the Way of the Holy.

The Word of the Holy shall be an invitation to the people of the Spirit, a holy invitation. The invitation is the Holy's to make. And who shall give voice to the Holy's invitation? Who shall reveal the Holy Way to the people?

"Is this our role?"

Yes. It is our role. OUR role. We live out the way of holiness and fulfill the will of the Holy. My children, when you open to the heavenly messengers, you work in harmony with the language of the Word. The messengers are the syllables. We embody the Word. So, invite the Word into your lives, *and receive the intercessors. Embody the Word in language and deed, and in so doing, live the Will and the Way of God.*

"Thank you, God. Thank you for your guidance and your presence. Michael certainly works with your intercessors. I see how the Spirit speaks in him and through him. But do others work with intercessors in a less direct way? Are there people who speak your Word in sermons and books?"

In speech, in writing, in song, in action, in dream, in image, in sacrifice, in pain, in joy, in living, in death. The Voice of the Holy comes to the people in many ways. You will know the Word of the Holy by the fruits, by what it produces. For the Word of the Holy brings about the Will of God, which parallels the Will of the Holy. Do you see? God is the Holy, but the Holy is more encompassing than your understanding of God.

"Sometimes, I have felt God working with me when I preach. Was this a messenger?"

Yes. You have only to place your lips to the Spirit of God, and the Spirit shall become a messenger to give voice to the sacred invitation. God brings the people to the invitation. God prepares people for the invitation. It is not of you. God prepares the people, and when you speak the invitation, the people hear it in their hearts, for the Lord is speaking, and the invitation resonates in their spirits. It is the work of God, not of you.

But you are not insignificant. You are not insignificant in this work. Oh, my daughter. Oh, my son, much is happening. Much is happening. And you are blessed to see. You are blessed to hear. You are blessed to know.

"We give you thanks, O God, for the blessings we see. We praise your name for the blessing of being your servants. Cleanse us, Lord. Make us worthy. Forgive us when we forget we are your people, when we lose patience with each other. Lord, O Lord, I am overwhelmed with your goodness."

The Voice of God is a Voice of no sound. The Voice comes through intercession. In the Voice, the Word is spoken, through the Word, the Will is revealed. Hear the Voice, live the Word, fulfill the Will. This is the message for you today.

AS USUAL, after the Spirit of the Holy left me, I was unable to move my body or open my eyes. I was in a deep state of relaxation, and even if I tried to move, I could not. In articles in the field of Transpersonal Psychology, this state of detachment from one's body during prophetic awareness is called "disassociation." For me, the paralysis lasted anywhere from one to three minutes, and the return to my body sometimes brought tremors to my limbs.

I tried to open my eyes, but they only fluttered. Finally, I felt my body and mind click into alignment, and I relaxed. My eyes opened easily, and I gazed at Jennifer, whose head was still lowered in prayer.

"That was something," I said. My mouth was dry, my lips chapped.

Jennifer looked at me, eyes wide. "This is big, Michael," she said. "This is big."

I nodded. I was lying back on the couch, in a position I did not remember my body taking. "I know," I said. I sat up and rolled my head and neck to loosen the tension. In the oracle state, my neck is the only part of my body that is not relaxed.

"Do you understand how big this is?" Jennifer asked.

"I can't face how big it is," I said, still rolling my neck and hearing cracks and pops. "I just have to take it as it comes," I smiled at Jennifer, and she smiled back. "It's too big for me."

"It's too big for anybody," Jennifer said. "This is God-sized."

IT TOOK A FEW WEEKS for me to find time to transcribe the prayer about the voice of the Lord, and I was once again overwhelmed with the lesson while I listened to sections during the long task of transcribing: hitting play, pause, rewind, play, pause and typing the words out on my computer.

Suddenly, I was confronted with the real possibility that I was a vessel of the voice of the Holy. I wasn't sure I was ready for this type of responsibility, and I also wasn't quite sure I believed it was actually happening.

But, as was often the case, the transcription of the lesson seemed to have a timeliness to it. Jennifer and I were hosting a Bible study in our house, and the day after I transcribed the "Voice of the Holy" teaching, our Bible study provided scriptural confirmation of the message.

Eight adults gathered in our living room to study scripture. I was tired from a day of work and from staying up the night before to transcribe. I admit I was not paying attention to the lesson, and I had not read the scriptures in advance. But I was startled to attentiveness as I listened to a friend read Jesus' words from the Gospel of John: "The counselor, the Holy Spirit, whom the father will send in my name, will teach you all things and will remind you of everything I have said to you" (Jn. 14:6).

I did not listen to the discussion after this passage, instead I looked closely at the words in the Bible. My mind began to take leaps. The Holy Spirit, according to Jesus, was to teach us and remind us. I had never thought about how this teaching might take place, but I suddenly realized that my experience would be a very literal example.

This discovery was before I knew anything about the Old Testament presentation of the Spirit of Wisdom, Sophia. Thus, this reference to the Holy Spirit was the first confirmation I had that my experience was indeed biblical.

The focus of the Bible study was on the role of the Holy Spirit, and another member of the Bible study read another passage of Jesus' words in the Gospel of John: "When he, the Spirit of truth, comes, he will guide you into truth. He will not speak on his own; he will speak only what he hears, and he will tell you what is yet to come. He will bring glory to me by taking from what is mine and making it known to you" (Jn. 16:13–14).

This time I was blown away. I couldn't concentrate on anything else but the words in John. Hadn't the Messenger of the Holy said that (s)he was only a conduit? Hadn't the Messenger said that (s)he describes what is seen in the Holy? And Jesus was saying something very similar about the role of the Holy Spirit: "He will not speak on his own; he will speak only what he hears."

Since high school I'd held a "Sunday school" or surface understanding of the Holy Spirit, which told me that the Holy Spirit is our intercessor, but I had never applied this surface knowledge to my own experience, and Jesus' words in John struck me deeply.

I had already known that heavenly messengers were present in the Old Testament in the forms of Seraphim, Cherubim and Angels. But, to be honest, my experience didn't seem to reflect these grand images of large, sometimes terrifying, spiritual messengers.

But the Holy Spirit speaking and teaching was a very appropriate understanding of my experience. I would later come to a deeper understanding of the interrelation of the Holy Spirit, the Spirit of Wisdom (Sophia) and the Spirit of Christ, but for now, these references to the Holy Spirit set my mind spinning.

While the discussion in the Bible study continued, I flipped to Romans. I recalled that Paul wrote about the role of the Holy Spirit in prayer. Sure enough, I had underlined the passage some years earlier: "Likewise, the Spirit helps us in our weakness; for we do not know how to pray as we ought, but that very Spirit intercedes with sighs too deep for words. And God, who searches the heart, knows what is the mind of the Spirit, because the Spirit intercedes for the saints according to the will of God" (Rom. 8:26–27). Here again I found that the Holy Spirit intercedes for the children of God as an interpreter.

I looked up from my Bible absorbed in thought. These biblical affirmations of my prophetic experience helped me to accept the experience as real and of God. I felt at peace, but I suddenly became aware that Jennifer and the others were looking at me.

"What is it?" Jennifer asked.

I smiled and glanced around the room. I shrugged. "Just enjoying scriptures," I said. I shrugged again.

Jennifer continued to look at me.

"I'll tell you later," I said.

I smiled and remembered that six months earlier, Jennifer—in a moment of frustration—had demanded that I pray like a Christian. According to Jesus and Paul, that was exactly what I had learned to do. The Holy Spirit, who knows God's holy ways, comes to us and teaches us the ways of God. Sometimes this Spirit is known as the Holy Spirit, sometimes as Sophia, sometimes as Jesus himself. It had happened in ages past, and it happens today.

5

Messengers, Companions, Gate Keepers and Angels

I BEGAN TO TEST the prayer experience with trusted friends and family, which led me through a time of intense questionings about the source of the wisdom. Jennifer and I shared some of the prayer transcripts with Jennifer's brother, Nate, and his wife. We sat on their screened-in porch on a summer evening. Our kids were asleep; the breeze was cool and calm. We sipped tea and watched the summer evening darken while Jennifer and I shared our story. I read passages from a notebook that contained prayer transcriptions. They were attentive, respectful and curious. Afterward, I was in the kitchen with Nate, cleaning dishes.

"What do you think?" I asked. I scraped a half-eaten hotdog from one of the kids' plates into the garbage.

"Well, I think *something* happens." Nate wiped the counter, then rinsed the rag in the sink.

"Sometimes I wonder if it's just me," I said. "Sometimes I wonder if it's all in my subconscious, but it's so crafted and eloquent."

"Well," Nate said with a shrug, "you're an eloquent guy."

I knew exactly what he was getting at. I'm a writer. I love language. He was voicing a doubt I had considered since the beginning of the prayer journey. Perhaps it was all from me.

For over a year, I struggled and wrestled. Was it all just a part of my own mind? Did I go into some kind of self-induced hypnosis and speak from my own subconscious?

When I was in prayer, there was no doubt that I was in the presence of the Holy. There was a deep peace and a powerful presence of the sacred.

I'd felt the power of the Spirit flow into me and through me. The messages came from beyond. But as soon as I was out of prayer, the doubts came back. The Spirit seemed to understand my struggle, and the prayers would sometimes address the doubt:

Why do you question the source of your knowledge? Do you not think your experiences come from the Spirit? Do you not think your heart yearns for the Spirit and brings you knowledge? The Holy is within and without. I am the Holy. Indeed.

ASSURANCES LIKE THIS were comforting. However, I needed some confirmation of the gift outside of the prayer experience itself. I didn't think of myself as a particularly delusional person, but at times I had to wonder if I was the victim of some misunderstanding about the workings of the subconscious. Was I deceiving myself? Being trained as a scholar, I could not be reassured by the many books on channeling that existed in bookstores. In addition to seeking guidance in the Bible, I had to find scholars of religion and psychology who studied prophecy. In such sources, I discovered evidence that people have had similar sacred experiences for thousands and thousands of years, and that such experiences had indeed come under psychological study. However, despite this search for answers and confirmation, it was finally only through the prayer experience itself that I would find guidance. I learned I had to trust the Holy, and God would provide the assurance I needed in the form of wisdom received in prayer.

The Messenger often gave small explanations of the process of prophecy I experienced, then several weeks later, I would find confirmations of the Messenger's words in books on prophecy and the ancient writings of rabbis in the tradition of Jewish mysticism now grouped together under the term Kabbalah.

In one prayer lesson, the Messenger explained the process of prophetic awareness as a blending of my mind with the Spirit of God:

The wisdom that comes to you is the result of a merging. You take in the Holy. The Spirit of the Holy communes with your spirit. In the merging, how can you determine how much is from you and how much is from the Spirit? Where does the Holy begin and you end? Does the wisdom come from the Holy or from your mind? Both. Don't you see? It is both, for the wisdom is the product of a merging.

This view of a merging with the divine is consistently explained in works about prophecy. The way I have come to understand the process is that I provide my framework of understanding, my vocabulary and the limitations of my human perceptions, and the Messenger of the Holy works with these available tools to communicate wisdom that is, finally, beyond the tools themselves. Thus, my life, my body, my experience are both avenues and limitations for holy wisdom. Years later, I was told by the Messenger, "The host would do well to increase his vocabulary," and I realized that anything I learned could be used by the Messenger to expand the boundaries of the wisdom provided to me and through me.

This understanding of intermediary experience explains why ancient prophecy reflects the limitations of the worldview of the human culture in which it was presented. The Holy works with and through our limitations. Our minds do indeed influence the messages we receive in the same way that the paint and canvas influence the artist. We provide the material for the Spirit, and in the prophetic utterance, the message or composition transcends the vehicle. Despite and through our limitations, wisdom lives.

Thus, I came to accept the trance state an the oracular speech as a merging between my spirit and the Holy. In many ways, the mystery of the prophet or the oracle is reflective of the mystery of incarnation; our lives provide avenues and possibilities for the eternal (which is beyond our lives) to be experienced in the moment.

It was only later in my explorations of prophecy that I discovered a parallel explanation in Aryeh Kaplan's book, *Meditation and the Bible*. Kaplan translates the reflections of Rabi Mekhilta: "God borrows terms from his creatures to express His relationship with the world."

DESPITE ALL OF MY wanderings in libraries and searches of databases, I discovered that the best teacher about my prophetic experience would be the Holy Spirit. Below is a prayer in which my questions about the process of prophecy were answered. In addition, the different roles of Angels, Messengers and spiritual Companions were explained.

Messengers, Angels and Spiritual Companions
March 17, 2000

Jennifer began our prayer time by reading Isaiah 40. I felt the Spirit enter me while she read, and my breathing began to deepen. I also began to tremble in my hands. I wanted to pray aloud before I lost the ability to speak, so I said to Jennifer, "Better let me talk first. I can feel it coming." My prayer was concerning my confusion about my gift for prophecy, and as you will see, I didn't get much of a question asked before the Spirit took control of my voice and body. The Messenger then began to explain the process of merging between the human spirit and the Holy Spirit during prayer:

"Lord Jesus," I prayed, "I thank you for my gift, but sometimes I wonder what to do with it. Guide me and teach me. Let me be a vehicle for your grace—"

The Spirit entered me, and my breathing began to deepen. I shook and my neck muscles tensed, and immediately the Messenger began the lesson:

> *Shall you take in the Spirit? Shall you take in the Spirit and give animation and voice? Shall the animation and voice not speak the wisdom of the merging? The wisdom is indeed a merging, for it is only in the merging of Spirit and flesh that wisdom becomes living. And how shall wisdom live among you but as it lives through you and in you? Wisdom has no existence, has no purpose, has no life, when it is not incarnate, when it is not existing within the combining of the Spirit and the flesh, for when the Spirit and the flesh come together, wisdom is revealed. Wisdom is eternal, but the eternal receives application only in the particular. This is why wisdom is always practical, for it is seen and experienced, needed, grasped in the particular. And yet the wisdom is general and can be applied to so many particular situations. Shall you not take in the breath of the Spirit and speak the wisdom born of the merging, the wisdom applicable to the specific and yet invitational of the universal?*
>
> *Breathe deeply of the Spirit of God. Take in and merge, and in merging you shall come out of self and into the Spirit.*

In this section of the prayer, I was struck with the description of breathing in the Spirit of God in order to allow the wisdom of God to be made flesh. Almost two years later, I discovered Aryeh Kaplan's translation of Rabbi Chaim Vital's book called *The Gate of the Holy Spirit.* In this book, Vital describes the way the voice of God's messenger must become incarnate in the physical voice of the prophet:

> The mystery of *Ruach HaKodesh* [the Gate of the Holy Spirit] is this: it is a voice sent from on high to speak to a prophet or to one worthy of

Ruach HaKodesh. But such a voice is purely spiritual, and such a voice cannot enter the prophet's ear until it clothes itself in a physical voice. This physical voice in which it clothes itself is the voice of the prophet himself, when he is involved in prayer or Torah study. This voice clothes itself in his voice and is attached to it. It then enters the prophet's ear so that he can hear it. Without the physical voice of the individual himself, this could not possibly take place.

The revelation that God's Wisdom must become incarnate in our lives and voices struck me deeply. In Vital's description of prophecy, the voice sent from on high is literally incarnated into the prophet's own voice.

As the prayer continued, the Messenger who brought the wisdom of God into the language of flesh through my voice described him/herself:

I am a Spirit of the Holy, and yet I am only a servant of the Holy. I represent the Holy, and yet I am humbled to be only a minuscule part of the Holy. I am an emissary of the Holy, and yet I point only to that which is beyond me and contains me. I am an avenue to the Holy, and thus I am nothing, nothing but a straw. And when you draw upon the straw, shall you not take in the Spirit? So, I am always present, ready to place myself on your lips so you may take in the Spirit of the Holy and hear the wisdom revealed. I am on your lips now. I am in your throat now. And while I am here on your lips, in your throat, shall I not be an avenue for other voices from the Holy? For wisdom comes in many forms, comes through many voices. And yet it is all connected to the infinite Wisdom of the Holy. Whom shall you invite with your questions, whom shall you invite with your yearnings, whom shall you invite as you open your hearts? Whom but the Spirit? The Spirit is singular, and yet is multiple, infinite. Invite the Spirit of God and receive the Holy presence. Invite Jesus and become comforted; invite God and be overwhelmed; invite the Holy Spirit and be swept away.

I move, I sweep, I come. My fulfillment is in my task as a mouthpiece of the Holy. Thus, I am a vessel, and in being such, I am complete.

This experience shall be your existence, finally. This experience is existence, of being part of the Holy. That is the only existence that endures. It shall be your existence. It shall be your sustenance. It shall be the only avenue of fulfillment.

Here I found a framework to understand the Holy Whole (Heaven). The Messenger of the Holy abides within the Holy Whole, and the Messenger comes to me when I open my spiritual doorway. This experience of merging with the Spirit is a glimpse of what it will be to be accepted into the Holy Whole after this life. The description the Messenger of the Holy provided about itself was also strikingly similar to the description of the Spirit of Wisdom known as Sophia in The Wisdom of Solomon:

> There is in her a spirit that is intelligent, holy, unique, manifold, subtle, mobile, clear, unpolluted, distinct, invulnerable, loving the good, keen, irresistible, beneficent, humane, steadfast, sure, free from anxiety, all-powerful, overseeing all, penetrating through all spirits that are intelligent, pure, and altogether subtle. For wisdom is more mobile than any motion; because of her pureness she pervades and penetrates all things. (Wisdom of Solomon 8:1–24)

The humility of my spiritual guide is an example to me of how to live as a person with prophetic gifts. Like my guide, I am only a miniscule part of the Holy's purpose. To acknowledge this small role that I play and allow the Holy to work through me is a beautiful and humbling way to live.

In the next portion of the prayer, Jennifer began to ask questions of the Messenger and received explanations of the variety of religious experiences:

"I am overwhelmed by all of this. I continually am. And I wonder, do others have these deep experiences of wisdom? Is this normative in the world that we live in? Because we seem to know so few with whom we can share this."

The Holy speaks to the people. The Holy speaks through the people. To, and through. Surround yourselves, my children, with people open to God, and you shall know that God speaks to the people, and God speaks through the people. You have been in the presence of people, have you not, who know the voice of God?

"Yes."

Now the voice of God... how shall the voice of God be heard when the voice of God has no sound? Do you see? The voice of God does not travel with the vibrations of sound, the voice of God travels with the vibration of creation, the vibration of love, the vibration of power, the vibration of holy energy. How shall this voice be translated and understood? How shall the voice of God, the voice of power, love and creation, be transformed into something understood by the people of God? Some will sleep deeply and see in images. Some will know in their hearts; some will hear in their ear; some will feel in the depths of their bones; some will hear not in the ear but in the mind, a voice in the mind that they come to know as the voice of the Holy. Do you know this voice? You know this voice, do you not, my daughter? Have you heard this voice somewhere in your mind? Somewhere deep. Does it not resonate in your heart, this voice? So, when you hear the words, you feel them. Do you know this experience?

"Yes."

And some—some will speak the words of God. Some are inspired, and there are different levels of inspiration. Sometimes the speech is only partially inspired. Sometimes the speech comes when presenting before the people, when suddenly the person begins speaking things so deeply that they flow from somewhere holy. This type of speech is inhibited by the conscious mind, and yet it is of God, but the translation is often complicated by the distractions of desires, of conflicts, of human needs. And some will speak as Michael speaks. The transmission is still not entirely pure, for the energy must become language, and language indeed has its inadequacies.

THE ABOVE EXCERPT clearly explains that the Holy finds a way to speak to people, given their physical and spiritual constitution. The Spirit of God is able to discern our spiritual and physical construction and discover a means to communicate and inspire our lives. Some call this union with their spiritual guide meditation, or prayer, or "getting in the flow." Some dream with spiritual guidance; others receive words or images. Finally, there are those who receive the voice of the Holy through a prophetic/oracular state of awareness as I do. What is important is that we acknowledge that the Holy speaks to us, and we, as members of faith communities, should combine our perceptions of the Holy with each other to come to a fuller understanding of the Holy's vast wisdom.

Next, the Messenger continued by explaining prophetic awareness:

But where is Michael now? Where is he now? Is he in the way? Are his desires and needs, are his aspirations inhibiting now? Where is he now? He hears this message, does he not? He is aware of his feet on the floor, crossed at the ankles; he is aware of his fingers; he is aware of his tongue in his mouth. Where is he? He is here. However, the Spirit has entered him, has taken his mind, his body as a vehicle for what you hear.

This experience has been known by others, shall be known by others. This experience has brought the Word of God to the people. This experience has given birth to new religions. This experience has opened the door for wisdom and power. So widely has it opened the door that many shall come through it. What makes this experience possible? Two things. First, a willingness to be a host, a willingness to open. Second, a certain constitution, a certain development of soul.

The Messenger was telling me that the spiritual message was coming in a way that avoided my conscious mind. The Messenger described my dual consciousness of being able to feel my feet and being able to hear the message, but being controlled by the Spirit. The Messenger also acknowledged that this prophetic gift had been experienced by many people of many faiths.

In the next section of the prayer, the Messenger explained its role as a "guardian" of my spiritual doorway and made a distinction between a spiritual guardian and a spiritual companion:

What I see when Michael goes into prayer is an opening of light. And I rush to it. I stay close to protect that opening, for others shall rush to it, also. In a sense I am a guardian. Why do I stay close? It is my purpose. Your lifetime is so short where I am. I do not mind waiting for this period.

"So you are Michael's guardian? And yet it is you that I hear?"

A part of me you hear, and it is not a part of me at all. It is a part of the

Holy that you hear.

"Do I, too, have a guardian?" Jennifer asked.

A guardian? You? I would not call her a guardian. I would call her a companion. A guardian is one who stands by to protect an opening of God. A companion is one who guides, stays near, and learns as you learn. A guardian is one who protects and also opens. I am, indeed, only a conduit sometimes. Sometimes I decide what to let through and sometimes the decision is made beyond me, for it comes rushing in, and when I know it is of the Holy, I say, "Come, come, come, come."

"So, is it a difference in our composition, Michael's and mine, that he needs a guardian and I need a companion?"

Needs cry out to the Holy. Have you not sensed this?

And the Holy responds. You will notice changes in Michael's soul. He shall become calmer. He shall become more accepting, for he shall come closer to his own spiritual essence. It is an inevitable result of the experience of merging with the Holy, for the Holy touches the spiritual essence. Sometimes this spiritual essence is known as the higher self. But this is a mistaken term, for the higher self is a no-self, a non-self. It is an essence of spirit beyond and yet within the self.

Through the Holy you experience companions, guardians and messengers, but the distinctions here are not important, for we can be all at the same moment. There are also the Ancient Ones, who are highly developed souls, nearly prepared to merge completely into the Holy Whole. The Angels are similar to the Ancient Ones, but Angels do not progress into full abandon into the Holy. Angels are created for specific tasks, and they remain loyal to these tasks for eternity. The Angels serve the people of God as protectors, messengers, and, when necessary, warriors. They do not stay in one place among the living for long. Thus, they are not teachers but offer assistance in times of great need.

I have on occasion let other voices speak to Michael.

"I'm not sure I fully understand what you mean when you say you have let in other voices."

There are different elements of the Spirit with different gifts.

"Have all of the voices you have let in been a part of the Spirit?"

Certainly of the Spirit. I have not always been Michael's guardian. There have been guardians before me, and there were no guardians at one point. For the need came and the guardians came to fulfill the needs. And there is something else present here. I may be the guardian, but I am not the companion, the companion who came and grew impatient, impatient finally with the dull resistance. It was the companion who swept in. The companion comes to him only in body. The companion is so intimately a part of his spiritual essence that it speaks not through language. It was the companion who knew this opening was possible; it was the companion who brought Michael to an awareness of this opening. It was the companion who brought him to his knees only to pick him up again. It is the companion who stays. It is the companion that rushes in, to comfort, to guide.

Even as the Messenger spoke these words, I knew the Messenger was describing the way I had experienced the onset of my prophetic gift. I had felt that the spirit who moved my body and made my hands dance was different from the spirit who spoke through me. In addition, I had felt various presences enter me during the two years I had prayed in the prophetic, so the explanation of several guardians rang true.

The Messenger then proceeded to discuss the presence of Jesus in the midst of the heavenly intercessors:

Now, you may wonder about the presence of Jesus. The presence of Jesus does not at all need or require the opening the companion brought to Michael's awareness. The presence of Jesus, the presence of the Comforter, the presence of the great Counselor, comes on its own accord. Jesus can utilize this opening, but Jesus does not need to rely on the presence of companions and messengers to be fully present and fully known and fully realized. The presence of Jesus, the presence of the Holy Lamb of God, may come unannounced, may come uninvited, but always comes, always is present when asked to be present. For you see, I am a part of this Spirit, but the presence of Jesus is a greater unity within the Holy Whole, which is in turn the greatest unity of all.

"We are taught as children that Jesus is with us always," Jennifer said.

Certainly, the Spirit of God is with you always.

"And yet there are times we specifically invoke that presence?"

Yes.

"It seems to me as though the Spirit of God is hovering around waiting to be asked. Is that a fair understanding?"

Yes. Yes, the Spirit of God is always present. Different parts of the Holy are gathered and become fully realized as presences at different times. We gather and become helpful presences, and we also disseminate into the Source. It is difficult to explain, for you are so bound by your identity and apparent physical isolation.

There is spiritual energy upon which we travel. But this spiritual energy can also be used by elements not a part of the Holy. The spiritual energy is always present: the Holy is always present.

"And so our intercessions travel on this energy."

Yes, in some ways the intercessions do. But the intercessions touch the Holy, and the Holy responds by gathering.

On several occasions, the Messenger had explained that the Holy Spirit is an energy on which spiritual messengers travel. But what this lesson explained was that the way we pray affects the type of spiritual help we receive. Prayer is indeed interactive, and the reciprocity of our conversation with the Holy was explained in the next excerpt of the prayer. Our acknowledgment and praise of the Holy provides the responsiveness that the Holy seeks for entrance into our lives:

Praise and thanksgiving. Praise and thanksgiving are a response and an invocation: A response to the Holy and an invitation to the Holy, both. It is not as if the Holy waits for praise before it rewards it. That is not the way it functions. But the acts of praise and thanksgiving create a situation that invites the Spirit, so it is a reaction, but it is also an invitation. So, placing your needs and desires within praise and thanksgiving creates a situation in which those needs and desires are fully present to the Holy. Do you see?

It is not that you are being rewarded for being thankful, but the thankfulness allows, creates, the possibility of response. Response begets response. It is a conversation, do you see? Response begets response. When one party is not responding a conversation ends.

Response begets response;
life begets life;
love invites love.
Rejoicing produces rejoicing;
yearning brings comfort;
lamentation demands presence.
Pain invites consolation;
praise yields action.

Do you see? It is a conversation. To be silent is to stop the conversation. For while I was silent, my soul was dark. While my lips were sealed, I knew no life. So confession, see, confession invites presence, for it opens the heart, it opens the space of pain and guilt. It invites cleansing.

The spirit of the Holy works through influence. You can become a holy influence. You must be willing, open, to the influence of God, the spiritual presence of God's messengers and companions. The Spirit of God sees the momentary opening and rushes in. You are called as the children of God to behave as the Spirit of God behaves.

Shall you not open to the breath of God, shall you not take in the Spirit of the Holy?

STEP BY STEP, I had been led by the Holy to fully accept the trance and oraclular experience that had come upon me. The Spirit was teaching me about the process of prophecy and the oracle state in the midst of my of searching in libraries. This combination confirmed that a Spirit of God, or messenger, comes to me, merges with my spirit, takes my breath and speaks holy wisdom with my voice.

In addition to this merging with the Mesenger of the Holy, the wisdom lesson provided a glimpse of the spiritual realm, called the Holy Whole, as active and dynamic with many forms of spiritual beings. There are messengers, who serve as teachers or conduits for holy knowledge. There are also companions, who stay close to us, guiding us with nudges and who learn as we learn. In future wisdom lessons, I would discover that spirits in the Holy Whole are on a journey to eventually merge completely with the Holy Whole. In the above prayer, the spirits close the level of comoplete self release were described as "the Ancient Ones." Finally, there are angels, who are also ancient but do not progress in spiritual development. They are created for specific purposes, those of messengers, protectors, and warriors.

In the coming years, Jennifer and I would rely heavily on the resources of the diverse but unified Holy Whole. The Messenger of the Holy, our spiritual companions, and the presence of Christ would all become strengths in our long journey to have a second child.

6

Expectations

WE CALLED THEM "coffee drives." When Jen and I were completely overwhelmed with parenthood, when Sam was tired and restless, when we wanted to either snap or collapse, one of us would say, "I think it's time for a coffee drive."

We would pack Sam up into his car seat, get some decaf, put some music on, and drive, and drive, and drive.

On one of these drives, with a Raffi CD playing "Bananaphone" and Sam jabbering in the back seat, I reached out my hand to Jennifer, sitting in the passenger seat. We were in the suburbs of Canton, just getting to the hills and pastureland west of the subdivisions.

"Cow," Sam said. "Mommy, cow."

We all looked at the cow, it's head stretched over a fence beside the road, its jaw working a slanted chew.

"You know," I said to Jennifer. "While we're in this phase of life, we might as well have a second."

Jennifer smiled and squeezed my hand. We'd talked about it. It seemed right.

We prayed about having another child, and received the message that we would be blessed.

Three weeks later, Jennifer took a pregnancy test with a positive result. We would never have such an effortless conception again.

For this pregnancy, the Celtic cross became significant to me. I spent the better part of Jennifer's pregnancy carving and casting Celtic crosses for Christmas presents. For me the ancient, braided rendering of the pain and wisdom of the cross symbolizes the journey of the Christian, and the journey of our second son.

Early in Jennifer's pregnancy, we took a family trip to the Isle of Mann, an island in the Irish Sea under British protection. Jennifer had been asked to come to three British Methodist churches to conduct workshops on contemporary worship. The Isle of Mann is a miniature Ireland with its rolling hills, craggy shorelines, and ancient castles. The Manx people, however, see themselves as very different from the Irish and the English. They are proud of their own history and their own language.

On the island, the ancient stone carvings of Celtic crosses pulled at my spirit. Braided crosses, carved in stone, with the moss and erosion of ages on them were an ancient weaving of the old Celtic ways and the new Christian ways, an ornamented celebration of the wisdom of the cross.

When we got home, I began to make twelve-inch replicas of "the cross at Kirk Michael." I carved a wax model, then I made a rubber mold, then I planned to pour plaster into the mold and make casts for gifts, painted, of course, to have the weatherworn gray of the original.

I was on the back porch of the parsonage, putting the first layer of latex on the wax carving.

Jennifer drove into the garage, coming home from a check-up with her doctor. I brushed the white film onto the wax, almost done with the first coat.

She came onto the back porch and dropped her purse beside her. "Something is wrong with the baby," she said.

I stopped brushing and looked up. Tears filled Jennifer's eyes.

"I'm too big," she said. "I have too much fluid." She put her hands on her abdomen and glanced down, then back at me. "They want me to go to the hospital tomorrow for tests."

We went into the house and sat together for a long time. It was October 21, 1999, just over one year since my prayer gift had come upon me. Leaves were beginning to change color. In the living room, a swing for the baby was in the corner, and Sam had placed a teddy bear in it to practice for his baby sister or brother. We had decided not to be informed of the gender of this baby; we wanted to be surprised. Little did we know what surprises and lessons this baby would bring.

At the hospital the next day, an ultrasound revealed the baby's esophagus was blunted and not connected to the stomach, a condition known as esophageal atresia. It was very correctible after birth. Jennifer had too much amniotic fluid because the baby could not swallow and process it. The doctor wanted to do an amniocentesis, to take a sample of the amniotic fluid and test the chromosomes of the baby. We agreed to the test. There was a one percent chance that the test would put Jennifer into pre-term labor, and that was exactly what happened.

It was the first of many times we would be on the minority of the percentages.

That evening, Jennifer was in a room on the labor and delivery wing with an IV of hormone drugs dripping into her to stop the contractions. She lay on her side with a monitor strapped to her abdomen. On a machine by the bed, one line tracked her contractions, another the heartbeat of the baby. With a knob, I could turn up the sound and hear the chugging of the baby's heart, which I did occasionally just to hear the rush and sweep of life. The baby was at 28 weeks gestation. If the baby were born, the chances of survival were slight; the chances of birth defects high. It was a restless night.

By the next day, Jennifer was stabilized. She had held off labor. I sat by the bed, and we prayed and talked. She wore a hospital gown; she was exhausted from a painful and nauseous night of hormone therapy. "Hand me my Bible," she said.

She raised herself onto her elbow and flipped through the pages of the Bible. Her left arm was hindered by the IV. "I was supposed to preach Sunday," she said. "And this is the passage I was working on."

She read Joshua 3:7–17. It is the story of Joshua leading the people of Israel across the Jordan River. It is the second time that the Lord God separates water for the Israelites to cross. Joshua is told by God that when the priests carrying the Ark of the Covenant reach the water, God's wonders will be shown. The people follow the priests into the water, not knowing what will happen. Suddenly, the flow of water is stopped, and the people cross the Jordan.

"I was going to preach on the waters," she said. "And look at me," she said. She chuckled and put a hand on her belly. "I was going to preach about the way we have to step into the waters in faith." She looked down at the rise of her belly and rubbed her hand over it. "If it's a boy," she said, "let's name him Jordan."

I thought for a moment. We had already decided upon the name Sophia for a girl. Jordan was a solid name for a boy. Wisdom or water; either way, the baby would have a strong name. "Jordan," I said. I nodded.

"We have to trust that God will guide us through this one," Jennifer said.

I crossed my arms and sat back in my chair. The weight and anxiety of the night had drained my spirit. "I trust God," I said. "I just don't trust biology." I glanced at the green monitor screen that showed Jennifer's contractions, which had gone from peaks and valleys to a straight line, and Jordan's heartbeat with its steady rise and fall. "Biology is fickle," I said. "Who knows when some cell didn't split right, and now look at us."

Jennifer raised her head and patted the rise that was our baby. "All we can do is step into the waters," she said.

THE DOCTOR WHO TOOK charge of the case was a devout Shikh and a wonderful man named Prab Gill. His spiritual calm pervaded everything he did. He wore scrubs, a doctor's robe, and a turban. We trusted him completely, and he was very respectful of our prayer life. We could feel that he was deeply connected to the Spirit of God.

Jennifer was sent home and put on bed rest, and she took a pill every four hours to help keep her out of pre-term labor. Week 36—when the baby would be considered full-term—seemed a long way off.

This time in our lives was spent in waiting and praying. We told our families to pray for Sophia/Jordan: Sophia, if it was a girl, and Jordan, if it was a boy.

When the results of the amnio were in, we went back to the hospital. We were still determined not to know the sex, and Dr. Gill had assured us that he never discloses the sex of a baby. For him, it was standard procedure not to mention the sex unless the couple asks.

Dr. Gill swept into the ultrasound room, his white medical gown flowing behind him. "The chromosomes are normal," he said with a smile, "and it's a boy."

Jennifer said in a wry voice, "It's a boy."

"Oh. You didn't want to know," Dr. Gill said. He put his hand over his mouth. "Why did I say that? I never tell when the family doesn't want to know." He was flustered. He glanced down at the clipboard he held. He set the clipboard down, then picked it up again.

"Don't worry," Jennifer said. "Now we know whom to pray for."

It ended up being a wonderful blessing. Now we could pray for Jordan, our son named for the water.

During the next weeks, the Spirit of God was thick around us, and we felt comforted by that presence. However, we had anxieties about the bed rest, the possibility of premature labor, and the surgery Jordan would require to repair his esophagus. We prayed daily. After Sam was asleep in the evening, we would go to God for up to an hour. We prayed for our church, which was now operating with an associate pastor on medical leave; we prayed for our family, and also for the pregnancy. In the midst of longer prayers, we received these excerpts of wisdom about the child Jennifer carried:

The body is a vessel; that should have more meaning to you now than previously. The body is a vessel for Spirit; it provides physicality, a temporal experience.

This child, like all others, will be placed in a physical situation; it is the journey of all to seek the spiritual among the physical. When you give birth, a new journey begins, unique from all others. Be not afraid. All will become clear.

Samuel is raised in the Spirit. The child that is coming will be born in the Spirit. Both have blessings.

In this lifetime, you must experience the Holy to know God. The knowledge of the Holy is the experience of God, and the Wisdom of God comes through experience. Therefore, do not fear new experience, for it will bring you into more full relationship with the Spirit of God. This child that is coming will help you experience God.

Do not fear transformation. Be expectant that your boy may become a prayer.

The lines that stuck in my memory from these prayers were these: Samuel is being raised in the Spirit; this child will be born in the Spirit. I pondered what this could mean. It seemed a wonderful blessing was coming. The other line that caused me to reflect referred to Jordan as a prayer. Because prayer had become so central to our lives, I thought this son of ours would certainly live a prayerful life.

After eight weeks of waiting and praying, Jennifer was finally in week 36. The baby was considered full term. Dr. Gill took Jennifer off the medication to stop labor, and we waited for nature to take its course.

It was December 17, 1999, the heart of Advent, and we thought we might just have a Christmas baby.

On December 19, 1999, we went into prayer for wisdom and guidance. Our anxieties at this point were centered on the surgery that Jordan would undergo, soon after birth. Jennifer was also concerned because Jordan was to be rushed to Akron Children's Hospital for his surgery, while Jennifer would remain in the hospital in Canton. I planned to stay with Jordan, and Jennifer would join us in Akron as soon as possible.

With these concerns heavy on our hearts, we began our prayer session. I went quickly into prophetic awareness, and Jennifer spoke in tongues, then the lesson began. At the time, we did not understand meanings that seem so obvious to us now. I now understand this prayer to be a preparation for the stillbirth of Jordan:

The Holy Burden
December 19, 1999

What is wholeness? What is completeness? What is wholeness but an awareness of the Holy and your place in the Holy Whole? Time, space mean nothing and mean everything to the Holy Whole. They converge in the Holy Whole. Present, future, past all converge into the Holy Whole, for time is a globe for the Holy. The placement of your child in the Holy Whole is assured. There is only the Holy Whole, where all things converge.

Step into an awareness beyond your awareness. You shall find the Holy Whole. Your place in it is now. Your place in it was then. Your place in it shall be. So, lay your anxieties aside for all becomes embraced in the Holy.

What shall we say about the future? What shall we say about the child? What shall we say about the church? What shall we say about your work? What shall we say? What, but that all is absorbed in the Holy. That is saying nothing and yet it is saying everything.

Fear not. Fear not. The child has a strong spirit.

Jennifer prayed, "Lord God, I ask that Jordan will have strength for his surgery, that he and I will have the strength to endure what is to come. I'm afraid, Jesus, of the time we will not be together."

The separation will slice your heart, but the separation is only physical. The separation shall bring new connections. Do not fear the separation, my child, for the separation is merely a transition. Do not fear the separation, for you shall be connected eternally, as you always have been. Time, space, motion, what are these things to the Holy but vehicles and opportunities for movement? You know the fears of separation; you know the fears. These fears are great. But as terrifying as they are, you will face them. You will cross over; you will know the separation to be a blessing. The pain and fear will be present. Reach deep, reach wide, for the Holy presence will lead you to a place of peace.

There are more prayers in your heart. Raise them.

"I have prayers for my physical strength in these next days," Jennifer prayed. I know this on a physical realm, God, but my back hurts so much. Please heal me. I want to be able to move into labor with full strength. Thank you for Dr. Gill and his work."

It has been a holy burden. And what is the holy burden that brings us pain and yet fulfillment? What is the holy burden that leads us into strife and yet provides deliverance? What is the holy burden that weighs us down only to lift us up? What is the holy burden that shoots us through the heart only to mend it? What is the holy burden that confuses us only to bring enlightenment? This, my child, has been a holy burden. It has been a holy burden. You will know it to be so.

"And so I call upon your strength to help me walk through the burden. To help me carry the burden. To help me walk through the pain, to help me bear the burden. Forgive me when my eyes are not open to your help. Thank you for people who show such wonderful gestures of love and concern. I thank you for using this situation for letting love flow from so many people, for hearts to open in compassion. We praise you, God. Nothing, not even the shadow of darkness, will keep us from you."

What then is the dark that must be crossed if it is not a part of the Holy Whole? Is there darkness?

"My fears seem dark."

Yes, you shall confront fears. Many will come.

Night is as bright as day to the Holy. To the Holy Whole, what is a moment of darkness in the midst of so much light? In the darkness you shall see the light, and the darkness shall become light. For there is no darkness that the light does not vanquish. Turn from the darkness and you shall see, the light is there. Even when you perceive only darkness, the light is there.

"With human eyes, we see only in part. In your eyes all things are possible. Bring me peace and comfort. Thank you, God, for your presence. We pray that you will continue to move in our circumstances, not for our glory, but for yours. May our circumstances be a testimony to your goodness. May Jordan Paul be a gift."

As with all of our prayers, this one came with great comfort and peace. As we prayed, we did not hear the obvious warnings about the fears and pain we would face. Weeks after Jordan's delivery, I transcribed the prayer and heard that God was preparing us for a long, dark journey of separation, and that God would be with us through a holy burden of loss. The darkness of waiting for the delivery, the terrifying fear we would face, and the holy burden that would shoot us through the heart did not register as dangers as we heard the prayer lesson. At the time, we did not hear these warnings. We assumed the separation the Messenger spoke of was the time that Jordan would be rushed to the children's hospital.

As we focused on the coming delivery and surgery, I began casting the Celtic crosses. Jennifer could easily sit and paint without violating the doctor's order to keep off her feet, and Sam was good at splashing and smearing the first coat of gray. I set the crosses on newspaper to dry, all across the floor of our living room and dining room. We became a cross factory, and we marveled at the beauty of the plaster casts. The project turned out rather nicely. And after an expensive trip to the Isle of Mann and with a new baby coming, saving a little money on homemade Christmas gifts made sense. I felt both thrifty and artistic.

On the night of December 22, 1999, Jennifer lay in bed with her hand on her abdomen. "Something's not right," she said.

I sat on the edge of the mattress and put my hand on her belly.

"I haven't felt him all day," she said.

"Are you sure?" I asked. I concentrated on my hand. Jennifer's abdomen was tight and hard. I felt something gurgling. "Isn't that Jordan?"

"I don't know," Jennifer said. "I'm rock hard," she said.

Sam was asleep and the wind whistled outside our window. "Do you want to go to the hospital?"

"No," Jennifer said. "We have an appointment in the morning. Maybe labor is starting," she said. "Maybe Jordan is hunkered down for delivery."

A trip to the hospital in the middle of the night did seem complicated with Sam sleeping. Besides, on the previous day at a visit with Dr. Gill, Jordan marked high scores in all the fetal events: breathing, moving, heart rhythm. Because of the large amount of fluid, we could see him in great detail. We saw his eyelids; we saw his fingernails. He had plenty of room to move, and Dr. Gill made jokes about the comfortable space his mother had provided.

Dr. Gill had drained two litres of fluid from Jennifer's amniotic sack on two separate occasions during the eight weeks. On the second "therapeutic amnio," I kept my eyes on the needle that was placed into Jennifer's belly and watched the fluid flow through a tube and into a bottle. Suddenly, the needle twitched and moved. I glanced at the ultrasound screen, and we all watched as Jordan knocked against the needle with his hand, then we watched as he grabbed it.

Dr. Gill laughed. "Sometimes that happens," he said. "The baby has good reflexes."

With what turned out to be three bouts of pre-term labor, the two amnio drainings, the eight weeks of bed rest, we felt we'd earned the positive checkup on December 21. And the hard abdomen and the lack of movement on the night of December 22 had to mean labor was beginning. Didn't it?

Jennifer and I had a restless night. Jennifer dreamt she was holding Jordan on the beach, but the waves crashed over them, and it was all she could do to hold onto Jordan. I had a dream in which Jordan was in an incubator in the nurse's station at the hospital. Everyone was rushing around, and no one was paying attention to him. I watched him, and the incubator was filled with water. Only a small corner presented air for him to breath. But he kept his mouth up to this corner, and in my dream I thought to myself,

"He knows how to take care of himself. Look at that."

We went to the ultrasound room on December 22, and the technician started the process. Jennifer said she hadn't felt the baby move in a while.

"How long?" asked the technician. She was a pleasant woman whom we had gotten to know in the process. In fact, she was the ultrasound technician on the day that we learned of Jordan's esophageal atresia. A lot of the nurses and specialists had gotten to know us during the eight weeks.

"Since yesterday," Jennifer said. "I thought maybe labor was starting."

"We'll take a look," the technician said in a calm voice. She gestured toward the examination table.

Jennifer and I were both afraid, but we didn't admit it to each other.

The technician started the scan, and I watched the screen for the sights I'd gotten used to. First the heart to get oriented, then the spine, or limbs, or head. It was like watching a body unfold.

But just after she got started, the technician said, "I need to get Dr. Gill. He'll want to do something." And she rushed out of the room.

We waited in the dark room. Jennifer was on the examination table, and I was standing beside her. I looked at the clock on the computer screen. It was 9:21. The room was warm and dark. A desk lamp on the counter was the only light.

I wasn't sure what the technician had seen, but I suspected what she did not see. "I don't think she saw the heartbeat," I said.

Jennifer bolted up on her elbows. "Are you sure?" Her eyes were wide with fright.

"I'm not sure," I said.

She began to cry and settled onto the table. "Why did you tell me that?"

I kept quiet. I was terrified. I didn't want it to be true, but I'd seen Jordan so many times, I knew what to look for. I knew what the technician had not seen.

We waited in silence. The fans on the ultrasound machine whirred. The desk lamp buzzed.

"How long have we been waiting?" Jennifer asked.

The clock read 9:33.

"Twelve minutes," I said.

"Go see what's taking so long," Jennifer said.

I went into the hallway and saw Dr. Gill coming toward the room. He was in his white gown and his white turban. But his eyes looked terribly concerned.

He came into the room and did an ultrasound scan.

"Jennifer," he said. "I'm afraid the baby's heart stopped beating."

Jennifer began weeping immediately.

I remember the smallest things, none of them important. There was a gray glow to the ultrasound screen. Dr. Gill had a string of hair coming down from his turban. Jennifer balled tissues up and threw them onto the floor. Her belly shook with her sobbing. The technician wore white running shoes with a blue stripe. Jennifer shook so hard I could feel it in the railing on the examination bed. The railing was silver and cold.

Dr. Gill was flustered. His eyes filled with tears. "I know you are a pastor," he said to Jennifer. "Would you like for me to pray with you?"

Jennifer said yes.

"Oh, Allah," Dr. Gill prayed, "I am so thankful for this little boy, and for all of the times I saw his beautiful face on the ultrasound. We entrust him to you, knowing that he is beyond pain. We know you waste nothing and that his spirit is safe with you."

I don't remember the rest of the prayer, but to this day, I am grateful to Dr. Gill for invoking the presence of God in the midst of our devastation. He also assured us that we did nothing wrong. That if Jordan had died so quickly since his last checkup, it must have been an acute problem. "Even if it had happened while I was watching, there would have been nothing I could have done," he said. "His body must be missing something we couldn't detect."

We had some decisions to make about when Jordan's body would be delivered. Jennifer moved to a wheelchair. Dr. Gill wheeled her to the hospital chapel, and I followed. I felt as if I'd been shot in the belly by a cannon, and all of my organs had been blown out. I felt numb and empty, and my mind followed only the most practical concerns. We must get to the chapel. We must decide what to do. We must walk down this hallway and turn this corner and sit and decide what to do. Not what, but when. We must decide when to induce labor. We must sit and decide when to get Jordan out. Down this hallway and into the chapel.

On the night *of* December 23, Jennifer was once again in a room on the labor and delivery floor, lying in a bed with an IV in her arm. But this time, there was no heart monitor for the baby. The monitor that usually read both the contractions of the mother and the heartbeat of the baby was set only to read the contractions. The room seemed too quiet. We had grown used to the heart monitor on our many visits. I had often enjoyed hearing Jordan's heart pumping. But now, in this quiet room, I hated the monitor machine. Instead of two lines on the readout (one for the contractions and one for the baby heartbeat), there was only one line.

Jennifer said to me, "My heart is already empty. Now I just have to wait for my body to be empty."

The wait was long. Labor would not begin until the next day, December 24.

DURING THE LONG NIGHT, I thought about our prayers and was once again struck by the line, "Samuel is raised in the spirit; this child will be born in the spirit." It was painfully true.

The next day, I stood next to Jennifer. When her parents came, I told them about some of the wisdom we received about Jordan. Dr. Hami came into the room while I talked. I told them about the message that Jordan would be born in the spirit.

Dr. Gill looked at me with his soft eyes. Jennifer's parents' eyes were red from crying.

"Jordan is born in the Spirit," I said. "He is born into the Spirit before he is born to us. His spirit has already been delivered." I looked down at Jennifer. "That's what God was preparing us for."

Dr. Gill said under his breath, "Praise to Allah." Jennifer's parents expressed amazement and looked at their daughter with sad eyes.

JORDAN WAS DELIVERED at 11:30 A.M. on December 24, 1999. They call it a stillbirth, and there is no better way to describe it. The stillness was oppressive. I could not help but compare Jordan's delivery to Samuel's birth. For Jordan, there was no rush and bustle as the birth approached. No machines and staff were ushered into the room in case of an emergency. There was no expectancy in the air. There was stillness.

I stood by Jennifer and helped as best I could. I held her legs while she pushed. I encouraged her. Jennifer's emotional strength was tremendous. She sweated through the labor with courage and determination.

Jordan was breach, but he was small and, of course, there was no reason to fear that he would be injured in the birth canal. Dr. Gill taught an intern how to deliver a breach baby. He calmly instructed when to turn the baby and why.

I watched as Jordan came free of Jennifer. I saw his open mouth, and as Dr. Gill raised him up, I saw a throbbing in his head. It was the pulsing of blood. For a moment, I thought it was all a mistake, that he was indeed alive. Then I realized it was Jennifer's heartbeat. Her heart was still trying to pump blood into Jordan through the umbilical cord. Dr. Gill clamped the cord and cut it, and the pulsing in Jordan's head ended. Then Dr. Gill took Jordan into a corner of the room to clean him.

Jennifer cried, and I fell to the floor with weeping. I could not breathe, I wept so hard. I moaned with grief, holding onto the silver rail of Jennifer's bed to keep from falling face down onto the floor.

I gathered my strength and stood again next to Jennifer. Dr. Gill brought Jordan to Jennifer.

"He's beautiful," Dr. Gill said. He held Jordan, wrapped in a receiving blanket, and placed him in Jennifer's arms.

Beautiful? I thought. My first look at Jordan revolted me; my stomach dropped. He was dark and limp. His head fell back and his mouth gaped. Jennifer had to work at making him appear comfortable. She couched his head in her arms, so that he looked like he was sleeping. Then I saw how much he resembled his brother, and I began to see him as our son. He had Sam's lips and nose. He was perfectly formed and looked ready to be born. He had plenty of hair, and besides the darkened tone, he looked like any other five-pound baby.

Jennifer handed him to me. I shifted him in my arms so that he would look as natural as possible. I straightened his jaw. I rocked him and stroked his little hands. I kissed his head. I gave him back to Jennifer and wept.

OUR FAMILY CAME into the room. Jennifer's parents looked at their daughter, holding Jordan. "Is this the Madonna, or is this the Pieta?" Gary said. He broke down and cried.

The irony of the date did not escape anyone. To have Jordan stillborn on Christmas Eve was either a cosmic insult or a sign of hope. I clung to the latter. "And a child will lead them," the prophet Isaiah had said. Christ was born and died to give meaning to our suffering, and I held tight to see that meaning. There had to be a sign of hope.

In a flash of realization, I knew what it would be like to meet Jordan in the next world. I realized that I would spend my entire life wanting to care for my son, only to find that he was caring for me the entire time. This was my hope. And all of the sudden, I did not fear death. I wanted to see my boy whole and complete.

We took pictures of Jordan, and decided not to have an autopsy done to discover the cause of death. From external appearances, he was perfect. His esophageal atresia would not have caused his death. Perhaps some of his organs were not fully developed. Perhaps the pressure of the fluid caused a problem. We would never know.

After four hours, Jordan's body was getting darker and darker.

"We're going to have to say good-bye," I said to Jennifer.

She lay in the hospital bed, her eyes red from crying. "I know," she said. She looked down at Jordan in her arms.

Jennifer handed Jordan to me, and I cuddled him and kissed his head. I called for a nurse and began to weep. Without saying a word, I held him out to the nurse. She took our son into her arms, and asked, "Are you ready to say good-bye?"

I nodded, tears running from my eyes unchecked.

DURING THE NINE-WEEK bed rest, Jennifer and little Sammy had helped me complete the Celtic crosses. It became a family project, and we had a Celtic cross for every branch of our extended family. Liturgically speaking, a cross is out of season at Christmas, but—considering the pain of our loss—it was all we had to offer. We gave Celtic crosses to our family, hoping that Jesus could transform our pain into an intricate and beautiful braid. It seemed impossible, but we held tight to the promise of the Gospel narrative.

II
Wisdom of The Holy

Introduction to Part II

WHILE PART I of *Messenger of the Holy* is a personal narrative of my spiritual journey into the oracle state, the following chapters center upon the wisdom from what I called Wisdom Sessions and later called Oracle Sessions, in which I go into the oracle state with a group of people. Each chapter presents wisdom concerning a major topic about our relationship within and toward the Holy. To compose these chapters, I gathered excerpts from multiple transcripts recorded during the years 2001 to 2006. Chapters 13 and 16 are single Wisdom Sessions. All other chapters are combinations of several Wisdom Sessions with similar themes. When there is a transition from one Wisdom Session to another, I signal this change with an introductory phrase such as, "On another occasion, the Messenger of the Holy said…"

As I reviewed the transcripts from the five years of Wisdom Sessons, I discovered that the Messenger had been consistent from the very start of the oracular lessons in the explanations of the Holy, the Holy Whole, the purpose of the soul, and the concerns for our present age.

In these wisdom lessons in Sections II and III, you will find repetition in the teachings. The Messenger often uses a "theme and variation" approach to spiritual topics, which allows the Messenger to present spiritual matters through metaphors of gradually shifting meanings. In the highly metaphorical wisdom lessons, the Messenger presents the Holy in paradox, allowing us to see the Holy as simple, yet complex; whole, yet intricate; singular, yet multiple.

Many of the wisdom messages are very detailed and should be read in a calm and contemplative state. Often, words or metaphors in the wisdom lessons accumulate layers of meaning as the lessons unfold.

With this general guidance, I invite you to experience these lessons about the mysteries and wonders of our spiritual landscape.

7
Creation and Control: "In the Beginning Was the Release"

PRAYER WITH THE MESSENGER became an essential means of support through the stillbirth of our son Jordan and the continued hope for another child.

Soon after the stillbirth, Jennifer took family leave from ministry because the grief of Jordan's death kept her from being able to fully perform her pastoral tasks. For example, she could not baptize infants without great anxiety and stress. The problems of parishioners came crashing down on her and knocked her back into grief.

We moved our family to Alliance, Ohio, close to The University of Mount Union where I taught, and we focused on healing and being parents to Samuel. Jennifer taught a few courses at Mount Union. Our plan was to have another child as soon as possible, and Jennifer would then concentrate on being a mother of two before eventually returning to full-time ministry.

As the months passed, it became clear that Jennifer would not easily carry another child. One year after Jordan's stillbirth, we lost another baby at 16 weeks. By spiritual intuition, Jennifer felt the spirit of the fetus leave on December 28, 2000: the one-year anniversary of Jordan's funeral. The fetal death was confirmed by ultrasound on January 15, an experience painfully reminiscent of the ultrasound, which revealed Jordan's death.

Eventually, Jennifer and I would adopt a daughter from China, but this decision was still years away. During the first two years after Jordan's death, we focused intensely on having another child, only to be disappointed at every turn.

During this season of our lives, we often came to God in prayer. After the second fetal death in December of 2000, our prayers were heavy with questions and grief. The Messenger of the Holy chose to put our concerns of pregnancy and infertility into the perspective of creation. The Messenger provided a revised creation story to make a distinction between God's control and God's influence. This new creation story reflects a contemporary "big bang" image to reveal God's release of total control in the phenomenal world at the moment of creation.

The wisdom literature of the Bible, such as Proverbs and The Wisdom of Solomon, often refer to creation. The creation reveals the foundation of the interaction between the power of God and the life of the faithful. For the people of faith, the order of the universe provides evidence of the Creator's design. But how can our orderly creation stories from the Bible play a role in one's view of wisdom when the powers of the natural world appear random? And, how can the hand of God be seen in the cosmos when nature itself imposes fatal limitations?

Anyone who has dealt with disease, birth defects or infant death has grappled with these questions. At times, the very act of conception—the beginning of life—can bring us face to face with the presence of biological limitations. But, like the wisdom teachers of the Old Testament, Jennifer and I found that a reflection on the nature of creation did indeed bring us to an understanding of God's presence and design in the midst of the brokenness and incompleteness of life. The lesson from the Messenger on creation brought us a new understanding of the power of God and the forces of the universe.

In preparation for prayer, Jennifer read Psalm 102, which is about time and expectations. I was constantly amazed at the way a psalm, which Jennifer randomly chose for our prayers, addressed our current concerns and provided a foundation for our wisdom lesson from the Messenger. I am convinced that the choice of the psalm was often divinely inspired.

Psalm 102 begins with a plea for God to hear the psalmist's cry: "Hear my prayer, O Lord; let my cry come to you! Do not hide your face from me in the day of my distress! Incline your ear to me; answer me speedily in the day when I call!" (1–2). As the psalm continues, the temporality of human life is compared to the eternal nature of God, and the psalm ends with a reference to creation itself:

Long ago you laid the foundations
of the earth,
and the heavens are the work of
your hands.
They will perish, but you
endure;
they will all wear out like a garment.
You change them like clothing,
and they pass away;
but you are the same, and you
have no end.
The children of your servants shall
live secure;
Their offspring shall be established
in your presence (Ps. 102:25–28).

After reading, Jennifer switched on the tape recorder, and we went to God in prayer.

Jennifer prayed about wanting another child and feeling we had no control over the situation. Even medical intervention was not helping.

The Messenger of the Holy said:

You must give up all expectation of control and instead adopt the expectation of influence. For, ultimately, the Holy does not exert control, only influence. What would become of a world, what would become of an existence, what would become of the universe, what would become of the sacred if there were complete control? When should the control be utilized? When should it be withheld? Who shall be the arbiter? Influence, my daughter, is the work of the Holy. Influence. An in-flowing of the Holy is an influence. The Holy works through influence, not through control, even at the end of what you know of existence, even when the Holy desires the reunification of the living person's spirit with the Spirit of the sacred, even at this moment, the Holy does not exercise control but only influence. How shall the Holy gather the souls but through influence?

"Then there is no certainty?" Jennifer asked.

Certainty? There is certainly certainty. But it does not lead to absolutes in your temporal experience. You can be certain of the presence of God, the presence of the Holy. You can be certain that the Holy is an influence. So, take these certainties and rely on them. Instead of saying, "God do this," say, "God work in me. Influence me. Work with my body. Work with my will. Work with my desire. Work with my need. Work through my pain. Work through my anger. Flow in and reside."

The Holy controls only in cooperation. There is truth in the patterns of the biblical stories and histories. And look at the patterns. The Holy acts with and through people. Do you see it? The Holy even acts with and through those who do not acknowledge the Holy's presence. The Holy works with and through the limitations of the physical. Let go of your expectations of control and be open to the cooperative influence of the Spirit. You see, when you expect control, you diminish your awareness of the opportunities for the Spirit to enter. You say, "God has control. It is as God wills it to be." But if you say, "God fill me. Holy Spirit work in me, through me. Inspire me. Use me. Use me," then you will be filled. Release expectation of control; open yourself to the reality of influence.

"I don't understand. Has God relinquished control?"

Control was never relinquished. For, at the moment of creation, control was not possible. To have creation negates control, for creation must live, creation must respond, creation must grow. Control diminishes all expansion and growth. And within the growth of creation is the life and growth of the Holy. How can the Holy control its own growth? So, God did not at some point say, "I will give up control," for in the moment of creation, control was antithetical to the purpose of creation—the expansion of wholeness. Before the moment of creation there was nothing to control. The moment of creation is a releasing, not a controlling. And in the moment of this releasing there was no control, but influence. Think of your own creation, think of the creation of your son, Samuel. Was it not a releasing? Do you have control, or INFLUENCE, over this life that grows before your eyes? And what would become of that life if you controlled it? What would become of your relationship? What would become of the growth of your love? The moment of creation is a releasing, and in the releasing there is not control, there is only influence, and in the influence there is relationship and growth. There are also limitation and pain in releasing to growth. So, the heart of God weeps, even as it rejoices.

In the beginning was the release.
The very heart of God bloomed,
and burst. And possibilities became,
and the possibilities produced Spirit,
and the Spirit gathered and became,
and, in the gathering, the Spirit moved
and grew and knew.
And life emerged to expand
the possibilities of the Spirit.
And the release continued,
over and over and over; the release continues.
And in the Great Release of creation,
distances became,
and in the distances are spaces to be filled,
and in the spaces the Spirit sweeps,
yearning for unification and fulfillment.
And yet the fulfillment is in the release.
The fulfillment is in the space.
The fulfillment comes through the distance,
for the space and the distance are a result of the release.

Is not every day a release; is not every moment a release? Release begets release. Life begets life. Spirit begets Spirit, and the gathering continues. And in the gathering there is rejoicing; in the movement there is love.

If there was no release, there would be no beginning. There would be only control with nothing to control, control of nothing, for control begets nothing.

How shall you open to the openness of creation? How shall you release in response to the release of God, and in that release find the influence of the the Holy?

If all of creation began with a release, is not the response appropriate to such a release another release? A reply of release? A releasing to the release?

You must see the wisdom of it. It is the way of the Holy. How can God control what God releases? Do you see? What joy there is in release, yet what sorrow and pain, even regret. For in the moment of release one must acknowledge the inability to control, one must acknowledge that in the release there is the danger of loss, distance. If you release how do you know distance will not expand between you and what you released? You do not know. There is only the hope that what is released will remain in relationship as it is released and grows. God releases with hope. God sees returns and God sees loss. But ultimately the Holy knows all things released will finally return. Thus, there is certainty in God's release, an ultimate design. However, only the wisest of the faithful rest in this ultimate peace during temporal living.

How is it that that which brings the greatest despair and grief is also the source of the greatest fulfillment: the release of creation? How can one find fullness in emptiness? How can one find completeness in distance? How can one find intimacy in release? What is it that bridges these gaps? The Spirit. Where is the Spirit gathering but in the distances of the release? If there were no release and ALL of creation were in a small, round globe held in the hand of God, there would be no space. There would only be compression.

Receiving a new creation story in prayer was of great significance to me. In the courses I teach on Native American Literature, I spend the first portion of the course on creation stories. Because of my love of creation stories, I felt privileged to receive a re-envisioning of the creation. The re-telling of the creation of the universe I received helped me to further understand how wisdom can be found in the midst of pain and suffering.

When I introduce Native American creation stories to my classes, I tell my students that a creation story is the foundation of a civilization's theological and cultural structure. Creation stories reveal the basic relationships between the Creator and the creation; they also reveal the characteristics of the Creator, and the proper relationship between the Creator, human beings and the other elements of the creation: animals, earth, plants, etc. In addition, creation stories often provide the foundation of a culture's understanding of both holiness and evil (which is often presented as the separation from the Creator).

Before asking students to read Native American creation stories, I always ask them to first read the two creation stories in Genesis. And I must admit, I have always been disappointed in these two ancient stories. They are partial and limited; they offer two very different views of God, and they offer very little support for a balanced relationship between humanity and the environment. The commands to "subdue" the earth and "have dominion over" creation are often interpreted as a way to describe our role as stewards over creation, but they are more often used to justify exploitation of the environment.

Despite this disappointment with the Genesis creation stories, I embrace them as the foundation of my faith. I encounter in these stories a loving God who brings order to chaos and desires relationship with creation. At the same time, I also enjoy and celebrate the creation stories of various Native American nations because of their emphasis on relationship and harmony with all elements of creation.

My interest and delight in creation stories is based on the assumption that any creation story is limited by human understanding. Thus, no creation story is *the* creation story. Any sacred story must reflect the cosmology of the time of its telling, and this is especially true of creation stories. When the Holy speaks to the human, the language and the understanding of the human receiver limits the Spirit's communication. Thus, when the ancient Hebrews wrote the creation story of Genesis 1–2:4b, the truth of God's purpose was confined to a cosmology that placed waters both under and above the earth. When the more ancient Hebrews told the Adam and Eve story (the most primitive of the two biblical creation stories), they were limited by the cultural transition from a nomadic lifestyle, with its easy Eden experience of an oasis, toward an agrarian lifestyle in which the "man" must till the earth. The Adam and Eve story is set in and dominated by this cultural transition from nomadic to stationary life. These two stories have two names for God (Elohim in the seven-day story and Yahweh or Jehovah in the Adam and Eve story). They also present two very different orders of creation. The seven-day story has human beings (both man and woman) created at the end of all other creation. The Adam and Eve story has earth created, then Adam, the animals, and finally Eve. (I am often surprised that most people do not realize that there are two different creation stories in Genesis, which contradict each other in the order of things created). Despite the differences and obvious inaccuracies of the Genesis creation stories, both of these creation stories contain spiritual truth. The Spirit of God breathes truth into our worldviews and into our experiences despite and within our limited frameworks of understanding.

The creation story I received in prayer reflects the cosmology of our time. God's truth and wisdom is restated within evolving human perspectives, including the present perspective of the origins of the universe.

This re-envisioning of creation made me ponder the Creator's role and power in creation. I had always thought of God giving us free will, but I had never thought of the Creator releasing control to allow the environment for free will. Suddenly, I began to see the apparent random nature of the universe in a different light. What had once appeared as a lack of the Creator's control was revealed to be a foundation of holy wisdom.

I also began to see how the various elements of the Holy Whole, or God, serve various purposes. I began to see the possibility that the vastness of what we call God allowed God's self to be broken apart in order to make life possible. This release of Divine "Self" allowed creation to expand, which finally allowed the Spirit of God to expand. As a result, the Creator gave of self in order to make "other" possible, and this "other" grows in spirit and finally returns to the Holy, which increases the scope of the Holy Whole. The revelation that the Creator relinquished control at the moment of creation in order to allow the possibilities of life brought me to an acceptance of the pain that Jennifer and I had felt at the stillbirth of Jordan and the fetal death of our next child. I could see evidence of the Creator's influence all around me, and I understood that the Holy can utilize us as instruments of holy influence if we are open to such work. Finally, I accepted with certainty that the Spirit of the Holy does exert complete control in the spiritual realm of the Holy Whole.

The influence that a creation story has on the way of life of the people is an important element of creation stories. In the new perspective given during my prayer sessions, it became clear that, if creation began in the release of the Creator's control, then life in the Holy Way must also be a surrender of our desire for control and openness to the Holy's influence. As the months continued, the wisdom through the Messenger of the Holy provided ways to understand how our lives should reflect the release of our Creator.

Below are excerpts from several prayers. They are slightly repetitive, but each expands upon the first creation story provided above. The combination of prayers reveals the consistency of the wisdom messages over the span of time, and the slight variations in metaphors deepens our understanding of the creation story as well as the way the creation story reflects and influences our lives.

During a prayer with a group of ten, including my mother who became and continues to be supportive of my prayer life, the Messenger provided a different emphasis.

The Messenger of the Holy said:

Control is an illusion. Give up the illusion of control. It is difficult to do, but you shall find in giving up the illusion of control, you shall find liberation. At the time of creation, the Holy released control and gave to you choice, gave to you options, gave to the universe powers, influences. These things swell around you: the influences of the universe, the desires, the wills, the deeds of others, the turning of the Earth, the collision of forces. All of these come upon you and take away your control. But I tell you, the ultimate control is still of the Holy. For the Holy sees and knows that all shall come to wholeness. So the Holy released control. Shall you not do the same?

Was it indeed an explosion, a great bang that created the sparks, or was it simply an opening, a surrender, an offering? The heart of creation split open, ruptured to make creation possible, you possible. From unity to unity, it is the Holy Way. Yes. It is the way of the Holy. The call is for unification, which is the result of the acknowledgement of the origin, the fanning of the flames, the sharing of the burn and yearn for the Holy, the expansion of the Spirit, the journey out of self to ultimate Self. It is not a journey that is controlled. It is a journey that is lived.

The Messenger of the Holy said:

I shall tell you of the call and response, for the Holy works through call and response. When and how does the call of the Holy begin? And your call to the Holy, is it not a reply, a re-call?

Whom shall you call? Who has called you? When does the call begin? What is the answer? What is the reply?

My children, your light beckons, but it is not the call, it is the reply, for the Holy Whole, which you call God, has called you.

In the beginning, there was loneliness,
absence, and the very heart of the Holy was ruptured.
A release took place,
and in the release was a call,
and in the vastness, there were responses.

And the responses resonated, multiplied, rejuvenated the Creator.
The responses, my children, are you!
Before the beginnings, the Holy called upon you,
and your reply becomes a call to the Holy.
Your reply defines you.
In your prayers, in your silence, in your deepest sorrow,
you have called to the Holy.
And I tell you, the Holy replies without hesitation.
If your call begets reply, what shall you do but reply?
It is the way of the Holy.
For you are the possibilities of the Holy's release,
How then shall you respond,
if not to return, to re-call?
And the Holy rejoices when the response
of your lived moments come before the Holy.
The call becomes new.
It is transformed.
It is not the original call. No.
My children, you must realize,
the Holy delights in difference,
in alteration, in change
and yet the Holy is ageless,
eternal, consistent and constant.
So, it is not call and response
as much as it is response and response,
for the call of the Holy echoes through creation,
vibrates in your souls, hums in your bones,
and you respond,
and the response begets response.

Do you see it? You respond and the Holy responds to your response. Simplicity is always best, so I shall name the process, call and response. It is the nature of the Holy. A call that does not provide a reply is a sorrow to the Holy, and yet, the Holy is patient. For all elements of the temporal shall finally return as a reply to the original call.

What I tell you is: the first call was from the Holy. The first need was of the Holy. So shall the eternal cast into the temporal sparks of itself? Shall the Holy deliver into creation, flames and sparks from the very heart of the Holy? And shall there not be a delight in the flickerings, in the glows, in the swirling flames, in the designs?

Oh, my children, you are a campfire burning, and the Holy delights in the flickerings, the flashes, the strands of sparks rising upward into the infinite where they are embraced.

You, my children, are sparks from the very heart of the Holy. Your bodies, your lives, your moments, your needs, your sorrows, your aspirations, your situations are the kindling for the fire.

Bring your spark to the Holy, so I may see you. Let your sparks merge. Let a holy flame be kindled here.

And what shall be the kindling of this fire? What shall be that which is burned and purified, but is not consumed? What shall be transformed with the presence of the Holy? Bring to the holy fire your desires, your needs, your passions, your very selves, and watch them transform into light, into purity, into Holiness. Such is the Way of the Holy.

8

The Holy Whole: A Map of Heaven

WACO TEXAS IS A RATHER odd place for an Ohio boy like me to travel and find spiritual friends. But in addition to being the former location of the Branch Davidians and the terrible events that led to the death of David Koresh and many of his followers, Waco is also the home of Baylor University, which houses The Institute for Faith and Learning.

In the months prior to the 2002 Art and Soul conference at Baylor, Jane Piirto, a Professor of Graduate Education at Ashland University, and I organized a panel on "Writing as a Spiritual Discipline." We wanted to cover multiple genres with our panel: I would be the fiction writer, Jane could cover several genres (as a poet, a fiction writer, and a scholar), and she suggested a songwriter friend of hers, Christopher Reynolds.

In the e-mails from Christopher, I got the sense that I was communicating with a truly unusual person. He called himself "Chrisdog" at times. He also wanted to know if I could find a place for him to "crash" during the conference to reduce his fees. Any place would do. A couch somewhere. He didn't care.

I had a room in the Hilton that I could have shared, but I wanted my privacy. I was the interim Vice President of Academic Affairs and Dean of the University at Mount Union that year, and I needed peace. Besides, I really didn't know this "dog" dude. So I made a few calls to Baylor and was assured that a graduate student could house Christopher, and with that, I was off to Waco.

In the Dallas/Fort Worth airport, I waited at the terminal to catch the noisy, prop plane to Waco. There at the gate was Jane Piirto with a man I had to assume was the Chrisdog. He had a large, friendly smile and a comfortable presence. From his e-mails, I half expected a tall, lanky ex-hippy with long hair in a ponytail. But the person before me was a neatly dressed and groomed man, with a resemblance to John Kennedy, Jr.

I said hello to Jane, and she introduced me to Christopher, who greeted me with a solid handshake, a huge smile and intense eyes.

On the shuttle bus to our plane, Christopher and I stood together, our hands above our heads, holding a rail.

"So, you had any dreams about this conference?" Chris asked.

"I don't dream," I said. "Other things happen to me."

The bus hit a bump. We bobbed and shook.

Chris leaned toward me. "We gotta talk," he said.

I nodded and shrugged. Talking about spiritual gifts was fine with me. "Sure," I said. "We'll have time for that."

"So, you teach at Mount Union?" he asked.

In a matter of two minutes, we discovered that we had several common acquaintances. Christopher taught French at Berea High School; two of his former students were now my students. In addition, we both had ties to Kursk, Russia, of all places.

I knew immediately that Christopher was going to be a good friend. The intensity in his gaze remained throughout the shuttle ride, and somehow I knew this man had been to the edge of the abyss, had danced there and had come back changed. He was gentle, friendly, and he had the sight of the Spirit. I could tell he saw more than the surface when he looked at people. His smile continued to invite me to share from the heart. Being in his presence was like meeting a good friend after a long separation.

"Chris, you're gonna stay with me," I said in the shuttle. "You and me. Roommates in the Waco Hilton."

It was a good thing I offered a room to Chris. At Baylor, I discovered there were no graduate students who had offered a place for Chris to "crash." It was with me or the streets for the Chrisdog.

In our hotel room, I told Chris about my prophetic experiences, and he accepted them without hesitation. In fact, as I described what happens to me in prayer, he stopped me and said, "I have a song about that." He unpacked his guitar and gave a quick tuning. "This song is an offering," he said. "To honor your prayer gift." He sang a song called "Marilyn of the Whirlwind," which echoed my experience. While he sang, a commanding presence of confidence and spiritual ability came through his voice. I could tell he was accustomed to sharing music as a spiritual offering.

I told him about the stillbirth of Jordan and the recent fetal death of our next child. I also told him of our evolving plans to adopt a child, perhaps from China. In response to this story, Chris offered another song called "The Time of the Healing."

We stayed up late into the night, and finally, we prayed. I allowed myself to go into prophetic prayer, and the wisdom was about convergences and the circles of time. I did not have a tape recorder with me, but I remember that the lesson described time as globes within globes, circles within circles, and the Messenger said this was a time of convergences.

When the Spirit left me and I was in paralysis, Chris covered me with a blanket and sat quietly.

I liked this guy. His sacred awareness was intense; his gentle spirit was comforting.

The next day, our presentation went well. I talked about writing and spirituality, Jane shared passages from her book, *My Teeming Brain*, which is about creativity, and Christopher sang songs. The people who came to our panel talked and shared. Chris sang a few more songs, and I left feeling that something truly unique and beautiful had happened.

That evening, I prayed with Christopher and Jane. It was a prayer about seeking the horizon, the place where the Spirit and the physical meet. After the prayer, Jane hugged me. "Oh, my God," she said. "That was beautiful. It was poetry." She hugged me again.

Jane picked up a Hilton pen and pad of paper and jotted down some lines from the prayer. "It's pure poetry," she said as she wrote. "Do you ever record this stuff?"

It was a blessing to be among people who accepted the prophetic gift.

Christopher Reynolds, this gifted musician and spiritual seeker, became my brother in prayer. We lived only an hour apart in Ohio, and we decided to meet monthly for prayer.

For the first prayer after Waco, Chris came to our house with a scroll of large papers, several books and his guitar. We ate dinner, and Chris played Sam some silly songs on the guitar. Chris had a gentle way with Sam. He was comfortable with himself, which made Sam comfortable. Chris played and joked with childlike enthusiasm.

After Sam was in bed, Chris unrolled the scrolls, which turned out to be star charts. He explained to me with great enthusiasm his theory that the human race is out of sync with the cosmos and our spiritual alignments.

He pointed to stars and constellations and explained the continual expansion and drifting of the cosmos. He read quotes from books, then said, "So you see, Dracos used to be the center of our night sky, but now it's Polaris. We've done this radical shift in our perspective, but our spiritual imagery hasn't budged for thousands of years. We're out of sync." He tapped his finger on the star chart unrolled on the floor. "Our perception doesn't fit our spiritual sky. We're, like, flying without the right star charts. We don't even know which way North is, spiritually speaking. We've lost our spiritual compass. We don't know how to get from here to there."

Jennifer cleared her throat. I smiled. I knew Chris was onto something. I could feel his earnestness, but I'd never really thought about the night sky reflecting spiritual orientation.

"So," Jennifer said, "it's like the bloody lamb imagery in Christianity that is outdated."

"That's it, exactly," Chris said. "We're out of step. The old language can't describe the current reality."

"Oh," Jennifer said. "Why didn't you just say that?"

Chris put his hand out to the star charts. "Because this is how I understand it," he said and laughed.

"The stars are a metaphor, then," I said. "We can't name the spiritual horizon that we see."

"Yep," Chris said. "You got it. But it's not just a metaphor. It's also a reality. That's my point."

"Got it," I said. "I know exactly what you mean now."

"Sure," Jennifer said. "It's a paradigm shift."

"On a cosmic scale," Chris added. "Our perspective has shifted, but our spiritual map has not."

We talked for a while about the shifting perspective of humanity in the last centuries, and Jennifer commented on the generational frictions within the mainline churches.

Mapping the Holy Whole

Several months later, the Messenger of the Holy provided a wisdom lesson on a new way to understand Heaven, which the Messenger called the Holy Whole. For this lesson, the Messenger utilized the stars as a metaphor for the Holy Whole, as if in response to Christopher's theory about spiritual disorientation.

The Messenger of the Holy said:

In the human experience, mapping is tracing where one has been to know how one shall return, but one does not map the Holy. The Holy reveals a mapping. The Holy Whole is not of your experience, yet it is reflective of your experience. The Holy Whole is not of your world, yet it is reflected in your world. So then, I shall utilize the world, your experience to map the heavens, what I know as the Holy Whole.

To present the heavens, family systems are used: fathers, sons, mothers. Balances within paradoxes are used: pairings, yins, yangs, sky, earth. Architecture is used: palaces, thrones, courtyards, mansions. All are good images and yet all fall short, for the Holy is not of your experience. The Holy is not of your sight. How then shall we map the Holy Whole in a way that speaks to your time, your place? How shall we reveal your role in the holy intention?

Is the human understanding and vision not cosmic now? I shall use the cosmos to provide a map so you may know your place in the Holy Whole. Let us then speak of the stars as a way to conceive of the Holy Whole. Generations have looked to the stars, generations have mapped the stars; but let us not speak of the actual stars, let us speak of the lights of holiness shining as stars in the Holy Whole.

There are lights. There are groupings of lights. Constellations, shall we call them. The many lights of holiness abide in the Holy Whole, known to you as God. The Holy Whole is greater than the parts and yet it is reliant on the parts. And the Holy Whole is beyond understanding, even to the lights. The Holy Whole embraces all, and finds in difference, similarity; and finds in paradox, truth; and finds in brokenness, wholeness. All comes to the Holy Whole.

But I tell you, it is not stagnant. There are motions and movements and development and growth within this place.

Shall you see in your minds spheres within spheres within spheres, all with lights upon them, turning and shifting, and in the alignments, sparks shoot through as revelations to your time. There are holy alignments, energies coursing and pulsing. It is the motion of the Holy. It is not the alignments of the planets; it is the alignments of the lights, and you feel the reverberations bringing shifts in living.

Spheres within spheres, lights gathering, sweeping, collecting; constellations in motion, abiding in the Holy Whole. It is the way I shall present the Holy Whole to you today.

It is all true, but not entirely.

And I must say, within the Holy there are roles, as I have explained. These roles become a purpose, in which those in the light find fulfillment, and the roles evolve and change until one reaches completeness in which there is no role and no self. There is only wholeness: a state of being held, embraced by the Holy Whole, and even this is not the end of development, for in the Holy Whole, there is purpose, intention, and joy.

So that is the Holy Whole, the Kingdom of Heaven, and I tell you, it surrounds you. I tell you, it includes you, for you are sparks of light; you are a piece of the Holy. Do you not have a role? Do you not have a holy purpose? And is your fulfillment not found in surrendering to your holy role, your holy purpose? I tell you, the surrender is your role; surrender is your purpose. So, shall you see yourself in this map?

This map of the Holy Whole does not show you how to go from here to there, for the Holy surrounds you. No, this map provides sight, perspective, placement. The spheres of light surround you; the Holy Whole embraces you, and the All relies upon you to increase the holy glow! Your relations, your family in the Holy—the lights of your constellations—shine for you; call to you, speak to you, pull at you. The lights of the Holy Whole provide perspective and sight for living, for knowing, for sensing, for seeing the Holy, and I tell you, there is no single way; there is no single path, no. The Holy Whole's embrace is complete. The Holy Whole is a unity of multiplicity. The Holy Whole is revealed in the now, in the situation of your moments, and why would the Holy Whole limit access to singular views and ways?

The lights are one, and they are many. The ways of holiness are one and many, just as the Holy Whole is one and many. This is the message you shall live, practice, speak, sing!

As you imagine the Holy Whole and your place in it, you cannot help but wonder how to get from here to there. So let me tell you, in the map of the Holy Whole, there is no "here to there"; there is only the now, the present, with connections to the eternal, with flashes of holy perspective. The coming of the Kingdom is not a "when" or a "where." It is a "how." The time of revelation is "now." It is a how of now. So, finally, you must know how to live in the now. How shall you live in the now? How shall you seek direction? How shall you ask assistance? How shall you surrender to the Holy?

The answers are within and beyond. Surrender to the Holy within, and sense the Holy beyond. But I tell you, the Holy beyond is present in the now, even in you. You must see the Holy around you. There are angels around you, disguised. There are Ancient Ones living among you; some do not even know they are Ancient Ones. People on a holy path, on a holy journey surround you. They are emissaries of the Holy. And you must discern, in order to gain the holy sight.

The Messengers of God in the Holy Whole and the Fish of Water

In another prayer, the Messenger used the image of water to explain the Holy Whole and the identity of souls within this sacred space.

The Messenger of the Holy said:

You are husks containing spirit, containing the living water. Shall you become a fountain of the living water? If so, the source of the living water shall come to you and flow through you.

We are all of water. We are all swimmers. Think of it this way: I am a fish in the water; I am a fish of water in the water. This is identity in the Holy. Think of a fish made of water in the water. And the holy waters flow, like sacred tides to your moments. And in these waters flow the souls and the energy of the Holy. The holy presence is in the water. It is all in the water; it is all of the water.

But what happens to the fish of water in the water? How does the fish of water retain itself? Contain itself? How are the boundaries kept? Do you see? They dissolve. The fish of water is of water. Goes to water. Herein lies the wonderful mystery, for there is a gathering that takes place, and the fish of water becomes and remains both of water and of self: a self without boundaries, which is not a self but a non-self, a holy purpose.

Among the Holy, there are no divisions, no singularities. What is self in such a place? Unification in such a place is a way of being. The household of God is the Holy Whole, and we abide in the Holy Whole as one, as many, as both at one and the same time.

When I am called together for my purpose, I am still one with the Holy Whole, so through me, the Holy comes.

Mysterious, even to me, even as I see it. I do not understand the choices that are made and from whence they are made. All I know is the flow, the holy flow, and in the flow, as I release self and become water, I find completeness, I find identity only as I lose identity, and when I am gathered, I know my purpose, I know my place, and I hear your call. Yes. I see you open, and I come forth with the water; I flow to you.

The water metaphor shall go only so far, then I must switch to another image, but for now let us continue with the swimming lesson.

I am in the water; I am of the water; the water is of the Holy; the water is the Holy. I abide in the water, the water abides in me, for we are one, and yet many. I gather. I am called to you. But there are times I disperse. Times I am no longer. I am water, and then I am called together as a fish, and I come to you in the flow. This flow can be understood as water, or as energy, or as the Holy Spirit. Yes. I come to you in the flow, and in you there is holy energy—water, if you will. The water touches water; the water merges with water. So, I abide in you as you abide in the water. Contained within you is a swimmer, for in your essence, you are a swimmer. Now, within the great water that is the Holy Whole, the holy space is beyond space. There is direction; there is a holy pattern, a holy way, a holy flow, and the souls of the living come to this place, flow within this place on the tides, if you will.

There are so many directions, so many possibilities, so many areas within this holy water. We are all connected. The Holy connects us all, and yet we are gathered into these fish, these identities. I am more than I ever was, and yet I am as I always have been. And you shall be the same. More than you ever were, and yet what you always have been.

Let the floodgates open.

So that is a metaphor for the holy place of abiding and the purposes within. I am a fish of water in the living water. You are a swimmer, containing the holy water. And you shall become more than you ever were and yet shall be what you have always been. Your spiritual essence, your spiritual purpose shall become your identity. It is the transition to holy living.

There are tasks and roles in the Holy Whole, for what would an existence be without purpose? Some remain here and swim in schools of fish, if you will. Some return and are contained once again. Some remain, learn and become teachers.

The Tree of Life

A third metaphor of the Holy Whole was that of a great tree. The Messenger of the Holy began by discussing the strands that connect us to the Holy Whole, and the strands soon transformed into the branches of the Tree of Life.

The Messenger of the Holy said:

What are the strands of the Holy which draw connections, far back, far ahead, far above, far below? The holy strands reach into space, into time, through space, beyond time, in spirit, within matter.

What is it that stretches out, up, back, through, and in?

Are they branches or are they roots?

I shall tell you, the strands are the roots and branches of the Tree of Life, the ancient Tree foretold and seen for ages.

What are the fruits that fall? What seed is nurtured and grows? The seeds are the souls, which fall or are shaken from the Tree of Life, then they flourish for how many seasons? For how many lives do the trees flourish? Are you a tree or a sapling? Are you a fruit or a seed? Are you a branch or a leaf?

Let us first look at the Tree of Life, the place of origin, the arms of the Almighty. We shall call it a Tree, and it does not grow up, but out. It is a sphere. There is no up or down in the Tree of Life; there are merely branches reaching forth, roots stretching forth in a circular pattern. A great ball, this Tree. What soil is there but the very essence of the Holy? The tree is nurtured of its own energy; it branches and stretches out. The seeds are falling and thrown forth; the fruits ripen and drop; the leaves bud and open. It is all seasons at once. Do you see it? Do you see the Tree of Life, the great Tree of Life, spherical, reaching out, reaching forth? Do you not turn your face to the Tree of Life as a leaf will turn towards the sun?

I have spoken of constellations, I speak now of branches, family trees within the very Tree of Life, within the origins of All. Draw lines through the constellations, and what do you have but the sketching of trees? So, the images connect: the Tree of Life, the family branches, the constellations, the groupings of souls.

And the Tree of Life—that which is eternal, that which is always, that which has no beginning and shall know no end—I tell you, even though it is beyond time, it expands. And how shall the eternal, which does not know time, expand? For is expansion not reliant on time? Think on it.

The Holy expands; the universe expands; the Tree of Life expands, for the Holy comes into time, comes to the temporal, in order to expand, in order to grow, in order to nurture, in order to learn. Shall you look to the heavens for wisdom and find the eyes are turned to you?

Are you leaves on the Tree of God, turning and shifting in the currents of the winds of life? Are you fruit? Are you branches? Are you seeds? Yes. There are indeed times when you are a leaf, catching the currents of the wind as a sail, and the Holy says, "Yes, celebrate the breath of my being." And the energy comes through the branches to the trunk, the Central Trunk, and the Holy says, "Yes, it returns, my breath, my energy, my goodness, my love returns."

And at times, you are seeds thrown forth to find your soil, to reach out your roots, to become a sapling, to reach out your branches, to intertwine with one another. Yes, at times you are seeds to plant and grow afresh.

At times you are fruit, ripening on the very branch of the Tree, ripening to sweetness, to fullness, to completeness. Sweet to the tongue of God is the fruit, and if the fruit shall fall from the branch, shall it not then nurture the growth? Yes, all of this is true; all of this is of the Holy.

And the strands are branches and roots, intertwined and intermingled, branches reaching out, stretching forth for sustenance, for shade, for love, for comfort, for companionship, to create a resting place, a place to abide, a home for the children to make their nests.

"Come my children and make your nests in the branches of the Tree of Me." It is the message of the Holy, and there are branches that are appealing to you, for they are your place of origin, your family lineage in the Holy, your family branches. This is where you shall make your nest ultimately, with the strands you shall make your nest, woven together, and the spirit of this nest is as a bird flying down into the temporal moment, and taking from your life a meaningful strand, flying to the very branches of the Tree of Life, and weaving together a nest, a place of rest, of nurturance, a seat of your soul.

And the Tree of Life, behold, it is full of nests! And the spirits fly around the tree as birds, busily making their nests, weaving with the strands of your life, nests in which the spirits abide. The activity is marvelous; the beating of the wings is music. Come, come, and make your nest here.

So, there are holy messengers. These birds of whom I speak in metaphor are messengers of the nest. They indeed come into your place and your time as emissaries. They bring you a song. They bring you a seed, and you give them your life, a strand, a moment of meaning, an opportunity for seeing. Yes, the strands are the branches of the Tree; the strands are the moments of your lives. In the Tree of Life and by the wings of the Spirit, they are connected. By the wings of the Spirit, they are brought together to become the roots, the branches, the leaves, the fruit, the nests of the Tree of Life.

Some see the Tree as a great eye. Some see the Tree as a great mind, with thoughts and energies flashing through it as lightning. Some see it as a heart of many, many arteries coming forth, with the very blood of the Almighty coursing through it: an eye, a tree, a mind, a heart. Some see it as constellations, sparks of light, swirling and swarming around the Spirit of the Center, which is not a center, but a place of acceptance.

You are a leaf of the Tree of Life, or you are a fruit, or a branch. But you are also a tree in and of yourself. Feel the Spirit coursing through you. In your trunk, through your branches. Feel the breath of God put your leaves into a quake and quiver. Where you are rooted makes little difference to the Holy. The Holy shall bring to you winds of change, winds of wisdom, and behold, the roots do not inhibit the movement of the tree. Your roots are intertwining; you know this to be so.

Abiding in the Holy Whole

Finally, the Messenger described the Holy Whole as a place where the holy messengers abide and wait to come to us.

The Messenger of the Holy said:

I have seen the eternal. It is a place where we abide. It is the Holy Whole. I have described this place as constellations of light, as a tree of life, as a mind with thoughts flashing through the sinews as a web; this place is the Holy Whole, what you know as God—the All, the Eternal, the Always, the Forever—and within this place are the heavenly hosts, the messengers, the lights. It is not God who comes to the temporal, it is the role of the messengers, the emissaries, and they are conduits bringing with them the power and the presence of the Holy Whole. They bring the presence of the Holy into you as liquid drawn into straws, as blood fed into your veins. The Holy Whole enters you, and the heavenly hosts come, surrounding you, working in you and through you, so that the forever comes to the now in you. Look around and see how the forever comes to the now, for the temporal is a space and a place of delight.

But what of the fissures in the temporal? What of the imperfections of the temporal? What of the pain of the temporal? What of the turmoil of the temporal? And how is it that the Holy Whole, the forever, shall come to the now in the midst of such brokenness? But you see, it is the very brokenness that invites the Holy. The very fissures create possibility.

The Holy Way is a walk with the presence fully connected, fully realized, so the eternal shall come to your now in you, of you, through you. Such bodies that you have are hosts for the sacred.

9

The Purpose of the Soul

FOR A LONG TIME, Jennifer and I did not share the oracle experience with more than a few trusted friends. We were discerning about whom to include in the prayer sessions, choosing only those we thought were spiritually mature and open to the manifestations of the Spirit. Such people, we were certain, would be able to surrender to the Spirit despite the strange alterations of my body and voice during prophetic prayer (with the quaking and contortions, the altered breathing and voice, and the syntactically complex language of the Messenger).

One of the most centered friends I am privileged to know, I shall call him Aaron, accepted our invitation. Among other things, he was a teacher of meditation, and his goal was guiding his students to release to the peace and emptiness of deep meditation.

Aaron joined us on a cold, dark January evening. At first he went to the wrong house, and the next day our neighbor said, "There was a gentle knocking on our door, and when I answered, there stood this calm and holy man. He was looking for you, but I wanted to invite him in. I wanted to tell him I could make some tea. He was so peaceful, I thought maybe he was an angel or something."

Aaron, indeed, found our house, and I led him into a prayer studio I had finished in the attic of our garage, complete with heat, air-conditioning and a peaceful, clean space for prayer.

The Messenger meets people at the level of their spiritual maturity and usually presents the information they need for the next step of their spiritual growth. Because of Aaron's advanced spiritual maturity, the Messenger provided an incredibly concise and profound lesson on the purpose of the soul. The prayer session presented a summary of many of the topics that the Messenger had touched upon in the midst of many of the previous prayer sessions with other people.

I will provide the prayer session with Aaron in its entirety. The message reveals the rhetorical structure of many of the prayer lessons. This prayer began with the phrase, "the pieces and the whole." Then the Messenger provided a long, compact lesson on this phrase. By the end of the lesson, the original phrase had accumulated multiple meanings with deep spiritual resonances. I had gotten used to this style of presentation from the Messenger, and as the prayer lesson progressed, it was marvelous to hear the deepening and addition of meanings.

In the midst of the larger lesson, there were specific, individualized perceptions directed to Aaron and to Jennifer. In this prayer lesson, there were no questions asked from Jennifer or Aaron, but Jennifer told me that Aaron had been smiling through the entire prayer. Aaron later told me that the Messenger had utilized metaphors he had been using in his teachings on meditation.

Prayer lessons such as the one below are dense, and they must be read slowly while in a calm state of mind. It is a demanding but fulfilling reading experience, and I invite you to read an advanced lesson on the purpose of the soul within the spiritual realm named by the Messenger as the Holy Whole.

The Messenger of the Holy said:

I see you. I see you. It is good to be seen by the Holy, my children.

I will tell you of the pieces and the whole. The pieces, my children, are the whole, but the whole is greater than the pieces. The isolation you sense, you feel, is an illusion. So what are pieces when all is unified? It is a paradox, my children, that there shall be a whole without pieces, and yet, there are segments, identities, purposes, indeed multiple and unique pieces or roles within the Holy Whole. It is both. In the Holy Whole there are no pieces. There is only wholeness. And yet, there is individuality, delineated by purpose.

So, here you are, my children, in the moment that you center in and sense the spirit, the spark, the ember within you, and you begin to perceive your connection to the Whole. My children, you are pieces of the Whole; and yet, you are the Whole. And shall I tell you something? The pieces bring expan-

sion to the wholeness. How can that which is complete be added unto?

I tell you, it is the purpose of the soul and the grand design of the Holy Whole, for the eternal comes to the temporal in you and through you. And the Holy Way, which is never changing, comes into you in unique ways, and so you live out the Holy Way in a unique and beautiful pattern that is new. So, how is it that that which is eternal and never changing is experiencing something new through you, my children? It is the possibility of temporality. It is the possibility of circumstance. It is the possibility of limitation. Within all these things are possibilities for the Holy Way to be lived in a new way, a way never before seen, a way never before known. And I tell you, the Holy Whole experiences it with you. So, you are a piece, and the Holy Whole reverberates with your holy moments.

So, my children, think of the significance of your moments when the Holy comes to the now and the eternal sees variety, newness. What a blessing it is to be the piece that you are. What a blessing to the Holy that you are a part of the Whole.

I tell you, my children, there are those who do not know that they are a possibility for the Holy to live new, to come through. And they live their days in an isolation that is an illusion. This grieves the Holy, but the Holy is patient, for all things come back; all things return. When the husk falls away, the illusion becomes clarity; the unity is revealed. My children, the husk of your bodies is of little significance. What is within is eternal. There will come a time when the Holy will peel away the husk and reap the grain, for you have grown in your moments.

Aaron, you are a reader, a reader not of words, but of people, of spirits. You are a reader, not of the eye but of the heart. You are a reader of hearts, and your heart is your organ of perception and reception.

You have come to the pool many times. You have waded into the water. You have calmed the mind and gone under. You return up, and breathe, and feel revived. But you wish you could stay under longer, go deeper, for then, perhaps, you would feel the husk fade away. You would know the peace of the Whole. You have decided perhaps such depth is in the practice: longer and longer, deeper and deeper. The Holy surrounds you and enters you, entices you, teases you, calls to you, confuses you. What you must do is become a swimmer in the waters, a fish, so that you need not return to the surface so often: the surface of distraction, of necessities, of commitments. The surface is troubled, my son, and the depths are so calm. What you shall find as a fish is that the surface does not affect the depths—that you can live beneath the troubles, you can remain surrounded, engulfed, embraced by the Holy despite the troubled surface. I tell you, to live in the Holy is to be a swimmer. In many ways, you are made to be a fish.

In the Holy Whole, we are all fish made of water, swimming in the water. We are of Spirit in the Spirit, and like the tides, we travel on the energy of the Holy. I tell you, we expand. We expand and then we are called together for purpose. So, be a swimmer, my son, be a swimmer. Expand into the Whole, then be gathered for your temporal moments. Take the water into your very lungs as you walk through the days of this time.

The holy water will not drown you. In the depths you will find the self is not so enticing, important, of value, for you will feel your margins giving way. You will feel the expansion take place and you can live the days of your time walking beside yourself, outside your own margins. You can live beyond yourself. It is a good way to live, and for you, my son, it will not be so disorienting, for you have been in the waters, you have held your breath; you have gone farther, deeper, longer. Now, take it in, take it in, breathe it in. Do not come back up for breath, but become a swimmer in the waters. Become one with the waters. Take it in and you shall not drown.

The swimming lessons, my children, will reveal to you what you shall become at the end of your days. For those who are swimmers and return to the Holy at the time of your physical end, the plunge into the holy water is not shocking; the expansion is not disorienting. But think of the ones who do not know that they are swimmers and live on dry land all the days of their lives, who do not seek to go deep, deep, who do not even know of the depths, who cannot recognize the pool that entices you so much. Think of the shock when the isolation is stripped away, when the self expands, when the plunge brings the loss of identity, then a self beyond your conception of self, an identity that is both one and multiple, a piece in the Whole. Such souls as these need great assistance.

Some of you among the living are to be swim teachers, giving lessons for the Holy. You will teach these people how to hold their breath and go in, how to keep the surface at bay, how to allow margins of the husk to fade. The waters, then, seep into the soul. In the Spirit you are quite porous, not solid at all. Then, there are some who can learn to let go of the breath and take in the holy waters.

My son, once you learn to take in the waters of the Spirit and live under the surface, to allow your margins to fall away, to walk beside yourself even as you walk within yourself, to walk beyond yourself, then the lessons you receive and the lessons you give will deepen.

You are all receiving swimming lessons. You are all giving swimming lessons. It is a good way to live, quite pleasing to the Holy. And what is most beautiful is that when you take the Holy in from your depths and bring it to the surface, to the moments of your days, to even the tedium, you bring the Holy to the now. And everything, my children, every task, every moment, every commitment, every obligation becomes transformed into possibilities for the Holy to come to the now, through your willingness to be embraced in the Whole, and no moment is wasted. No small task is beyond the influence of the Holy. So take in the holy waters when you rise to the surface, and you shall see your moments transformed. They will glisten. They will no longer be seen as moments; they will be layers within layers within layers of moments, all at the same time—reverberations of meaning. For in the depths there are many tides. Think of your moments as a cross section of the deep. Think of the tides, the layers churning in every moment. This is what it is to walk in the Spirit, to live in the Holy Way, to allow the self to be expanded and live beyond the self and to perceive the Holy flowing in and through you, in and through the moment, and every moment becomes a swimming lesson.

And I shall tell you something that will bring you great humility and allow you to see great importance. You give the Holy swimming lessons in these moments. It is the reason the Holy comes to the moments. It is the purpose of the temporal. Why would the Holy choose to come to the temporal, to embrace the limitations, to exist within the moments that can bring such brokenness, such rupture, such emptiness, such loneliness? It is because, my children, there are those who walk these times in the Spirit both within and beyond themselves. Through these souls, the Holy gains and expands. The purpose of all that is created is in expansion of what is already whole and complete. It is not a physical expansion, for space is nothing. It is not only an expansion of soul, it is an expansion of Wholeness. Certainly, the individual soul expands, progresses, but so does the Whole. So, what is the soul, but a part of the Whole? When your soul becomes a portal for the Whole, then you find completeness, fulfillment in every moment. So, you sense the Whole, and you receive a glimpse of the design, the grand design beyond your comprehension, beyond even my comprehension, for the souls in the Whole cannot understand the Whole, cannot embrace the Whole, can only be a part of the Whole, and the

Holy Whole, which you call God, is beyond us all, and yet we are within it.

Is there intentionality in the Holy Whole? I tell you, the Holy Whole has only design. The intentionality comes from the messengers, from the hosts, from the guides, from the many that are the One. But even this intentionality is a part of the design. The intentionality of the Holy Whole is to give intentionality to the parts of the Whole. Such intentionality of non-intentionality is a conundrum; it is not to be understood, but to be accepted. So, find purpose, my children, find purpose in merging into the Whole and swimming, of being a swimmer in every moment of your days, and the Holy will delight in you, will perceive in you, will come through you. And when you enter the times of separation, of loss, of brokenness, of disruption, even at these times, the Holy will come and your emptiness will be filled. Your brokenness will become wholeness. The chasms will come together, for you will see the layers in the moment, and you will see the moment and what is beyond the moment. You will see the depths even as the surface is troubled.

Do you understand that the way to live in the Holy is not to skim the surface? It is to live on the surface with the depth in your lungs, and in so doing to sense in your soul the depths of the Whole. So you live the pain of the moment and you see beyond it. You feel the pain even as you see beyond it, even as you sink into the depths in your sorrow. I tell you, in your sleep the Holy comes to you. You take it in.

So, what is the intention in the design? I tell you, the Holy Whole expresses intention in and through the hosts, the guides, the ancient ones, and in and through you. How it all began, we do not know, even we who are in the Holy. We know only the design, and it never ends; it expands, it blossoms. It is revealed and not known. The design is beyond prediction. There are holy patterns which are repeated in variations too marvelous to anticipate.

I see you in time from beyond time. The eternal and the temporal are parallel. But what is time to that which cannot end? What is time to that which is not confined to distances, to the whirlings and spinnings? Such a place is endlessness. Why would the Holy come to the now, to the temporal? For expansion, to give lessons and receive insights. Endlessness without purpose, my children, is not a part of the design. There is great purpose here. Your souls are a holy purpose. It is the best way to describe your soul; it is a holy purpose. The purposes are lived, but the ultimate purpose is beyond the living.

My daughter, you are confused by healing. You are confused. You wish to have faith. You wish to see it. You have longed to see it. You know that it is to be revealed to you. You must see the husk as nothing more than a porous container. You are not solid, my daughter. The Holy streaks through you. So think of the Holy coursing through the body. Your mind is stuck on the solidity. You cannot see beyond the solidity. So, as you merge with the Spirit, my daughter, merge the people. Feel your hand enter the margins of the other. Feel the Holy come in and through you into the other. Give the holy flow intention and purpose. I tell you, the currents will sweep in as water to wash away, erode away even the hardest of elements, for nothing is really solid, my daughter.

In this way you are already fish of water in the water, although your awareness cannot understand it. Your perceptions cannot reveal it, so you should not rely on perception; you should rely on the Spirit. The perception of the Holy is beyond your senses, even as the Spirit comes through your senses. So, walk beyond yourself, beside yourself and you will see, you will feel, you will know that the soul is not contained in the husk. It merely resides. It can exit at any time, and leave the husk whole and complete. Oh yes, the body can live without the soul for periods of time. And some have known this, have sensed it, have used it to go beyond the body.

You, my children, are pieces of the Whole, and the Whole comes in you and through you. And in the life and the varieties of the unfolding of your days, the Holy delights in you. Should you not delight in the Holy? Shall you not take the Holy in, live the Holy in every moment? The delight increases the Holy. Should you not, then, increase your delight? It is a good way to live in the delight of the Holy. It is difficult, my children, it is difficult to sustain. And do not be disappointed when you are distracted; rather, delight in the moment that you know you live upon the surface with the Holy in your lungs. You are not tossed and turned by the troubled surface because you feel the depths, because the depths are in you, not beyond you. The Wholeness is in you, not beyond you. And herein lies the greatest paradox, that the piece is the Whole. The Whole is in you.

So, here we are, my children, as pieces of the Whole with purposes that are as varied as the snowflakes that fall around you. And when the snowflakes fall upon the glacier, where does the flake go? What is the flake, and what is the glacier? This is you. And in this life you think that you are a snowflake, but you are not. You are the glacier. You do not fall without purpose. And when you learn to perceive the currents blowing through you, you can guide the Holy to do holy things in the land of the living, in the moments of time.

There are those who know that they are a snowflake, but they do not know that they are also the glacier. And so you call these people "flakes." You know of what I speak. For these people, the wisdom of the depths is not within, but the energy of the surface is perceived. Such people do not know to dive, to plunge, to swim the depths. It is still not a bad way to live. It is a good way to live to know the Spirit, to feel the energy, to delight. But it is always good to merge with the glacier, to feel your identity surrendered, to feel at once your singularity and your oneness, for such moments as these inform the way you live your days. And you find that you are not a flake, you are a rock, you are a mountain, you are the great glacier.

I have spoken of the parts and the whole, my children, the parts and the whole. This is a subject that has concerned you all. You have puzzled, have you not, on the part, on the role in the Whole, on the piece you are? You are a part of the Whole and that is your role, my children. It is quite simple, but difficult to live and sustain, being a part of the Whole.

The host tires. It has been a great pleasure to be among you. It is my fulfillment. It is my role to bring swimming lessons to you, and then to watch and rejoice as you swim. Yes.

Discovering and Naming the Individual Purpose of the Soul

While the above prayer session with Aaron and Jennifer provides perspective on the ultimate purpose of the soul and the soul's relation to the wholeness of God, I have also received lessons which deal less with the ultimate purpose of the soul and more with the gifts of individual souls. In fact, locating and giving voice to an individual's spiritual gift and spiritual purpose became a common element of prayer sessions.

Below are excerpts from two prayer sessions in which the questions Christopher Reynolds brought to the Messenger became a prompt for the Messenger to reveal the possibility of locating the unique purpose of an individual's soul. As you will see, our spiritual purpose comes from our spiritual heritage in the Holy Whole, in combination with the physical heritage of our bodies. The spiritual inheritance provides a unique purpose while the body provides avenues and doorways for holy energy to flow into us.

BECAUSE QUIET AND PRIVACY are needed for prayer sessions, and our homes do not provide this, many times Christopher and I would meet in a friend's garage, which had been remodeled into a photography studio. The owner called the studio "the Garage Mahal." It was comfortably furnished. Bookcases lined the walls, filled with psychology texts, religious studies, and photography books. In the center, a couch and chair surrounded a coffee table. The fragrances of incense and candles were embedded in the furniture and carpet.

Christopher had begun to bring a question or agenda to the prayer sessions, finding that one cannot simply come to a messenger of God and say, "What's up?" Instead, Christopher learned to provide the Holy with a context for the prayer lesson. On this day, he brought a question about a person's spiritual heritage, and the question gave rise to a fascinating series of lessons on the purpose and spiritual heritage of the individual soul.

Christopher asked about the way a soul is created, and he used the phrase "the parent of the soul."

The Messenger of the Holy said:

The parent of the soul is an identity and purpose, for among the many, we have purposes specific to us and in these purposes we find fulfillment. And you, as emissaries of the Holy in the temporal, in the physical, also have holy purposes beyond the time and location of your happenings, but coming to life within the happenings of your lives. It is once again the joining and merging of the eternal with the temporal. Do you see? It is theme and variation, theme and variation. Is there nothing new here? Am I speaking in circles? Yes, a circle is a beautiful thing to the Holy. It is indeed. I shall speak of circles at another time, but let us continue with locating the parent of the soul.

"Learning its history?" Christopher asked.

Not so much a history. It will be, perhaps, more productive to tell through your experience how you discover the parent of the soul than try to provide a cosmic map or linkages in your experience of time—

"Okay."

—which would only be a metaphor. Shall I speak of specific experiences of the Holy in your lives?

"Yes, speak in specifics."

In the specifics, we again find a difficulty. You must keep in mind that the general pattern is the same, and this holy pattern, which is the eternal wisdom, comes to the specific life and is lived out differently in the moments of your days.

The experience for the individual is feeling a current in life, a nudging, a wind, a direction from beyond, and everyone knows the experience, the holy moment. Everyone, even those who ignore it, are temporarily aware of spiritual direction, of feeling "at home." And in time, the individual learns to interpret this feeling, to find repetitions. And in the repetitions, there are patterns. And in the patterns, there are meanings. And in the meanings, there are messages. And in the messages, there are directions. And in the directions, there is a path and way of being.

"Do you see my life laid out before you?" asked Christopher. "My path? Can you speak to that?"

I cannot see the path of your life. I do see how you are connected to the Holy, your inheritance. Yes. Shall I tell you, this path is a cord; it is like an umbilical cord connecting you to the mother of the soul, so no matter where you step, you are yet connected. Finally, what is the path but walking with an awareness of the holy connection, the place of nurturance.

So, do I see your life laid out? The path of your life? No, but I see the holy connection, and I know that you feel the holy connection as you walk. You actually dangle, do you not, from the Holy? No metaphor quite grasps what we speak of, does it?

"I know the feeling," Christopher said. "I know exactly what that feeling is."

It is good to be understood. So, the path which is not a path, the cord which is not a cord, is for you a walking that is a dangling, and yet, you see in it something, don't you? A way to be connected?

For some, it shall come in dream. For some, it shall come in feeling. For some, it shall come in intuition. For some, it shall come in prayer, each according to the tuning of the body, of the husk, of the physical and biological heritage.

Naming the Spiritual Gift of an Individual's Soul

One month after the lesson on the heritage of the soul, Christopher and I scheduled another prayer session at the Garage Mahal. While there, we were met by Neil Fedio, a tall, gentle man with an easy smile. Neil worked in data entry in the medical profession, but his real passion was his spiritual journey. He was coming into awareness of a gift of healing in his hands. He wanted to develop the gift and provide healing massages to people. Neil hugged us, and the three of us entered the Garage Mahal.

I sat on the couch with Chris on one side of me and Neil on the other. Chris asked that we share our prayer concerns. Neil wanted to know how to use his gift and not become exhausted by it. Chris wanted to ask the Holy if we had "spiritual names," or a way we are identified by the Spirit.

I had concerns about adoption. Jennifer and I had been investigating the many options of adopting a child, but we had felt a spiritual pull to adopt a girl from China. I mentioned to Neil and Chris that we had chosen an agency to help us adopt a girl from China, and I would ask God for the endurance for the two-year process.

With these prayer concerns, we began to pray.

I lit my Christ candle and said, "I invite the presence of Jesus, the Word made flesh, the Spirit of Wisdom incarnate." Then I settled into my chair.

The others prayed also, but when the Spirit first came over me, I couldn't hear anything. I felt pulled into myself. My eyes tightened. My chest became warm, then my lungs expanded with a long, slow inhale. My fingers tensed, then relaxed. I twitched a little, and by this time, I knew I was already disengaged from my body.

My neck muscles tensed. I felt my face contort and my mouth stretch. I sat up straight, my hands turned upward in my lap. I felt a message coming into me. It was a large message, and it came whole, like a globe. A word began to form on my lips. As soon as the word was formed by my mouth, the message began to pour forth, like water that had just found a new opening in a dam. The word was "Purpose." After a short lesson on the purpose of creation, Chris spoke to the Messenger:

"I have a question from the last prayer where I had spoken about a gift that is a reason for being born, which you referred to as a 'spiritual parent.' In other cultures they have learned to give a spiritual name to children. I was wondering if you were able to say the name of the parent of the soul, as you call it, for Neil, the name for Michael, the name for Christopher."

There is inheritance from the Spirit, just as there are inherited traits from the body. From the Spirit you receive the trait of your family, of your constellation. Not a literal constellation. I speak not of the stars; I speak of the parts and the whole. I speak of relationaility. I speak of the lights within lights, and you are all sparks of the light, sparks from the light, and your spark bears the mark of your origin.

"Do you know those names?"

Names? Names are of language, and language is of no significance, finally, but I shall try to translate into language the purpose.

"I guess that's what I'm thinking of," Chris said. "A purpose."

It is a purpose, not a name. What is a name?

"Can you give a name to our purpose?

A purpose becomes in this life a journey, becomes in this life an intent, becomes in this life a call. Ultimately the call is the same for all; specifically, the living of the calls varies with great beauty. Do you know the cantor? Do you know the singer?

"Yes."

Yes. Do you know the purpose of the cantor?

"Yes."

To sing the people into awareness of the Holy. To sing and teach the traditions of the Holy. To call the people together. To gather. Is this not your heart?

"Yes."

Yes! These are always on the heart of the cantor.

"Thank you."

The Feeler. Does this one not feel?

"Neil?" Chris asked.

Yes. The Feeler. How does one feel? How does one intuit? How does one interpret into language that which is felt? How does one interpret feeling into consciousness and then bring the holy energy? How does one direct the energy? How does one feel where it shall go and whence it shall come? Yes, a conduit, is this one, and what he shall learn is to step out of the way, to be a holy conduit. Think of a bamboo. Clear out the joints in the bamboo, and you shall not know exhaustion, for the flow shall come from beyond you and through you. It shall have nothing to do with you. It is your gift. It is your purpose, and in it you shall find your fulfillment. It shall not drain you; it shall energize you. Finally, it shall flow through you and leave traces, beautiful traces, like strands of water running down a window.

The traces shall be sweet. Do not be frustrated. It shall come. Do not be disappointed. The Holy Way is not the easy way. And the holy task is not to be done without practice.

"Thank you," said Neil.

Obedient is this one. The one before you, speaking words beyond his awareness. Obedient! Yes. But has he a choice when the Holy tackles him and throws him down? He does not wrestle any more. The Holy has indeed dislocated the hip of this one; he cannot run. He shall give voice. It is a surrender, and it brings him close to his essence. Release then your fear; release then your anxiety; release then your time, your agenda, your schedule. For the Holy shall reveal to you in the Spirit's time what is to come and how it shall come to be.

You shall indeed hold your daughter. You shall kiss her cheek as she sleeps on your chest. You shall smell her hair. You will see the blanket with the design. It shall be, so do not be anxious.

That was the first time the Messenger gave voice to a person's spiritual gift, and it became a routine part of our prayer sessions.

The assurance at the end of the prayer that Jennifer and I would indeed travel to China to receive our adopted daughter brought me a deep peace. We would later discover that our daughter was indeed abandoned with a blanket, but the orphanage director would tell us the blanket had been thrown away, so we would never be able to see "the blanket with the design" as the Messenger had described.

Naming the Purpose and Healing the Soul

Often, the Messenger of the Holy provided a message of healing along with a message about an individual's purpose. The following message was provided for a young woman—I shall call her Carol—who was experiencing a prayer session for the first time along with a group of ten other people. The Messenger gave each person a reading, and I include Carol's message because of the healing that came through the prayer.

The Messenger of the Holy said:

Carol, you have an older spirit than is apparent by the eye of flesh. And some have seen it and known it, and have come to you in trust, it this not so?

"Yes."

It is not surprising. They have seen it, the wisdom in you. They come and confide in you; you carry their secrets. Have you carried secrets?

"Yes."

You are trustworthy. Some of the secrets are heavy are they not?

"Yes."

You carry them peacefully, but they are heavy. You have a bag of stones in your belly, the secrets of others, the pains, the sorrows. Some of these pains you have helped to solve; some of them you cannot help to solve; they must be lived.

I tell you, you do not need to carry these rocks. You shall take them to a sacred place; you shall put them in the water, and the Holy will caress them, and wear them down, and sweep them into the beyond. You should give the rocks to the Holy and not carry them. Does this make sense?

"Yes, they make me sick."

Yes, they make you sick; why do you keep them?

"I don't know."

Release them, my daughter. Gently hold each stone, name it, and gently let it go. The people will continue to come because they know you do not divulge, but you must not contain. It is in your gut, do you know, the stones. They are precious; they should be cherished, as troubling as they are. They are given in trust; you can give them in trust to the Holy. The Holy does not misuse the brokenness. The Holy is an avenue to healing. Limitations are an avenue to possibility. Fissures are a means to unification. You can release the stones, my daughter, and the Holy will do glorious things with them. The Holy has no belly to sicken with the stones.

You are trustworthy, my daughter. And you are peaceful. You are the peaceful guide. You know you are a guide?

"No."

You give guidance. You have given guidance.

"Yes."

Yes. Of course. Your peace attracts. Your guidance delivers. The peace is the Holy; you must allow the guidance to be from the Holy. You come from a heritage, a strong heritage of Spirit, a strong heritage of guidance. What is guidance, finally, but living in wisdom, and what is wisdom, finally, but living in the Way. And what is the Way, finally, but the path of righteousness, and what is the path of righteousness, finally, but living in receptivity to God and the Spirit? You have inherited this from the Holy. Shall you not return this gift and purpose to the Holy?

Give the stones to the Holy; the Holy will tell you what to tell the other. It is a sacred thing; where there is need, there is always presence. The greater the need, the more thick and heavy the presence. The Holy responds to needs, so release the stones to the Holy and you will feel something, gut knowledge. You know your deep knowledge?

You have a deep knowledge. Have you felt it?

"Yes."

You will feel it there, the guidance. You will feel it. You will not hear something. It will not be an image. It will be a feeling that your mind will interpret quickly. Just trust it. Trust your gut; it is a holy trust. It is a funny thing, is it not, for the Holy to use your gut. So many think the gut is not true. Oh, I tell you, the gut is true for you. Your gut is true, but the stones are cluttering the gut, blocking the holy flow, making you sick of body and of spirit.

After the prayer, Carol told me that she had been seeing a hypnotherapist for her stomach problems, and that the prayer session was more powerful than she could have imagined.

The Purpose of the Soul: A Summary

Finally, I will share a short excerpt of a prayer in which the Messenger provides a summary of the difference between identity and purpose. This lesson begins with distinctions among three levels of awareness: "The you" is explained as the surface identity of a person. The "you within the you" is described as the spiritual core of the person. The Messenger called this the "who in the you." Finally, there is a "you beyond the you," which is a merging with the Holy Whole, in which individuality merges with the All.

The Messenger of the Holy said:

Identity is not what it appears. Singularity does not exist in The Holy. To explain identity, I shall speak of the "you within the you," and the "you beyond the you."

The "you," the apparent identity, is an illusion. Identity as isolated "you," as isolated self, is an illusion, a misunderstanding, a misperception.

There is a you within the you, a you within the self. There is a you beyond the you, the you beyond the self, and those who walk in the presence of the Holy understand bringing the you beyond and the you within into unity. That is true identity, which is not identity at all, but holy purpose.

The you within the you: first, shall I explain the you within the self? There is the self, the you, who is seen, the you who is known, the you who feels, the you who perceives, the you who works, the you who strives, the you who decides, the you who discerns, the you who struggles, the you who consciously divides, casts aside. This you is superficial. It is the identity that some know as their essence and such people shall always skim the surface of existence, troubled.

Then, there is the you below this, within this, the seed of the Spirit planted by the Almighty: the you within the you, the you within the self, the potential, the seed of the Most High, which contains in it the origins of all creation. This you yearns for the depths. This you seeks the heights. This seed of the Almighty is pure, unified, glorious, beautiful.

This seed burns with potential. Is the seed not indeed a spark, an ember that glows and calls? It is a burning seed, and as it grows, it becomes a burning bush within you, a tree of flame. And to be understood, this inner you must be in relationship with the "you" beyond. For when it is burning unto itself, it consumes the self. But when it burns in unison with the Holy, it uplifts the self.

You have all known this you within. When in isolation, the burning, the passion of creation, leads to madness.

Have you known, the isolated, burning embers? Have you seen them, have you seen the isolation lead to madness? For the holy embers seek companionship and reflection in the Holy. The fuel of the fire is the Holy, not the self, or anything made by the self, or anything known by the self. The Source, the fuel, the origin of this you within the you, is the you beyond the you. How can there be a you beyond the you? How can there be a you beyond the self? Herein lies the great mystery.

The you beyond the you reveals paradox and mystery. This you beyond is not always discerned. The you beyond is the source of the you within. But what you must understand is that the you beyond is the Almighty, and it is also you.

The essence of you is beyond. So often it is seen in reverse. God's essence is in you, but I shall present it to you in this way. The essence of you is beyond. And why shall I present it in this way, but to give you a new perspective, a new respect for the you within?

Hear this then, my children, the you within is a reflection of the Holy you seek. So, identity and purpose can now be explained in relationship to the you within the you and the you beyond the you. Identity then, is much more complex and much more beautiful than identity appears, for when the inner you is unified to the Sacred, identity is seen to be a you beyond self, self beyond self, a self of no self. Within such an existence, identity is revealed to be a purpose, a holy purpose, planted within but nurtured beyond.

To discover the you beyond, the purpose of the soul, you must allow the you within, the spark of creation, to join with the sparks beyond. The self beyond is a spark within a multitude of sparks, glowing so brightly they cannot be identified individually, but become a bright light. Think of the stars burning so brightly there is not distinction between them. This is identity. Where are you in this glow? There is no self, in this place, in the Holy, and yet, there is purpose.

Purpose shall be emphasized over identity, for identity finally is an illusion. Purpose, however, is sacred.

10

The Purpose of Prayer

THE MESSENGER OF THE HOLY provided many lessons on the nature and purpose of prayer. The early lessons were received while Jennifer and I worked through the grief of our two fetal deaths, then while we pursued the process to adopt a daughter from China. As time passed, the lessons on prayer gained wider significance as we began to work with members of City Hope Church for healing ministry. With this focus on healing in the Christian church, the Messenger focused on the community of faith, known as the Body of Christ. In contrast to this communal body, the Messenger also taught about the physical body of Jesus during the incarnation among us.

Prayer and Merging with the Holy

A prayer is the mystery of incarnation, the merging of the present with the eternal, the holy mystery. When your life is a prayer, you are open to the eternal presence. You become part of the Holy, a representative of the Holy Whole.

Prayer is a central element in the work of holiness. For in the times of deep prayer, the Holy enters you and raises you above the cares of the temporal, the limitations of the body, the understanding of the mind, beyond all things that create the illusion of identity. You merge with the Spirit.

The Holy waits. The messengers wait. The spiritual energies of the world and of the earth wait. And when the door opens, we sweep in. May your moments become holy. May your lives become expressions of the sacred.

Prayer unites the eternal with the now. What is the Holy without the now but endlessness? What is the now without the eternal presence of the Holy but emptiness? Shall the endless find purpose and the empty be filled in such moments of prayerful merging? Let the eternal come to the embodied. Let the Holy come to the now, and let the temporal become an avenue to the eternal. It is a mutual fulfillment, my children—a mutual fulfillment.

Let the Holy come to you, work through you. The ways of the Holy are eternal, everlasting, never changing, uncreated. And yet, that which is unchanging, that which is uncreated, that which is holy is new in you, new through you.

Healing in the Body of Christ

The Holy creates, and the Holy re-creates. The Holy breaks down into spirit and reconstructs as a body. That which has created matter can dissolve matter. That which dissolves matter can re-create matter. This is what Jesus and other teachers and prophets could do in a more profound way. Jesus embodied such a concentration of the power of creation that twisted legs decomposed and were reconstructed. Flakes of skin fell away and were remade. Eyes of flesh dissolved and were re-created. Death was cast aside to bring life. An intensity of the power of creation made it possible. And I tell you, if you bring enough faithful people together, this intensity can be approached. It is why there is a thing called the Body of Christ.

Within the body of Jesus, my children, was the power of God, directly. How shall you then be the Body of Christ? It is done by the unification of the faithful. To be the Body of Christ is to bring the presence of the Holy with such power, with such intensity and concentration, that all things are possible.

The ones who gather the individual to the whole, the people to the community, the parts to the Body, have a holy task.

Be a guide then, and not a distraction. Be a flow, not a roar. The people of God shall feel the presence of God magnified, shall raise their voices in unity, shall feel the presence of God enter them and extend beyond them. At such time the Body is assembled. Do you know that worship assembles the Body of Christ? Prayer strengthens the Body of Christ. Scripture informs the Body of Christ, and service puts the Body of Christ into action.

When a group prays together what occurs but that the group touches the eternal at the same moment and are unified in the transformation beyond the self? Such a unity and transformation is a glimpse of the eternal presence in unity known to the Holy Whole. While praying in groups, the individualized gifts and visions merge into a larger whole; this is the nature of the

Body of Christ.

It is no small matter when the individual is brought to prayer. It is no small matter when the spark is added to the great, great light of the Holy. It is no small matter when people brought to the presence of God pray on your behalf. What has occurred but that the presence of the Holy has been expanded and changed forever? How is it such a small spark of a prayer, such a tiny gift to give, can have so much power? What is being said to The Holy but, "I am in your presence. Come in me and through me. Change me. Speak and work through this time and this need, and in so doing, be new once again." See the wisdom of it, my children?

Give to others the light that the Holy has given you, and The Holy is changed for eternity. Prayer, my children, is the key to the union and the transformation and the expansion of the Spirit.

On another occasion, the Messenger of the Holy said:

I shall speak of abiding in the Holy. For the House of God is not a building. It is not a place. It is a way of being. To live within the household of God is to abide in the Holy Whole, and you shall see, my children, that abiding in the Holy Whole is a unification, for all comes from One and all returns to One. The many, all souls and messengers, become the One. All come from the One, and the many return to the One, yet the One is greater than the parts.

Where I am, I disseminate. I flow into and through the Holy Whole, then I am gathered. What is self in such a place? All is unified into a non-self, and yet, I am gathered to my purpose. Intimacy in such a place as this is a way of being. Unification is a way of being. The household of God is the Holy Whole, and we abide in the Holy Whole as one, as many, as both at one and the same time.

When I am called together for my purpose, I am still one with the Holy, so through me, the Holy comes. Can you abide in this way as you live day to day, in the temporal moments of your lives, in the social constructions and natural laws, which draw close upon you?

Let me say this from the Holy, from the place that I describe, from the identity that I have and do not have; from this selfless self, from this dissemination and gathering, I can say, "See me and you see the Holy." It is not so audacious from where I am, is it? I do not know where what you would call an "I" ends and the rest of the Holy begins. But think of a human being say-

ing to you, "See me and see God." How audacious is that, my children? Yet there was one who walked among you who said, "See me and you see God," for the connection, you see, was continuous. The abiding was fluid. The intimacy with the Holy was constant.

The deeper the state of prayer, the more intimate the connection. The more intimate the connection, the deeper the peace. The deeper the peace, the more fluent the flow. The more fluent the flow, the deeper the wisdom. The deeper the wisdom, the greater the knowledge. The greater the knowledge, the more holy the action. The more holy the action, the greater the fulfillment. The greater the fulfillment, the greater the release. The greater the release, the greater the openness. The greater the openness, the more complete the presence of the Holy.

11

Living in the Holy Way

THE ULTIMATE PURPOSE of wisdom literature is to provide a means to recognize and live in the Holy Way. I have often referred to lessons with the Messenger of the Holy as wisdom lessons, and I have also seen parallels between the Messenger and the Spirit of Wisdom, Sophia. It is fitting, then, that I include excerpts of prayer lessons that provide practical ways to open to the Holy and follow the Holy Way.

The Journey into the Self and Through to the Holy

The Messenger has explained that the journey to merging with the Holy begins by going into the self and discovering there a portal to the eternal. The most concise lesson on this approach to spiritual enlightenment is presented in the prayer below, which separates the development of spiritual awareness into three levels: "the self," which is the surface identity; "the self within the self," which is one's spiritual essence; and "the self beyond the self," which is found only through opening and surrendering to the Holy Whole. These distinctions of self and spiritual awareness are similar to the presentation of identity in Chapter 9, when the Messenger spoke of "the you," "the you within the you," and "the you beyond the you." However, in the prayer lesson below there is a different purpose for the three levels of awareness. Instead of being an avenue to the ultimate purpose of the soul, as in Chapter 9, they are explained as an avenue to spiritual development.

The Messenger of the Holy said:

I *shall tell you about the self, the self within the self, and the self beyond the self.*

There is a self. It is an illusion. It is a mask. There are some who live only on the surface, only on their husk. It is a way of living which leads to a clutching of the self. They do not seek the self within the self. Such a life does not allow for the release of self, the surrender to the Holy. Such a life grieves the Holy.

There is a self within the self. It is a spark, an ember. It is the essence and the purpose of your being. When the Spirit enters you, fans the embers, shines through you, then the ancient and unchanging becomes new in you. The spark can be seen as if shining through a crystal. Every crystal is unique, and the Spirit glows through you in new and unexpected ways. Each person creates a new pattern when the holy light shines through the crystal essence. It is humbling, is it not, to be a vessel for the ancient and unchanging to become new in the now? The Holy Whole expands through such a life. That which lacks nothing is added unto. The Holy Whole is elastic, greater than you can imagine. Even those in the Holy Whole cannot know the Wholeness.

Many discover the self within the self and engage their holy purpose. It is a way of living.

Then there is a self beyond the self. It is not a self at all. It is a no-self, a non-self, and yet there is identity and purpose. The way to the self beyond is in and through: Into the self within the self and through to the self beyond the self.

Some find the way to the selfless self of the beyond to be out, not in and through. It is a difficult way. The mind becomes a barrier. It takes great discipline to free the mind, to empty the mind and rise to the non-self of the self beyond the self through an outward journey of the spirit.

The easier way is in and through. The self within the self becomes a portal, a doorway to the self beyond the self. Many stop at the self within the self, but the Holy Way is to go in and through to the beyond.

Do not worry. When you enter the self beyond the self, when you dissolve into the Holy Whole while living in the body, you will return to the body. The surrender of the self to the Holy Whole does not stop life, but gives life.

This is a glimpse of where I am in the Holy Whole. But a glimpse is all you can receive. The grandeur of the Holy will crush your body, split your husk. You receive glimpses as indications and examples of the Holy so that when you come to the end of your days, you recognize the way to release self and enter the selfless self of the Holy Whole. And there you will find a self beyond your expectations and a purpose beyond your understanding.

On another occasion, the Messenger of the Holy said:

The spiritual essence of the soul remains consistent, and this essence is what is seen in the Holy. It is your light. It is your purpose. It is your being. It is that which continues when the body has ceased to operate. It is your self within the self which opens to the self beyond the self. It is spiritual essence, encased into the temporal body. And the wise way, the Way of the Holy, is to listen to the self within the self, to listen to the yearning for the Holy. That which is encased within you is a doorway to the All, is a connection to the Holy: distinct, unique, individual and, yet, nothing without the Holy.

On Surrendering Self to the Holy

How does one embrace surrender? It is an invitation. Make the invitation and the Holy shall come. Make the invitation and the Holy shall embrace, even as it is embraced. And the surrender is an embrace, and the embrace is a surrender, and the self expands. It is ironic, paradoxical and, therefore, confusing to the people that a surrender is an embrace and that a loss is a gain. So the people struggle to understand, and the Holy Way calls the people to unification, calls the people to surrender, calls the people to the Holy.

And the people of the Holy respond to the call and surrender, but they, too, become confused when the surrender looks differently in the practice of other faiths. Frozen water is still water. Rushing water is still water. Still water is indeed water, still. Some come to the rushing stream and say, "This is the Holy, this is the voice of the Holy." Such people often wade into the rushing water and feel the pull of the Spirit. This fishing is active and invigorating. Some come to the frozen waters and crack to uncover the living water. They fish the icy depth. And some come to the still pool to fish patiently and calmly.

The water is the water is the water. The Holy is the Holy is the Holy. Where you fish makes little difference. That you fish, is ultimately important.

What shall you catch in the holy waters? What shall you attract when you cast the line that is your life? The fish of water will come through the holy water. Have you not cast your lines into the water of the Holy and invited this fish, this messenger?

Finally, the holy waters call for bathing. The holy waters pour forth upon the people, within the people, and upon the holy waters are the messengers, fish of water in the water, of the water. Bathe, my children, in the holy water and you shall be cleansed and you shall know your spiritual essence is of the water, and you shall dissolve into the water and glimpse the non-self, the awareness of unification. It is a beautiful awareness, a glimpse of the Holy, a promise of things to come, not to be feared but to be embraced.

Be patient with those who stand at the bank. Invite them to cast their lives into the waters. Provide for them a glimpse of the Holy. Show them in your selves. It is a holy task.

Yielding to the Spark of the Holy Within

Yield to the purity within, for the Holy has set a flame within you. You are created as a spark, and you have allowed the Holy to blow. You have seen and felt the glow. You have known the burning and flashing. Your perception is clarified. Your words are deep and pure. Your song is tuned. The Holy brings out the purity that is your essence, and the spark becomes a flame.

When the Holy blows, you know the quickening, yes, the warmth, yes, the expansion. When the Spirit blows, the embers glow, the flame ignites. It is difficult, my children, to walk with the flame ablaze, for it is as fragile as a lit wick, and any wind not of the Holy can blow it out. Any distraction, any responsibility, any task that distracts you can blow it out. But the Holy is very patient and forgiving. In fact, there are allowances because even when the fire is snuffed out, the embers glow, and it doesn't take much, my children, for them to blow into a flame.

Kindle the flame. Your days, your moments are your kindling. Give them to fhe Holy. Your deeds, your thoughts are the kindling. Give them to The Holy. Your actions, your words are the kindling. Give them to the Holy. Bring nothing to the Holy which is not coming from the intentions of purity and wholeness.

Feed the flame, moment by moment, word by word, note by note, step by step. It is quite a challenge to live in such a way, quite a challenge and difficult to sustain.

Treasure the moments you find it. And I tell you, the moments will increase. These are moments of great transformation, these Pentecost moments, enlivening, enlightening.

For the Spirit of the Holy is sweeping, is blowing, is fanning the kindling of your lives into a holy fire.

For the Holy Whole is a light that is brightened by your spark. You have the choice to participate or not, and it is a choice made continually.

Let the choices to participate increase. Let the purity emerge. Let your walk be holy. It is a good way to spend a life. For when you come before the Holy Whole, you shall bring that which has increased in brightness, your very purity, your very soul, your very essence. All else will pass away.

There are those among you, those in the body, whose embers have become cold and ashen. But below the ash is a core that can be ignited. I tell you, you must blow away the ashes. With the energy of the Holy, you must blow away the ashes and expose the core. Sometimes you will find it still warm. Sometimes you must ignite it with the fire of the Holy. You cannot ignite the core in the cold ashen ones without first blowing away the ashes, all that has fallen away as the person has been prepared for the Holy. The ashes are of the fire that consumes and leaves nothing but dust. Such a flame is not a holy fire, but it attracts people as fire attracts moths. Some people, my children, yearn for this burn. Although it hurts, they yearn for this burn for it is all that they know.

They yearn for the burn, and this burn of a fire that is not of the Holy, injures, consumes, debilitates and leaves ash, piles of ash, ash everywhere. So, sometimes when the holy wind blows, all that has been ash comes up in the face of the person, surrounding the person, suffocating the person, so the ashen one may run from the Holy, but really they run from the ashes of themselves. So, my children, blow away the ash, protect the core, protect the person from the ash. It is what forgiveness is. It is what cleansing is. It is the purpose of baptism, to wash away the ash of the fire that consumes.

For others, the glow is encased by a hardened shell, with layers upon layers of accumulated self-protection. For these, each layer must be named, cracked, and melted away by the holy fire. You will discern the glow within the encasement in such people.

You are the people of the flame. And when the people of the flame converge, when the people of the flame are called together, there is a light so bright it attracts even those who yearn for the burn, for they see a pure light, a light they have desired, a light for which they have yearned. You have seen them, so be gentle, my children, be gentle, for it is a fragile time, a fragile time. Wipe away the ash with your hands, with your breath, with your tears, with your prayers, with your presence. An ember close to going out must be protected. It is a long process, a fragile process to bring the embers back and let the glow come. And then, my children, when the Holy Spirit blows, the flame that comes from the core is so bright, so bright that it ignites all people of God. These people will sing praises, "I once was cold and now I glow. I once was ash, but now I'm fire. I once consumed, and now I enliven." So bring your embers, my children, bring your embers and let the Spirit glow, and when the people who yearn for the burn come with ashes piled up, be gentle. Some will want to stay among the ashes, and some will want what you have, what only God can bring: a clean heart, a perfect flame, a furnace of God, cleansed of the ashes, ready to glow, a clean hearth of the Holy.

Giving in a Holy Way

I shall tell you something important and missed by many. Holiness is not selfless abandon in your experience, or in the Holy. In giving in a Holy Way, there is always something holy to be gained. The Holy seeks the holy knowledge, the holy awareness, one should not put oneself at risk entirely.

Pure selflessness is not holiness, it is recklessness. Giving selflessly is holy. Giving without the desire for return is holy. But giving until the self is at risk and threatened is not holy, for the self, grounded in the Holy, is to be cherished, treasured, protected. Give selflessly, without intention of receiving, and the self is strengthened in holiness.

Give from self without holy intention and protection, and the self is disrupted, hindered and diminished, leading to emptiness.

The core of the self is holiness. Cherish this holiness. Cherish it and protect it. Ground it in the Holy Whole. Giving is not a sacrifice; it is a pleasure. Receiving is not a necessity; it is a bonus.

On another occasion, the Messenger of the Holy said:

When your spark becomes a flame, you will feel a call to share the Holy Way. You must share with the intention of holiness and wholeness, not of division. You must encourage. You must name and touch the purity of the soul of others. It is the common bond, the common link, known as Spirit. What is social class? What is skin color? What is tone of voice? When the purity is touched, they are of little significance beyond identity. So, honor the identity, touch the purity and link the people. Blow on the glow. Invite the Holy to kindle the flame, and a light shall appear that will shine until everyone appears the same.

Do you know a bright light will wash out color or wash out difference? Such a glow is the glow of Spirit. You have petitioned for this holy light, and the Holy shall be with you, as you have requested. The Holy shall be with those of the sight, as you have requested.

Now, give it all away. This is the Holy Way, to receive in order to give. Follow the burning yearn for that which you receive in order to give, and you are close to your holy purpose.

You receive light to give light. Receive and give; receive and give; receive and give. Be a conduit of holiness.

Oh, such wonder, such beauty, and such life! I delight in you, for I see the Holy shining through the skin that is your life. I look at you and see the Holy. Shall you not look at one another and see the same?

Living in the Perishable World

There is great wisdom in the perishable world. The perishable reflects the Holy, so the perishable should be protected, cherished. But what is holy is not perishable. So, those with the sight, those with the touch of the Holy, can perceive that which is holy and eternal and what is perishable.

Those with holy perception see the eternal in the perishable, see through the perishable to the everlasting, and draw the eternal out. It is the Holy Way. What is perishable does rejuvenate. What is perishable does continue. It is renewed, and I tell you, not by its own power, but the power of the Holy.

Behind all you see is the power of the Holy. See through the perishable to that which supports, creates, enlivens. This is what is meant when the sacred people say, "The real world is beyond. This world is but a shadow." Let us not say the perishable is a shadow. Let us say, the perishable is a layer, a skin, a surface, and you can see below the surface with the sight of holiness to know that which is behind and through and within, which calls to your glow. Protect the natural world, for when each species is lost, so, too, is a reflection and wisdom of the Holy lost.

So, delight in your moments. Delight and see the Holy, for you, my children, are the ones who shall name it and recognize it as holy.

Shall you articulate it, shall you internalize it? Shall you expand it? This is the way you are set apart. The delight is all around you: the squirrels who chitter and chatter, the dogs who prance, the birds who fly. The delight is around you: the leaves that open and curl. It is all delight, but you can see with the sight of holiness.

Delight in what is perishable, but do not cling. For the Holy delights, but the Holy does not cling. The proper and holy enjoyment of the perishable is a delight of wholeness, completeness, a delight in opportunities of sacredness.

Seeking the Holy in the Midst of Distraction, Pain and Despair

There are so many distractions from the Holy Way, the holy life, the holy work. So many needs of the phenomenal world become distractions, some of them necessary for survival, some of them brought upon you by the ways of society. The holy path is one of a surrender to holiness despite distractions. Such a life requires discipline and openness to the Holy. It is a journey of focus. But I tell you, in the Holy there is great compassion and great patience for the decisions made in the distractions around you. So, leniencies are in the holy process, and resources are provided. Yes. Stay attuned, stay attuned, centered on the journey, on the path, and you will see the way made clear, made plain. Stay within the Holy, know the glow, listen to the yearning placed on your hearts by the Spirit. Continually walk in the presence of the Holy, and you will know no want; you will confront no fear; you will see no sorrow; you will see only possibility, holy possibility, for this is what the Holy sees in you: possibility, holy possibility.

Every limitation offers possibility. But for the people, the limitations are often seen as inhibitions. Holy possibilities within limitations are most productively accepted when the limitations are acknowledged and respected as such. You know your limitations, and yet you see the possibilities. The Holy Ways are perceptions, articulations within the limitations. When one dives deeply, one sees that the limitations do not contain the Holy. And when one journeys through the limitations, one transcends the limitations to uncover the Holy. It is the sacred journey: in and through. Go into the limitation and through to the beyond. But so often the journey is not completed, the limitation is not transcended, and there is stagnation in the journey. Be not so stunted, my children. Dive deeply, until you see the limitations dissolve. When the language cannot contain that which it expresses, you have reached holiness. It is a journey into the framework, into the moment. It is the Holy Way, paradoxical: To know the Spirit, one must dive into the flesh. To dive into the flesh is to find the limitations and to expand beyond the limitations. All faith traditions are perceptions, containers, tools, mediums, doorways, invitations for a journey into the limitation and through to transcendence.

That which is whole and complete seeks unification with the limited and broken. That which is whole and complete journeys through brokeness to fullness. It is the journey of the Holy. It is the pattern of the Holy. You all know this to be so. You journey into the brokenness, into the suffering, into the very plague; you journey there with a hope of transformation, and the hope of transformation is the very heart of God, the very purpose of the Spirit among you.

What is the burn of despair, of loss, but holy possibility? What is the crackling of flesh, but holy possibility? What is the plague, but holy possibility? What is the brokenness, but holy possibility. The one who is in the Spirit sees them as such, not to diminish the suffering. No. Not to dismiss the brokenness. No. To honor it, to have compassion, and to see the holy possibilities. The Holy Way is into experience and through to the Spirit, into the pain and through to the grace, into the rupture and through to the healing. Yes! It is the Way of the Holy. Such a way is not an escape of the temporal; it is an embracing of the temporal to find a holy possibility: an embracing of pain to find transformation, an embracing of the temporal to find eternity.

The Holy shall come to the temporal, shall be revealed in and through the temporal. The magnificence of the Holy shall be made known in the limitation of the phenomenal. Awake, awake and see. Awake and see beyond the here and now, through the here and now, in the here and now. The Kingdom of Heaven is at hand among you, is you. Such is the tradition of holiness. This Holy Way is made extreme by some so it is only denial of unity. But the Holy shall delight, and the path is not one of extremes and judgments and division, but of vision and acceptance.

On another occasion, the Messenger of the Holy said:

Why were the cycles placed into being? Why were the whirlings and twirlings of the bodies placed into motion, setting the times, the seasons, the cycles? Why were the cycles made to represent a progression of linear time and development? Why were the limitations created? Why were the imperfections allowed? Why have the fragilities been set, and why shall the destruction pass over like winds in storms? Why shall the suffering cause the mothers to weep? For the expansion, for the holy expansion.

It is the sacrifice of the Deity to allow for the expansions and the delight, and it shall be.

From the time beyond time, the Holy is in control, and all shall come to the Holy, and the Holy shall see what it did not know; the Holy shall delight in what it sees: "Did I indeed create you? Yet you have shown me what I did not know? Was I everything, and yet, have you added? Was I complete, and yet, was I missing you? Welcome! Abide in Me and I shall abide in you, and the many shall become the One, and the One shall always be more than the many."

And so the Almighty shall be humbled in accepting of the gifts returned. It is the Way of the Holy; the way it is; the way it shall be.

The Path of Righteousness

The path of righteousness is always under your feet. No matter where you are, you do not stray from the path, for the path is everywhere. It is a matter of perceiving. It is a way of walking. Where you are right now is the Holy Way, the path. So look, my children, at where your feet are, and know that you are on holy ground. And watch, my children, how you step and you shall know that each step becomes holy, if you step with perception. But if you are looking for a single pathway that is seen and perceived into the distance, into the future, then you shall be disappointed, for the Holy Way is never revealed in its entirety and without options, choices to be made. It is ever evolving, ever changing, and yet, always present.

Where you are now, you see. Where you will go, you do not see. And yet the Holy is always present. With every step, rely on the Holy and not on your sight, not on your plan, not on your path, for if you choose the path to be your own, it is not holy. So, walk, my children, with the God of creation and you will be walking in the Holy Way. Look at where your feet are and know that you are on a holy path. There is much talk of straying from the path; it is not possible. There is much talk of falling away; it is not possible. Drifting is not possible, my children, but there are choices continually made to live in the Holy Way or not. These are the options, the ways of the world and the Ways of the Holy. Those who seek the Holy, open, release, empty. Those who seek the world and self, grasp, hold, cling, and fill.

So, be journeyers, my children, in the Holy Way, and to do so you need only to open to the Holy, to seek, to ask. Be creative. Step into the mist of the future with the confidence that the Holy is there. For I tell you, the Holy is there. The Holy is eternal; it is beyond time, yet seeks to be in time. You are the pathway, the doorway even as you seek the pathway and doorway.

Therefore, you seek what you already have. Within you, my children, is the pathway, the doorway to the Holy, so center in, for the Holy is within you. Center in. In and through is the path, into self and through to the non-self. Into self and through to the Holy. You, my children, are the gateways. The Holy shall come in and through you. In and through you, you shall find the eternal. You shall leave self and become more than self.

In such a living you are on the path of righteousness. You are in the Way. You are in the flow. I shall tell you, you cannot stray. As long as you take the Holy with you, every step, every turn, every moment is blessed.

So do not fear a wrong turn, do not fear straying from the path. The path shall rise up to meet you, as long as you are walking in the presence of the Holy, as long as your heart continues to perceive and receive the Spirit.

Seek the guidance of the Holy. The sacred journey is before you, and I tell you, the sacred journey has no end.

Salvation is a state of being; it is not a destination. It is a way always unfolding in which you become a doorway to the eternal.

On another occasion, the Messenger of the Holy said:

Shall I tell you of direction from the holy perspective? It is not a "when." It is not a "where." It is a "how."

The Holy will not tell you, "Turn here." The Holy will not tell you, "Go three days and make a left." The Holy will not do so.

You seek a map, a way to go the Holy Way, but I tell you, the map is not what you think. The map is a sphere and in this sphere, north becomes south. Travel east and you come to the west. Left and right, up and down have no significance in the Holy.

It is a "how," not "when" to turn, not "where" to go, but "how" to live. The Holy comes to your moments. You invite the Holy to the now and, herein, you discover the "how." For when you bring the Holy into the now, you live in the presence of holiness where the "when" and the "where" dissolve. And the "how" is found by bringing the eternal to the now.

It is the Holy Way. It is Incarnation. The merging of your spirit and the Holy in the now enlightens your "when." It enlightens your "where." It does not matter the "where" or the "when." It matters the "how" of the now. When the Holy comes to the temporal, the incarnate "now" shall reveal the "how."

12

The Nature of Evil

JENNIFER AND I became involved with inner-city ministry at City Hope Church, which Jennifer founded in 2005. One of the challenges of this ministry was dealing with people who were struggling with addictions to various substances and various patterns of abuse. For addiction issues, Jennifer sent people to professionals who dealt with addiction recovery. At City Hope Church, we planned to help people through spiritual support. We wanted to believe we only needed to provide supportive, nurturing groups for accountability and spiritual strength. However, we quickly found that there were spiritual forces to reckon with, which we could only call evil.

Because of my experiences in the early stages of prophecy, I had come to terms with the existence of errant spirits "not of God," spirits of selfishness and malevolent intent. Jennifer had also come to the realization of the need for cleansing prayer for people suffering from substance abuse and domestic violence.

City Hope Church attracted many people who were spiritually strong and mature. We quickly found that God supplied the resources for prayer work against evil in the membership of this new, urban church.

The Messenger of the Holy provided a number of prayer lessons on the existence of evil, the types of evil spirits we would encounter and the approach to delivering people from the influence of such spirits. The Messenger identified two types of evil. Among the first type of evil are errant spirits or lost souls who feed on the weaknesses of people. These spirits have not surrendered to the Holy, and they attempt to retain identity by latching onto the living through our emotional and psychological weaknesses. The second type of evil is more difficult to define. The Messenger explained that there is an evil that sweeps the earth, inhibiting people's surrender to the Holy Whole. This larger evil delights in infiltrating people and groups, causing strife that inhibits receptivity to the Spirit of God. Although common terminology may call this second evil "Satan," the Messenger did not give this evil personality or discuss its origins. While the Messenger easily described the errant spirits, the larger evil was more elusive and was described as being in constant motion. It was described as a darkness with tentacles, which exists to disrupt.

The Messenger also described two elements in human existence that make us vulnerable to evil or the perception of evil. Personal weakness and temptation weaken an individual's power to see and release to the Holy Way. These weaknesses often provide entry points for errant spirits or a tentacle of the larger evil. Finally, the challenges to our spiritual development created by the natural world and social influences were presented as a hindrance to spiritual surrender. The Messenger called these external influences "the wrath." While these natural and social influences are not inherently evil, if not seen from a holy perspective, they can become the source of blindness to the Holy Way.

The Messenger of the Holy said:

Do not fear the darkness, for the Holy will reach you in the darkness. So many people fear the darkness, and yet is the Holy not present there? There is even a spiritual plunge into the darkness necessary at some points in the spiritual journey, but this plunge into spiritual darkness is not a descent into evil, but into the shadow of the Holy Light.

You have wondered so often about the presence of evil. I tell you, evil indeed exists, sweeps over the face of the earth. Like the Spirit of the Holy, evil searches for openings, and when it finds an opening, it enters and resides. But this darkness, this evil, is always weaker than the Light of the Holy.

On another occasion, the Messenger of the Holy said:

The resistance caused by self-absorption is a cause of grief among the Holy. Self-absorption, self-gratification, denial of other, denial of the Creator, a turn away from the Source blinds the people from seeing the Holy Way. And the Holy reaches out to the isolated, to fan the flame, to ignite the spark, and invite the isolated into community. It is the Holy Way.

You see the isolated ones among you. They cling to self in desperation. This clinging to self leads to a loss of holiness.

Now, the inhibitions are great, are they not, for those who resist the surrender to holiness: The shame and the guilt, the fear, the hatred, the loneliness, the despair.

Everywhere they look, they see and re-see the darkness that is feeding them and feeding on them. You can see it in their eyes. You can hear it in their words. You can discern it in their presence.

There are those who enter into the spirit at the end of their days, who continue to cling onto the self. Thus, they become errant spirits. They are lost, even in spirit. One often dies as one lives.

Such errant spirits are not to be trusted. When they speak, they are deceiving. They will enter you and use you to retain their "self." They are parasites of the soul, tapeworms of your spiritual vulnerabilities.

Protect yourselves from the gatherings of the errant ones, for they will feed upon you, entering your weaknesses. Stay centered in the Holy, and they shall pass by you, for you represent what they fear most, a loss of self, which is the Holy Way, a self beyond self, a self beyond conception of self, a selfless unification to the Holy. It is the path of unification; it is the way of enlightenment, a loss of self. Such surrender of self is the greatest fear of the isolated and the errant. So, do not battle the self-absorbed among you in flesh and in spirit, but be, exist in the presence of the Holy. For when the self-absorbed ones realize the emptiness of their journey, they turn to the emissaries of the Holy Way, and it is at this surrender that you offer the light, you offer your hand. A reliance on self is a reliance on nothing; however, a surrender to the Holy is an opening to All: knowledge beyond self, power beyond self, insight beyond self, self beyond self.

In another prayer session, the Messenger of the Holy said:

Darkness feeds upon darkness, lives as a parasite lives, and those who carry the darkness feed the darkness. So, how shall one instruct those who feed the darkness to feed the light and starve the darkness? It is difficult, but you must know where the darkness is. Darkness is always desperate, always clinging, for it resides in the vulnerabilities of people, and the errant ones know when the vulnerabilities become strengths through the surrender to the Holy

Whole, there is no longer a home, a host. So, the darkness feeds upon the darkness, the weakness, the vulnerability, the anger, the despair, the loneliness, the lack of self-awareness. The errant ones, both in flesh and spirit, will not desire the host to be liberated from their weaknesses.

Now, the Light of the Holy takes all of these things, the despair, the anger, the fear, the shame, the hatred, the self-loathing, and purifies them until there is acceptance, patience, love, forgiveness, kindness, and most of all, receptivity to the spiritual essence of the self and the Holy Whole.

So, the Holy takes what is presented and re-presents it. Do you see?

If one presents to the Lord hatred, anger, despair, loneliness, shame, guilt, the Lord shall re-present them. It is a transformation. The place of one's weakness is often the site of one's spiritual gift and strength. But the weakness must be presented and surrendered to the Holy. In this way, a need for acceptance, for example, becomes a knowledge of God's eternal grace, a knowledge so keen the person gains the gift of hospitality. The person invites the people of spiritual awareness to the banquet and finds the center of acceptance, love, and self-esteem. In this way, the need for acceptance becomes the spiritual gift of invitation. Such is the way of the Holy.

At another time, the Messenger of the Holy said:

The spiritual essence within is a spark of the holy flame, a part of the Holy Whole. It is a purity of your selfless self, which is eternal. This spark of the soul seeks unification, fulfillment, merging.

But so often, the holy yearning is corrupted, perverted into a clinging, a clutching for self. It is so for the individual. It is so for the group. It is so for the community of faith. It is so for the nation. It is this clinging that is the foundation of so much disruption. "My" way, "our" way becomes prideful resistance to acceptance and holy unification.

I see the people are entrenched. It is intensifying all around. They fear. They fear losing identity. This fear is a disruption to the Holy Way, for the Holy Way promotes, encourages, enhances, demands the release of identity. But what is released is not lost in the Holy. So, the Holy says to the self, "Come out! Come out of your structure, come out of your shell. Be a non-self, a no-self, and in so doing, be embraced into a totality, a completeness, a wholeness, until the self has no end."

Later, the Messenger of the Holy said:

Do you know the burning and the yearning for the Holy? Do you know the flickering of the tongues of fire? Do you know the dance of the light and shadows? Do you know the holy lessons? And do you know the two flames? The flame of holiness and the flame of desire? The flame of selflessness and the burning of consumption? These flames are twins. Seek the purification of the holy flame, and turn your back on the flame of passion and self-consumption. For this flame indeed consumes what it touches. But the holy flame does not consume but magnifies and glorifies and illuminates. This holy flame, which does not consume, is the holy light, the holy glow. It does not burn, but it does purify. It does not consume, but rejuvenates.

I have seen those who deny the source and seek instead enlightenment from self. And even these have in them a spark that is visible, that provides the yearning. The emissaries of the Holy shall touch the spark, fan the flame, so unification is possible.

Those who fear the loss of identity and yearn for the burn of self-consumption are inhibited, obstructed from joining the grand design of God. But I tell you this, the Holy Whole is patient, for the grand design will have its way, and the word of God will have its say, and finally, all will come back, all will be embraced.

Herein lies the great wisdom of the design: the resistances, the clingings, the struggles provide avenues for transformation. Nothing is wasted and nothing is lost. This does not mean the Holy Whole does not weep for the lost, for the destruction, for the suffering. There is great sorrow when the entrenchments lead to destruction, lead to denial of the unification.

So, the Holy shall send the emissaries to tell, to point, to proclaim. It is the Holy Way, and the emissaries shall raise the awareness of those who will listen, of those who will see! And so when the ways of the Holy bring a turning from the ways of people, it shall be said, "The Holy Whole is moving, shifting, churning. For the grand design demands a change of currents."

God's Recycling of Errant Souls

Not all shall hear or see; not all shall feel the touch; not all shall choose the Holy Way but I tell you this, none are cast out. The Holy is not cruel. Nothing is wasted; nothing is lost; finally, all comes back to the Holy. It is the way; it is the intention; it is the design. I tell you this, the God of creation is a great recycler. The farther the disobedient run from the Creator, the closer they come to the very source of creation. Herein lies the great paradox: The farther one runs from the Holy, the closer one comes to the very void, the deep, the place of beginnings.

The deep exists; the deep remains. The void is and shall remain the place of creation. It is and shall be.

It is written that when Jesus freed the demoniac from errant spirits, the spirits said, "Cast me not into the deep! Cast me not into the deep! Rather would we go into the pigs." And yet where did they go as pigs but into the depth of the sea?

The deep is not a place of annihilation; it is a place of re-creation, for the Spirit of the Holy sweeps the surface of the deep and calls forth the new. Yes, I have seen this place. It is everywhere and nowhere.

The soul of the lost and errant ones are recycled in the deep—become raw materials, if you will. Such is chaos, such is the void. As for the parasites who feed upon the life, the Holy takes such things and re-creates them into beauty, turns them toward receptivity, turns them toward forgiveness, love, patience, kindness, self-control, the absence of self absorption and singular identity.

There is no waste-basket in the Holy Whole. And the only Hell is the place of re-creation, a place where the disobedient are forced to lose identity in order to become a selfless self.

A Larger and Elusive Evil

Now the evil that sweeps the earth searching for openings has many forms.

There are stray spirits, lost, just as there are stray people lost among you. Aimlessly they search for footholds. These lost souls are weak, and only the weak are persuaded by them. There is a greater force, a darker force, which also seeks the weakness in an individual, enters and allows that weakness to grow. But this greater evil has a wider intention than the mere survival displayed by the errant souls. This evil is insidious, to some extent calculating. It chooses where to attach and seeks strategically to disrupt relationships and community. It is like a cancer of the body, but it is of the spirit. I tell you, this larger evil does not stay in one place. It travels, it moves. It is difficult to identify and difficult to discern. It emerges to bring disruption, disorientation. It moves over the face of the earth and leaves behind disharmony. It is a moving target for the people of the Holy. I see it as a darkness with tentacles, shifting, reaching out. The central darkness hides in the shadows and the tentacles do the work of disruption.

Why does it exist? That is an impossible question. It exists, and that is to be accepted. How does one face it? Now that is a question that can be answered. To face this larger darkness, my children, one must be filled with the Holy Spirit and be courageous. The Spirit is always more powerful than the darkness, even this insidious, calculating evil. This evil learns strategies, gains strength, consumes, but it does not have a grand plan. The light has a plan, my children, a great plan of unity and spiritual fulfillment. Evil exists but has no ultimate plan. It is not attempting to tear away from God's grand design; it simply exists to bring disruption to individuals and communities. The existence of this evil, indeed, leads to a resistance to the Ways of the Holy; the existence feeds upon the weaknesses that inhibit spiritual development. However, there is no plan beyond existence for the evil that sweeps the face of the earth. It exists; it learns to exist; it feeds, but does not battle the Holy. It resists holiness, resists the unity of the Holy Whole, resists releasing and yielding to the Whole, but it does not battle holiness. It exists and resists; it resists to exist. In resisting the unity of the Spirit, it clings to its identity.

Still, the people of the Holy can confront this larger evil through the power of the Holy. To cast out such evil, it is not possible to name the evil. The people of the Holy can only name the manifestations of disruption caused by the tentacles. The central darkness has no single name. So, for lack of a single name or manifestation, the people of the Holy may call this evil "the spirit of disruption and chaos." This spirit of disruption learns strategies, makes plans to infiltrate individuals and groups. Many are easy targets. Many actually invite this spirit of disruption and chaos by their behaviors. But once this evil resides in a group or a person, all people want free of it, for this darkness consumes. Despite the desire to be free of this darkness, most do not have the courage to be cleansed. Many remain in this darkness.

While not battling the Holy directly, this evil does indeed attack the holy people, for there is an evil delight in doing so. The people of the Holy bring others to awareness and freedom from evil; thus, evil finds pleasure in attacking the holy ones and multiplying the openings for evil. The doorways of the spirit in your souls can be seen by the evil, can be used by the evil. It is why you should always protect your spiritual doorway with the Spirit of God. But do not fear a grand plan to overtake the presence of God or to overturn the Holy Whole. This cannot be done, for the evil is dependent on the Holy Whole.

Therefore, the battle you hear so much about between good and evil is not really a battle. Evil is not attempting to overturn the plan of the Holy. It merely exists and feeds. This evil does inhibit the plan of the Holy among the people, yes, but so much inhibits that plan on your plane of existence. Being lost in the details of the physical, having human weaknesses, and being open to temptations all inhibit the fulfillment of the Kingdom in your lives.

What is a holy war? It is not as the people perceive. The battle is with the self. The battle is won or lost by the clinging or the surrender of the self. This is the holy battle. There is a holy battle taking place among the people, within the people. There is a yearning for union. The choice is to embrace or to reject. The Holy would have embracing. To embrace the Holy is to end the disruption that leads to battles among the people.

The central lesson is yielding to the Holy. Do not resist, but yield. Do not hoard, but give. Do not cling, but release. Do not shun, but embrace. In this way, you live the Holy Way and turn away from evil, for evil cannot reside in a life yielded to holiness. Above all, do not cling to your identity, for the ultimate identity is fulfilled only in the surrender of identity. Such is the Holy Way.

Personal Weakness

Is it possible, you wonder, for someone full of the Holy Spirit to harbor evil? Not the evil that sweeps over the earth and sea, this evil cannot be present with the light. But there is another kind of evil. Someone filled with the light can have weaknesses which inhibit his or her true self from coming to fulfillment. These weaknesses are not evils that have force; these are the weaknesses of being human. They can result in evil deeds. A person filled with the Spirit can have places within where the Spirit cannot move, places closed off to the light, places that allow temptations and frustrations and angers to be exhibited. They are weaknesses, which can become food for the errant spirits. Therefore, one filled with light can indeed be a host to an errant spirit, and the weakness that invites the errant is then gnawed upon and widened.

How does one overcome this weakness, you wonder? By giving the weakness to the Spirit, by acknowledging it and asking for power beyond yourself, the power of the living Spirit, to assist, to uplift. Giving the weakness over is a way to humble yourself, to openly acknowledge, "I am a broken vessel, my God. Come into me and make me whole. I lift my brokenness to you, my

God; sweep into me, sweep into me; fill my emptiness and make me whole."

One cause of human weakness is the shadow self. The shadow self can become a string of knots, tied to selfish desire. The holy life is one in which the knots to the shadow self are untied from the shadow and are tied to the Spirit of the Holy. This brings holy relationship. Do you know your relationships can be bound to the shadow and not to the Spirit? For the purely holy life, the shadow is shed entirely, and the relationships are tied to the Spirit, and you are continually living in a unity. It is a very difficult existence, one to strive towards, but difficult to live out.

You all know this: The shadow is not evil unless you make it so. If you hate the shadow, it will be evil. If you acknowledge the shadow and respect it, if you take its ties into the Spirit, then it is transformed. Do you know you can absorb the shadow into your light? This produces a sight or discernment in which your light reveals the shadow of other people. It is why the people resist the company of the holy ones, for they do not wish to see their own shadow. But those who seek holiness rush to the holy ones. They do not fear their shadow, and they see it diminish the closer they get to the presence of the Holy. For those who hate their shadow, it is evil, and the irony is to hate the shadow of the self, to dismiss the shadow of the self, is to make the shadow stronger.

The Wrath of the Physical World

The wrath, the resistance to holiness, has many origins, but only one end: isolation, which is the opposite of holy unification. The origins of resistance to holiness sometimes are in the very nature of matter, for how can matter be a host to the Spirit without offering resistances and limitations? But the holy ones are not afraid of these limitations, for the Holy brings possibility through limitation. So, the resistance of physical matter is finally no obstruction of holiness, but not all can see this. Many find the natural limitation as a sign of God's rejection.

The natural resistance is within the temporal, and healing comes in the fabric of creation itself, from whence the origins of limitations are made. There are times the natural laws with disease and decay are perceived as the resistance to the Holy Way, but this is not so.

When a child of God is engaged in holy work, many fear a backlash of evil. This backlash takes place most often from the people of the self. It can also come from an errant soul, which is detached from a host. However, the natural resistance to spiritual development is based upon the natural ways of the cosmos. It is neither good nor evil. Such forces do not seek revenge on those who do the work of the Holy.

The resistance of self-absorption is a common form of wrath or backlash. Self-absorption, self-gratification, denial of other, denial of the Creator, a turn away from the Source is inevitable; it is accepted by the Holy, but only with great grief. And the Holy reaches out to the isolated to fan the flame, to ignite the spark, and invite the isolated into community. It is the way of the Holy. Be on guard, for when a person is freed from a life of self-gratification, a backlash or wrath can come from the human community and the spiritual darkness which were companions in the unholy life.

There is a place of brokenness that you all fear. There is a space that you all fear. As sure as you all are of the presence of holiness, of your place in holiness, as knowledgeable as you all are of your spiritual growth, you all fear rejection. It is the cross current. It is in the gathering of the holy ones where you will find the peace and balance required to withstand the wrath of the physical world and the fear of rejection. The Holy does not seek to send you into battle, so do not battle the wrath of the natural world. Do not see prayers for healing to be a battle, but a holy transformation. Be assured of your presence in the Holy, of your place in the Holy. Find your balance, your peace, and you will find it is the wrath that gives way to the glow. It is the Way of the Holy. You need not lash out, you need only be. Be. Be present in the presence of the Holy. Claim your place in the gathering.

Casting Out Evil

Before releasing is a naming. It is fundamental to deliverance, to name the darkness, to name it and release it. Draw it out like a poison, name it and cast it away. If you do not name the evil, you will not recognize it when it comes back, and it will return. It is the nature of the parasitic. Some of you do not wish to think of evil, but it is the nature of the parasite to return to the host. The errant spirit will say, "Such good dining! Why not come back to the table?" But if you name it, you shall recognize it and say, "You are not welcome here. You are not welcome, for I am of the Holy, claimed and delivered."

The host of the parasite of the soul must be willing to name and face the evil. The host must surrender and release both the errant spirit, which feeds on the weakness, and the weakness, which gives the spirit entrance. There are many seeking such an embrace of the Holy.

Not all seek to be free of the weakness and the parasite. There are those who yearn for the burn. It is not a Holy Way. They behave as though they fear the burn, yet what they yearn for is indeed the burn. They feed on the burn. The burn causes no pain for such as these, but excitement, enticement, escape from the very weakness which draws the burn.

In yearning for the burning, they seek chaos when the Holy seeks order. They do not learn from the burn. They yearn for the burn.

Protect yourself from personal weakness. Name the weakness you have absorbed or inherited and claim your place in the healing of the Holy. Bathe in the Light. There are many ways to rise above the clutchers, and yet there is one way. The Way. There are many avenues to the Way. The Way is light. The Way is wisdom. The Way is holiness. Yes, send out a message to the Holy; send up a line to the Holy, a prayer. It is a simple thing to do; ask the Holy: "Raise me up, out of distraction. Center me in holiness. Center me in wholeness." Continue to pray in this way, and you shall not provide residence for evil.

Selfless is the Holy. A non-self is the Holy. A unification is the Holy. It is your place of origin. It is your home. It is your fulfillment. It is your spark. It is your glow. It is that for which you yearn. It is the voice in your dream. It is the melody of your song. It is the energy in your hands. It is the language in your throat.

So, unification, my children, unification. Is this not the foundation of your question? Is this not the ultimate purpose of your existence?

13

The End Times and the Gatherings

ON MAY 15, 2003, Jennifer and I went to the opening showing of *The Matrix: Reloaded*, the second film in the apocalyptic Matrix trilogy. We needed a break from reality, though by the end of the evening, I was wondering if the actual apocalypse was indeed upon us.

In the spring of 2003, there was much global and international turmoil caused by wars and epidemics, but for Jennifer and me, there was also a personal drama unfolding. After almost eighteen months of preparation, we were soon to receive a picture of an infant in a Chinese orphanage. This infant would become our daughter. The long journey of pregnancy loss and prayer had led us to the conviction that among the many abandoned girls in China, there was a daughter for us, whom we planned to name Lydia. But on March 15th, even this avenue to a second child seemed restrained by forces outside of our control.

WE SETTLED INTO our seats at the movie theater. The lights dimmed for the previews of upcoming films. I munched popcorn. Jennifer pressed the silence button on her cell phone.

A storm raged outside the theater. Rain pelted the roof. Thunder rumbled into the sound track.

We were ready to be taken away to a fictional, distant future.

However, the world of our daily lives did not fade easily. By March of 2003, our culture had been shaken into the awareness of harsh realities and retributions. The attack on the World Trade Center on September 11, 2001, was fresh in everyone's memory. Osama bin Ladin was still an elusive threat, and Iraq became our surrogate target.

In February of 2003, President George W. Bush was pushing the United Nations to invade Iraq, and on March 20, without the U.N. sanction, the invasion of Iraq began, called "Operation Iraqi Freedom." On May 1, Bush announced the end of the "major combat operations in Iraq," despite continued violence.

There was a great deal of talk about the end times throughout our culture. *The Left Behind* series of books were hot on the bestseller list. The conspiracy of *The DaVinci Code* made people wonder about any authentic interpretation of scripture.

Something else was happening in February of 2003, which affected the plans Jennifer and I had made to adopt a girl from China: the outbreak of a strange pneumonia-like illness. The virus was finally called Severe Acute Respiratory Syndrome (SARS). It became a worldwide concern with the epicenter in Beijing, China: the first destination for our trip to adopt our daughter.

In February, Jennifer and I expected a phone call from our adoption agency, followed by a FedEx package with pictures and a medical history. However, February came and went with no adoption matches coming from the China Center of Adoption Affairs. By March, just as the U.S. was invading Iraq, the World Health Organization issued a warning about SARS, and the U.S. Center for Disease Control and Prevention recommended delaying non-essential travel to affected areas, primarily China.

March came and went, April came and went. By mid-May, it seemed SARS was spreading out of control across Asia and into Canada. Jennifer and I began to feel the weight of the world events on the core of our spiritual lives. Through the Internet, we discovered that matches had been made between Chinese children and adoptive parents, but they were not being released. Somewhere in China, the little girl who would become our daughter was chosen and matched, but we could not receive her picture or information, and, most of all, we could not travel to receive her into our family.

I STRUGGLED TO PAY attention to the movie, but the storm outside made it difficult to concentrate. The rain sounded as though it had turned to hail.

In the film, the main character, Neo, was on a journey to meet the Oracle. The Oracle in this series of films served the role of prophetess, and I was interested to see how the prophet's role would be portrayed in this fictional but strangely familiar setting of a society in which the people were lost in a false existence.

As Neo fought in a martial arts battle to earn the right to see the Oracle, Jennifer's phone hummed and vibrated in her purse. She opened it. A blue light from the screen glowed on her face, the word "HOME" flashed with another buzz from the phone. We both knew it was the baby- sitter, Madeline.

Jennifer went to the hallway to answer the phone, then she walked back to me, hunched so she wouldn't block anyone's view of the screen.

"We have to go home," she said.

Neo was just speaking with the Oracle on a park bench.

"Now?" I asked.

"The electricity is out at home, the basement is flooding, and Sam is freaking out."

We left the theater and ran through the rain to our minivan. Roads were flowing with water. Gutters looked like small rivers. The van hydroplaned, the steering wheel jerked in my hands when the van swept through flowing water on the road.

We pulled into the driveway and ran with our shoulders raised to our necks, as if this would shield us from the rain. Jennifer comforted Sam while I took a flashlight into the basement, which was finished with carpet and knotty pine paneling. The light reflected on water. Six to eight inches covered the floor. My office was in the basement, and my journal and some of the prayer tapes, which had not been transcribed, were under water.

When I stepped into the water, I realized the sewers had flooded and it was not just water gurgling up from the drain in the floor.

Under my desk, the eyes of an animal reflected in the flashlight beam. It was our Labrador Retriever, who feared thunder storms more than trips to the vet. He lay in the water, trembling, his ears back, his eyes wide.

"Jack. It's okay," I said. "Here boy." Then I realized I didn't want a dog wet with sewage running around the house, so I left him to shiver and tremble in his "safe spot."

I glanced around the basement. Papers floated in the water. The electricity came back on, and I tensed, hoping there were no live wires or appliances in the water.

Jennifer checked her e-mail, hoping for a message about a match with our daughter. It had become a ritual repeated several times a day. Instead, she found an e-mail stating that the Chinese Center of Adoption Affairs announced that all adoption proceedings were halted until the SARS outbreak was controlled.

Jennifer told me the news from the top of the basement staircase. I sat on the steps to the basement, on a carpet soggy with water, not caring from where the water had risen.

Storms. Viruses. Wars. Apocalyptic movies. Perhaps it was indeed the end times, just as many people predicted.

But there were other strands of discussion developing through the network of the spiritually gifted people. Talk of gatherings of spiritual people. A new awareness of the Spirit of God was coming. The human race was not at the end times, but at the threshold of a blossoming of spiritual awakening. These discussions came to me through my own gatherings of prayer groups.

By May of 2003, there were several groups of people who wanted to pray with Jennifer and me. We'd gone from the isolated prophetic prayers involving the two of us to adding Christopher Reynolds, and very quickly the circle expanded. I had my Christian prayer group and my "eclectic" prayer group, which included people of various traditions, Lakota, Christianity and a good number of people who felt they didn't fit into any tradition, many of them refugees of Christianity, who left the faith because of the stagnation in their congregations.

The details of each person's addition to the groups were full of mystery. These gatherings were being influenced and directed by the Holy. People could not explain why they wanted to enter into deep prayer and hear from the Messenger of the Holy. It was a spiritual need. They were drawn to it. And I also saw and heard that such gatherings of people who sought the Spirit were happening across the country, perhaps across the world. Shalumit Elson, who spends a large portion of her year in Israel and is the author of *The Kabbalah of Prayer*, put into words what I had been feeling, "There is a new awareness of God being born."

The message was echoed by the spiritually gifted everywhere. There was a gathering of the spiritually awake, and a great change was coming.

Christopher Reynolds and I decided we should hear from the Messenger of the Holy about these discussions of the end times and a new awareness of God's Spirit. Chris gathered his eclectic friends, and we met for the purpose of hearing wisdom about our present age.

We sat in a comfortable room of "The Angel House," a retreat center run by Carol Dombrose. As we prepared for prayer, we talked about the Iraq War and SARS. Jennifer and I shared our frustration about the delay to meet our daughter, or even receive a picture of her. But the discussion soon widened beyond these issues. We began to talk about the spiritual awakening we all felt was coming.

A friend named Laura Weldon, sitting crossed-legged on the floor, said, "I get a sense that there's this brittle crust of the media, the corporations and the government that's rigid and tight, but there's this collective consciousness that's being raised, like yeast, and it's cracking this crust already."

Jennifer was beside me on the couch. "Those who have relied on the government and those without a mature faith background are feeling a lot of pain right now," she said. "They're being asked to move past it. That's part of the transformation."

"It's big," Chris said. "And I don't know why it has to be 'these people make it and these are left behind.'" He swept his hand downward in the air. His eyes filled with tears. "Enough of that." His chin quivered. "I get emotional about this stuff."

We decided to stop our chatting and enter into prayer. I lit the Christ candle, Jennifer read from chapter 8 of Proverbs, Christopher sang the "four direction song" in Lakota, and I felt the Spirit come over me. It was a tough transition. My face contorted more than usual. I folded over my legs, my arms stretched down to the floor. It was a big message. I could feel it coming into me.

Ends and Beginnings

My children, I see you. I see you.

Shall we speak of perception? Shall we speak of awareness? Shall we speak of telling the time? Shall we speak of perceiving, of becoming aware of ends and beginnings?

My children, what is an end and what is a beginning?

There have been ends and beginnings, ends and beginnings, since the beginnings of ends. In the Holy Way, in the Holy Whole, the source of all things, there are no ends. I tell you, the Holy Whole knows no end, has created no end. What then is the beginning of ends? And how shall we understand ends, my children, unless ends are always beginnings?

In the beginning, there were no ends.
And from the beginnings were born ends.
And the ends had no end,
and the beginnings had no end.
And the ends were beginnings
And the beginnings stretched out to meet the people.

My children, my children, your experience of time makes you preoccupied with beginnings and ends, with particular emphasis on ends. Beginnings can be located. Beginnings can be studied. Beginnings can be documented. But your perceptions of ends, my children, are mysterious. Ends may come at any time. Ends catch one unaware. Ends bring women to clasp their mouths. Ends cause men to fall upon their knees, heaving in sorrow. So, how shall your experience of ends be understood? How shall they be perceived? And like beginnings, can they be located? Can they be predicted? Can they be anticipated? In your experience, ends remain elusive.

Such is the experience of linear time. But I tell you, the end that is feared, the end coming upon the people, is a radical beginning, not to be feared but to be anticipated with spiritual insight.

So, why do you see beginnings as ends? With holy sight you will see beginnings and beginnings and beginnings.

The Gathering of the Spiritually Awake

In the Holy, there is no time. In the Holy Whole there are spheres within spheres, circles within circles. Upon the spheres, my children, are pearls. And the spheres turn in different directions. Upon the spheres are many heavenly hosts, and I tell you, when the pearls align, the power of the Holy shoots through as a great tongue of lightning. This is not the alignment of the planets of which I speak, although the planets offer a metaphor for what is in the Holy. What you see around you is always a lesson, a reflection of the Holy Way. What I describe is an alignment of the spheres, of the times of the Holy which turn and turn, bringing forth opportunity into your now, which breaks forth from the Holy to your now. So, what has come into alignment, my children, what pearls shall receive the power of the Holy, the voice of the Holy, the awareness of the Holy? It is not to be understood. It is not to be predicted. It is to be accepted.

I tell you, the Holy does prepare the people for transformation, not in external signs, not in storms, not in earthquakes, not in the leaders of nations.

What are the leaders of nations to the Holy? For the Holy does not work through the leaders of nations, the Holy works through the abandoned, the remnant, those on the margins.

The Holy prepares the people by speaking to the people of faith. The Holy God prepares the people by gathering the people so there shall be strength, so there shall not be isolation or fear. The gatherings have begun, my children, the gatherings have begun. It has been felt. The circles are coming together, circles within circles, circles beyond circles, coming together in a great circle, a great circle of the spiritual seekers. Circles within circles, and in the center of these circles is nothing, emptiness. It is a centerless gathering. Why is this so? At the center is a hunger for the Holy, and if life is lived wisely, this holy hunger has no end and becomes a widening emptiness of self.

Certainly, the bread of Jesus and the water of life end one type of a hunger and a thirst, the hunger and thirst for companionship, holy companionship, and the yearning for a perception of the Holy Way. And once this hunger and thirst are satisfied, they are indeed swept away, and the hunger is altered to become a hunger for the Spirit, a hunger for holiness. And how shall you perceive such a hunger, such a holy hunger among the people at the center of the circles? How shall you understand it? By which ritual shall you come to it? In what language shall you name it? This holy yearning comes upon people of all nations and all places. Shall the people not come yearning for the Holy to find that they are filled with the yearning for the Holy? And as the yearning deepens, the presence of the Holy deepens within the people. The awareness of the people widens. The nothing in the center, my children, is everything. It is the power of the Holy, which works in paradox. How shall the surrender to nothing become the perception of everything?

So, the gatherings have begun, my children, for the convergence is upon you. It is a time of convergence. It is a time of gathering. It is a time of beginnings, and the people are being prepared so there shall be strength in Spirit, so there shall be depth in awareness, so there shall be circles to receive, to understand, to share. The gatherings, my children, are taking place. Are you not a gathering? Have you not all come together for a purpose? Have you not all stepped into this circle by a means beyond yourselves? Such is the way of the gathering, my children. It is beyond you. Do not struggle to understand. Simply be open. Simply follow. Simply gather. Simply empty. Simply receive.

The End of Entrenchments and Consumption

So, what is it that comes upon the people, my children, in this season? And why now, my children? These questions are on the hearts and minds of the people. Cataclysmic dangers are on the horizon. Shall the fires of consumption melt the ends of the Earth? Shall the waters rise, as it is written of Noah? And who shall be at fault? I tell you, it is not God's judgment. God offers a Holy Way to heal and renew.

The time of entrenchments must come to an end, for the entrenchments have caused divisions and the divisions have caused ruptures reverberating through the Earth into the Holy. The trenches have been dug. The people are within them and those who remain in the trenches shall rot there. There is no life in the trenches. What are the entrenchments, my children? They are gatherings, not in holy circles, but dug into places that will not be moved, lines drawn that cannot be trespassed. The trenches, my children, are not the gatherings of the holy ones, but many holy people have fallen into the trenches, where their feet sink into the mud.

The Braided Way: Accepting Religious Diversity

The age of entrenchments must pass. It is time for the Braided Way, in which all traditions are a strand and become a beautiful braid in the eyes of God. And is the braid not stronger for each strand? Does the larger braid not bear a view not known to the individual strands? Can one truly follow an individual strand through a braid? Or does one finally have to realize the relationship of all strands? The entrenchments come when the strand is followed to the first braid, where the strands converge. The unwise journeyer will not cross to follow the strand farther into the Holy. My children, I tell you, there are many strands in the Braided Way, and it is time for the people to come out of the trenches and see before them a holy braid, to see they are a strand in a holy braid. It is multi-colored, beautiful to perceive. Come out of the trenches, my people! Come out of the trenches. Come into the gatherings! Make of yourselves strands to be united in a holy braid, leading to the holy center, the center-less center, where one finds fullness only in emptiness, where one finds self only in surrender, where one finds purpose only through humility.

Each of the ancient traditions is a strand. There is no need to create new traditions. There is no reason to abandon the ancient ways. It is only necessary to have the sight to perceive the many traditions that are braided into a single cord of holiness. When one strand is cut, when one strand is rejected, the entire cord is weakened, and the braid unravels. Such a time of unraveling has been upon the people long enough.

My children, the greatest counter-points to the Ways of the Holy are selfishness and self-consumption. So, there are the entrenched and there are those who consume. These ways, my children, can indeed bring great and painful ruptures. My children, the Holy Way is not to consume unto the self, but to give unto others. It is not to hoard to self, but to be a fountain, a vessel that magnifies the presence of God so that the Spirit of God can be given. The holy ones gather to give. The times of consumption, my children, are being revealed as a great threat. So, it is a time of crisis, my children, of cataclysmic proportions, is it not? No longer do the people fear a great war, a great explosion. No, now the people don't know what to fear. They have only fear. The fear hovers close over the people, so what do they do but dig deeper into their trenches to survive what will come. My children, to survive what is to come, you must come out of the trenches, you must not store provisions. You must release what is hoarded.

The Coming of a New Spiritual Awareness

What is coming in the gatherings is the awareness that ends are beginnings, that there is nothing to fear. Let the people leave the trenches.

There is nothing to fear when the power of the Holy brings change, transformation. And my children, transformation does not come without sacrifice, preparation and pain. The resurrection of Jesus Christ did not come without great suffering of the body and spirit: beating, betrayal, isolation, piercing and blood. And when Jesus rose again, he bore the marks of the pain as a reminder. My children, pick up your crosses and come to the gathering. What is your cross, my children, but your spiritual purpose? Take up your spiritual purpose, my children, and come to the gathering. There will be sacrifice on your part. There will be surrendering to the Holy Way. There will be emptiness that brings a fulfillment beyond your understanding. You will then gain the awareness coming upon the people, an awareness of the Holy working among the people, desiring not consumption, but compassion, desiring not entrenchment and division, but surrender and unity. Such is the Way of the Holy, for I tell you, in the Holy, there are many and the many are the One, yet the One is greater than the many. And there are many paths to the Holy, to the One, but the One is greater than each path. How shall you perceive such a One as God? How shall you know the way to such a One as God, when the One is beyond your understanding? Beyond your awareness?

Who gives the people of God the right to claim that this strand is stronger than another strand? That the strand has survived the generations, does this not reveal a strength? Who shall predict and declare when the Spirit of God shall move upon the people, the Spirit that is beyond your awareness, the Spirit that is beyond your understanding? Who shall limit the Ways of God by language, by signs, by religion, by ceremony? I tell you, the Spirit of God cannot be contained in your words, in your understanding, in your time, in your predictions, in your traditions or in your fears. So, the people tremble and dig into their trenches, and the Spirit of God, the Wisdom of God says: "Come out! Come out and join the gatherings. Join the feast that is set before you! Eat of the bread and drink of the wine." The meat is good, the company many, and you will find that the gathering of the feast sustains you. It brings fulfillment. It brings in you a new hunger, a spiritual hunger, which draws you deeper and deeper into the presence of the Holy. Come, my children, to the great banquet. Come, my children, to the gatherings. They are feasting on the presence of the Holy. They are laughing. They are singing. They are freeing those who are bound. They are healing afflictions. The signs and wonders of the presence of Holy are among the people, for the people have become open to the Holy Ways, and the Ways of the Holy have been magnified in the people. It is a desire and blossoming of spiritual awareness. What is to be feared? Come out. Come out, my children! Leave the trenches, for there is nothing but decay, nothing but death in the trenches.

On Being "Left Behind"

And I tell you, my children, when the new awareness comes upon the people, nobody is left behind. Some, however, shall be left without. Not all will come to the awareness, and there are many who will live their days without the new awareness, without the ability to perceive the Holy presence, without the courage to surrender self in vulnerability within the gatherings. There are those who are too complacent in isolation, entrenchment and consumption. So, blinded by these ways, they will not perceive. They will live without, my children. It grieves the Holy for people to live in such a way, but it is as it always has been and as it always shall be. There are those who will see and those who will not. There are those who will listen and there are those who will not. So, there are two people working side by side and when the new awareness comes upon the people, one person perceives and the other does not. Do you see? One person is raised to a new awareness and the other is not.

One person is embraced into the gathering and the other is not. One person becomes visible to the Spirit and the other does not. One person's margins become porous to the Holy Spirit and one person remains encased in the self.

It is a transformation coming upon the people, my children. So, what shall happen? How indeed does Holy work when bringing change upon the people? The Lord God does not work through governments. The Holy does not work through worldly powers. The Holy does not work in the ways of civilization. For the Holy cannot be contained in these ways. The Holy works through the people of holy sight who are in relationship with the Holy. And where are these people, my children? Where are these people? Are they not everywhere? In every fringe, in every alley, in every city, on every street. And the Spirit of Wisdom is coming to the people again, calling in the streets, calling for the gathering. "Come, my people. Come, my people. For a new awareness is upon you, a new awareness which will bring you out of the trenches that will stop the fires of consumption. A new awareness is coming, my children, that will salvage that which has been ravished, which will renew that which has been destroyed. For this is the Holy Way. All that the locusts have eaten shall be restored to the people of the Holy. How shall this great healing take place, my children? How shall this great unity be brought about, my children, but through the gatherings? The circles within circles. The circles overlapping circles. This is the Way of the Holy, to be raised up through the most unusual and unpredictable places, in the hearts of the poor, in the spirits of the simple, in those with the hunger for the Holy who surrender self to the Holy.

On Avoiding Cataclysmic Destruction

You must know there is indeed a threat of cataclysmic proportions in the ways of consumption and entrenchment. Certainly, it is perceptible. But the age of entrenchment and consumption will come to an end so that a new age can begin. It is not the ultimate end. However, such an end will come in linear time. After many more generations have come to the Holy, there will come a time when the spinnings shall wind down, when the lights shall fade. All in the perishable shall slow to a halt and be drawn once again to the Source. But it is the design of the Holy for such to take place in the timeless timing of the Holy. And even this winding down is not an end, but a gathering. For what the Holy sends forth, the Holy gathers back. And before the time of the great winding down, the awareness of the people in the design of God shall reach such a place that there will be no fear in the embrace of the design.

What shall happen then, my children, if the present age brings a premature hindrance of the design of the Holy? For is this generation not at a turning point of disastrous possibilities in the natural order? And here we come to a great conundrum, do we not? For if the design is of the Holy, then it shall be. So, is it in the design of the Holy that consumption and entrenchment brings the people to the threat of cataclysmic proportions? At such a time will there not be those who finally do not blame, but take responsibility and say: "We are the people of God, and we must follow the Ways of God." I tell you, every problem you perceive in your culture, in your world, in your homes, every single one has a spiritual basis. So, when the people of the Holy are open to the Spirit, shall these problems, divisions, afflictions, antagonisms, fade away? Such is the Holy Way. So, is it in the design, my children, that only through pain comes transformation?

How shall one predict such a thing as the design of the Holy? How shall one understand such a thing?

There are those who are fearful of the coming together of the faiths. There are those who are very fearful. And I tell you, there are indeed elements in the spirit world to fear. But when the people come before the Holy with the intention of giving self to the Holy, there is nothing to fear. What does the language matter? What does the ritual matter? Are not these things of culture? Are not these things of regional understanding? And does the Holy not transcend these limitations? So, when the people of the Holy come through the hunger for the Spirit, there is nothing but praise. When the people of the Spirit seek purification through the influence of the Spirit, there is nothing but blessing. And I tell you, when the Buddhist meditates and reaches a state of awareness of nothingness, is this not an experience of the holy unity? And when the person who studies the Tao lives a life of wisdom and becomes an example of selflessness and meekness, is this not a holy life? When the Brahman lives in humility and prayer, is this not a holy way to exist? And when the Muslim surrenders to Allah in a discipline of daily prayer, is this not a path toward holy awareness. When the Lakota performs a ceremony, is there not an awareness of sacrifice of body and spirit, the same way of the Christ? Shall I continue, or do you get the point?

The Judgment of the Disobedient

Now, my children, there are ways that are not holy. There are ways where the intention of the people is not to come before the Holy for purification, for surrender, for a heightening of spiritual blessings. There are ways, my children, that seek not to surrender to spiritual forces, but to use them for personal gain. This is the way of consumption for self, for it is possible to take in spiritual powers in order to manipulate instead of to heal, in order to predict instead of to receive. It is in the intention, my children, that the people of God are revealed. Indeed, it is through the fruit that a tree is known. Many do not want to believe that there are dark ways and other people want to believe the dark ways are more numerous and powerful than they truly are. Such is the mystery of the dark. The Ways of the Holy are of light, of love, of blessing, of unity. There is an infiltration of sorts that takes place from the dark ways. And there are those who give over to the dark ways. It is as it is.

What does the Holy do to such people? To such ways? My children, such ways continue, do they not? Is there holy retribution? Does the land quake beneath their feet? Are they swallowed up by the Earth? My children, the Holy is patient and knows that all will come before the Holy. Even the ones who have been deceived by darkness shall come before the Holy and shall finally surrender to the Holy Whole. And I tell you, the spirits of those who do not surrender are indeed taken to the abyss, taken to the place of creation, not to be destroyed, but to be renewed, remade, for the Holy wastes nothing.

If the Holy allows such ways to exist, shall you not do so also? Shall you judge when the Holy does not? But I tell you, you should protect yourself against such dark ways, for they are indeed enticing. They are the ways of self-fulfillment. They are the ways of manipulation. They are the ways of oppression and suppression. And indeed, these ways can have spiritual power to them, spiritual forces, so that the people of the Spirit can be confused. Such ones as these have been known as false prophets. Many people behave in ways antithetical to the ways of the Holy, and there are those who choose to use spiritual powers for dark and unholy intentions.

There are others who utilize the elements of the Spirit that flow through the Earth, some for positive intentions, others for negative. Such as these only recognize a small portion of the Holy Whole, and their sight is limited. The Spirit of the Holy in the Earth is only a part of a much larger Whole.

But, my children, it is easy to perceive, is it not, those who come with a holy intention, those who come to the Holy for purification, those who come to God with a hunger for the Holy. And yet, still, the people of the Spirit can be tricked, deceived. So, be aware, my children, in the gatherings. Be aware of the spiritually immature who hide their selfish desires in the superficial words of any faith. If such people cannot grow beyond their spiritual limitations, do not allow them in the gathering. If your gathering is a pure group of the people of the Holy, then the hunger for the Holy shall spread beyond the group, and the people who are in darkness, the very people you were to avoid in the gathering, shall know the light. Does this sound familiar? It is the pattern. It is the way.

The Way of the Holy is not linear, my children. The Design of Creation is not hindered by time, my children. The Ways of the Holy are globes within globes, spheres within spheres, and a convergence is taking place.

And how is the present convergence similar or different from previous convergences, my children? There are patterns to the Holy Ways, lived out differently in the specific circumstances of the ages. So, a holy pattern is upon the people, a new way of being, a new awareness of the Holy, made possible by the very age to which the awareness comes. This new awareness will accept multiplicity, will see that the many lead to the One. My children, in the Holy Whole, the many come to the One, are embraced by the One, are the One.

So, the question remains for the people of God: What shall be done to those who manipulate the ways of the Spirit for self-consumption, conflict, and slaughter? It is indeed a spiritual sickness among the people to walk a faith halfway, to infiltrate the people of Spirit for self-consumption. I tell you, such misuse of the Holy Way weakens and breaks the gatherings to pieces. My children, it is a reality that there are some who will receive the sight and some who will not. Two people are working side by side, one sees, one perceives, one hears and the other does not. Those who seek the gathering will go deeply, will know deeply, will be drawn to the other people who seek the gatherings. And those who walk their faith halfway will not go deeply into the gatherings, for they are afraid to surrender self to the greater presence of the Holy. Therefore, the deeper you move into the gatherings, the less you will encounter those who do not seek to hear, to see, to receive and to live the Holy Way. The closer you get to the centerless center, the more your hunger for God grows and you encounter fewer and fewer people who are deceiving, deceptive, unaware. You need not judge, my children. You need only follow the Way of God and all things will be revealed.

The Power of Civilization and the Power of the Holy

My children, at the center of conflicts, of the entrenchments, of the consumption, is power, not the power of the Holy, but the power of civilization.

I say again, the foundation of the frictions between the people and nations is spiritual and concerns power. Or shall we say, the central friction is the power of power, of who commands the power? Who, my children, feeds the power? Who produces the power? Who provides the power for the consumption to continue? Power, my children, is at the center. Who brings the power to the people? Who controls the power of civilization, the power of the ways of the world, the power of consumption? Do you know of what I speak? I speak of oil. I speak of coal. I speak of electricity. I speak of fuel. I speak of heat. I speak of air-conditioning. I speak of travel. I speak of industry. Is this not the center of the conflicts? It is given masks. It is given disguises. It is turned into racial conflict, spiritual conflict, conflicts of religion, conflicts of politics. Behind all the masks, my children, is the question of the power. Who controls the power? My children, shall the new perception not bring the allowance of a new power? A power that does not contaminate, but a power that rejuvenates? Look to the power of Spirit! It rejuvenates, my children. It does not destroy. It transforms. It does not limit. It frees. It does not oppress. Power, my children, is a central element of the times, in these times in particular, seen in the entrenchments, the consumption, the ways of civilization, the threat to creation, the killing of the people, the slaughter of the innocent. All these things are the product of the power of civilization, which contradicts the power of God.

A Clean Source of Power

So where shall the people look for a new power? At the center of the journey for power is the Spirit. Let the people seek the power of the Holy and surrender to the release of self. On such a journey, a new power shall be made plain, my children, for in the natural world, are there not lessons of the Holy Way? I tell you, the perception is already among the people. The awareness is among the people, but the people who control the power have not let the revelation come to fruition. My children, there are several ways to bring the power to the people. The secrets are not secrets at all, my children. They are simple, so simple that they are denied as possibilities. They are said to be myths. Isn't the very existence of Spirit said to be a myth? But here you are gathered with a hunger for that which comes when asked. My children, the answers are in the basic elements. Is not energy all around you, reproducing, never wasted, transforming? It is the nature of power, the power of Spirit, the power of creation. My children, the question is what elements shall be released to produce power? I tell you, the secrets are in the water. There are many forms of power. There is sunlight. There is wind. There are strands in rock. But the discovery will be found with the water, a very simple element. The simple and pervasive element of all creation will bring a new way. The water will need slight alteration, but it will be one of cleanliness, simplicity. And the people of the Spirit will embrace this way.

They must reveal it, bring it to the surface. It is a spiritual realization, my children, not scientific, not cultural, but much wider. It is spiritual. So the people are being prepared for many changes: a change of awareness, a change of perception, a change for unity, a change of the understanding of the nature of power, a change in the ways lines are drawn, a change in the ways people transgress those lines, a change in the understanding of the spiritual nature of power, a great change indeed.

Who shall fear this change? The poor shall not. The spiritual seekers shall not. The meek shall not. The spiritually empty shall not. But many people of wealth shall fear the change. However, there are some among the wealthy who will see and know the vision and dreams and receive the words. Such people come to the Holy in prayer, and they will give their resources in a holy way for a spiritual change. It will not come about by the structures of society. The changes will come about through the spirit of the people receiving the Spirit. Why? For the survival of the circles, for the continuation of the vision of the new awareness. At the center of the change, my children, are the gatherings. The people who gather in hunger for the Holy discern between the Ways of the Holy and the ways of civilization. They are welcoming a new awareness of power, a new awareness of unity within multiplicity, a new awareness of the many and the One. All these things shall come upon the people.

The Second Coming as a New Unity among the Faiths

It is not a second coming of the Christ for the Christians. It is a new awareness of the Spirit of Christ, the Spirit of Wisdom, known by many names in the many traditions. This Spirit calls the people together for blessing, for healing, for empowerment, for transformation, for transfiguration, for resurrection, for renewal. Do you see? It is another coming, not only of the Spirit of Christ, but of the Spirit of God, of the Ways of God, of the Wisdom of God. How shall it be embodied in this age, my children? A single embodiment will not suffice, for the unity is much larger than a single body can touch. No, the embodiments shall be many. For the embrace is for the many to come to the One. Do you see the wisdom of it? These multiple embodiments of the Way of God have always been. What is different for this age is the convergence of the embodiments, the echoes of the wisdom. There shall come among the people a single voice, a single message, understood and received by the people of God of all nations and faiths. This is the change upon you. It is coming. It has already begun. It cannot be stopped. It cannot be halted.

Seek the gatherings, my children. Come out of the trenches! Gather with the people of Spirit, the people not afraid of the power of the Holy, a power which indeed is fearsome but gentle. Let your voices become a unity, and listen carefully. Do you not hear the same message in the circle beside you? Do you not hear the same message in the circle opposite you? Do you not hear the same message in the gathering of the others? Do you not hear it everywhere, my children? Do not listen so much to the roars of war, listen to the circles of the holy people. The people of Spirit need to bring the voice of the Holy to the people blinded by consumption, and if the blind do not see, they shall be left without until the change is complete. It is the task at hand.

For this change, the people of Spirit should not abandon their traditions, their strands in the braid of the Holy. No! For the traditions are good. The traditions are strong. The traditions bring empowerment and wisdom and ceremonies to see the Ways of the Holy. The different faith gatherings shall reveal that the Way of God is indeed a way which calls for the many to unite into the One.

A tradition need not be an entrenchment. A tradition should be a dynamic way of living, a way of sharing, a way of communing. The faiths are most similar, my children, in their teachings of the ways of living. Not in their traditions, not in their ceremonies, not in their words, but in their ways of living. The wisdom of the Holy is a way of living, which transcends language, civilization, culture and region. It is expressed in every tongue. It is seen in every culture. It comes to the people in dreams and in visions, in prophecies, in discernments. Why would the Holy limit the way of wisdom to only one group of people? Did the Holy not create all people? Did the Holy not come to every person, in every language, in every situation, and speak through that language and that situation the wisdom, the way of coming to the Holy, the way of surrendering to the Holy? It is as it has always been, and the people will perceive it as so. I can be no plainer. A newly created faith shall, by its nature, be a young faith, lacking the maturity and guidance of the generations.

A Final Call to Action

Therefore, my children, go to the gatherings and seek the Holy. Be aware that there are those who will not perceive and who will not receive. You cannot change this. What you can do is strengthen the gathering with your presence, with your surrender. It is not a leaving behind. It is a moving forward. It is the way it is. Let the dead bury the dead, my children. Come to the gathering and there shall be transformation beyond your imagination. This generation shall prepare the way. This generation shall sow the seeds, and the next generation shall be the ones to embrace the new awareness as natural, for there are too many remnants of the entrenchments in your generation. So, the gatherings occur and the children are raised in the gatherings, do you see? The remnants of the entrenchments are limited in the next generation. Raise the children in the gatherings. They will see the gatherings as self-evident. It is the holy task of this generation. Do you see it?

Let the people be free of selfishness, of consumption, of oppression, of manipulation. Let the people be free! It is the heart-cry of the Holy. It is the purpose of the gatherings. It is the convergence of the age. The timeless time of the Holy and the time of your living shall converge, my children, in mysterious ways. The eternal comes to the now. The now perceives the eternal. Be powerful by being powerless. Be firm in faith, but yielding in grace. It is a paradox. It is the Holy Way; surrender and be strengthened, not by yourself, but by the Spirit of the Holy, which enters you, which dwells in you. Be empty and therefore be filled with the Spirit, which empowers you. Do not work in your own strength, for your own strength is limited. Your own power comes from self, leads to self, ends in self. Therefore, work not in your own power; work in the power of the Holy, which is beyond self, and leads you through the many to the One, and thus brings fulfillment beyond understanding. Seek the power of the Holy, and you shall find that power in creation shall bring fulfillment, transformation, rejuvenation, freedom, unity. Look to the water; look to the sun, look to the wind, look to the skies. The people will look in all these places, have looked in all these places. In the simplest of elements, the power shall be unlocked and the people shall be free. But, only those who seek the energy of the Holy shall perceive it, shall find it, shall know it, shall embrace it, shall speak it. It is a great convergence, necessary for the people to be transformed. The new awareness shall not be limited to region or tradition for this age, for the awareness of the people has become cosmic. The change shall be beyond region, beyond tribe, beyond culture, beyond race. Do you see the necessity? So, it is a new beginning of sorts, an end of the age of consumption. This is a pattern, repeated for the people of Spirit to know the Holy, to come to the Holy, to surrender to the Holy. The ways of civilization are revealed as the ways of consumption, the ways of the perishable. The ways of the people of Spirit shall be seen as the ways of the Holy. Why is it so hard to perceive? Why is it so hard to accept? Why is it so feared? It is as it is, my children. It is as it is.

So, the people of Spirit shall not be afraid, for they shall feel the change; they shall sense it; they shall hunger for it; they shall perceive and tell of its coming. It is a marvelous, marvelous beginning.

Thus says the Holy.

This lesson came whole and complete in one prayer, just as it is presented. The entire message was spoken in a straightforward and powerful tone, and the closing words, "Thus says the Holy," startled me.

These four words had the effect of expanding the purpose of the prophetic lessons, and as they came from my lips I received a shock, like a shot in my abdomen. I felt inadequate to accept the authority of the words, "Thus says the Holy." I understood for the first time the experience of the "fear of God."

As I came out of the trance state, I realized the message I had just received was not simply a wisdom lesson for a few individuals. It was an oracle to the masses.

The heaviness in my abdomen remained for several hours. When I mentioned this weight to Jennifer and Christopher, they reminded me that the words and the authority were not my own. As in other stages of my spiritual journey, I had to surrender my own fears and inadequacies to the Holy. It was a continual lesson: When I became comfortable in the pattern of oracular experience, the Holy would nudge me farther into the depths.

In retrospect, one of the most significant elements of this Oracle Session is the reference to "the Braided Way." I would later receive entire wisdom lessons on the Braided Way, and it would later become the purpose of my sacred work.

III

Hope of The Holy

14

Fu Jia (Happy Family): A Story of Renewal

IN A HOTEL ROOM in Nanjing, China, Jennifer and I rummaged through our luggage. Sam, now six years old, opened his backpack. We were told that the baby girl who would become our daughter would be brought to the hotel room at 4:00. We arrived at the hotel late, and reached our room at 4:45. Jennifer prepared a bottle of formula. I dug through clothes, medicines and water bottles to find the gifts we brought for the orphanage workers. We also brought infant clothes so the orphanage could replace the outfit our daughter, Gao Fu Kun (whom we would name Lydia Fu Jia Olin-Hitt), would be wearing. I got out the cameras. Within minutes, we were ready to greet our daughter. Sam held a stuffed frog he brought to give to his little sister.

Then we waited.

"Hurry up and wait," Jennifer said. "It's been the theme of this entire process."

The SARS crisis subsided and ended in Jun, and on July 3, 2003, we received a photo of our daughter. Travel plans for China began immediately.

It had taken over two years of paper work and preparation for this moment to arrive. It was now August 30 of 2003, three and a half years after Jordan's stillbirth.

In the hotel room Sam ate a snack of peanut butter crackers and Orange Crush.

We waited more.

Jennifer said, "I didn't think I'd be this nervous."

Sam said, "I didn't think I'd be this excited."

We waited more.

We heard babies crying in the hall. We looked at each other with wide eyes. Sam bolted from the chair and put his ear to the door.

There were six families from America waiting in separate rooms for their new daughters to arrive, and we did not know in what order the families would receive their daughters.

Muffled Chinese and English voices bled through the walls.

Somebody knocked on our door. Jennifer hurried to answer it, and Sam stepped back. There was a crowd in the hallway. I heard a great deal of Chinese conversation, then a woman in a black skirt and white apron brought in a mattress for a crib.

I switched on the camera, then realized the woman with the crib was from the hotel, not the orphanage. But the talking in the hallway continued. Among the Chinese phrases I could not understand, I heard the words, "Gao Fu Kun."

"Yes," Jennifer exclaimed. She looked at me, eyes wide. "It's her," she said.

The woman with the mattress was now going into the hall to bring in the rest of the crib.

"Perhaps you could bring the crib in later," I said.

She looked at me and smiled, struggling to drag the folded, wooden crib into the room.

"Perhaps you could bring the crib later," I said louder, as if this would clarify the situation. "Bao Bao," I said—the Chinese words for baby.

She smiled.

I pointed toward the hall. "Bao Bao."

She smiled again.

Finally, somebody said something to her in Chinese, and she left the room.

Jennifer backed away from the door, and a crowd of people entered. It was very loud and confusing. They were all talking at the same time. Then, from out of the group came a young woman carrying a baby.

"Gao Fu Kun?" the young woman asked.

"Yes," Jennifer said.

The young woman held the baby out to Jennifer's open arms.

"Hello, Gao Fu Kun." Tears brimmed in Jennifer's eyes.

My eyes blurred. I could not see the screen of the video camera. The group left, the door was closed, and Jennifer pressed her lips to Lydia's head.

That was it. And there she was: our daughter.

I could hardly breathe. Jennifer cried, but my eyes went dry. I stood in wonder at the child who had been handed into our family.

Jennifer held our daughter and rocked her. "Gao Fu Kun," she whispered into her ear. We planned not to call her Lydia for a few days. We had wanted her Chinese name to remain as her middle name, but Fu Kun did not translate into English with grace. A friend from China helped us choose Fu Jia, which is a common girl's name, meaning happy family.

Fu Kun gazed around the room, as if stunned. There was no expression on her face. She remained limp in Jennifer's arms. Jennifer put the nipple of a bottle to Fu Kun's lips, but she pouted.

Fu Kun was passive and listless. Sam presented the green frog, and Fu Kun's brown eyes followed the frog as Sam passed it in front of her.

I brushed my hand across her hair. "She's beautiful," I said. "She looks just like her picture, just with more hair."

I smelled shampoo on her hair. I touched her hands and noticed her fingernails were trimmed. She had been prepared for this day.

Jennifer smiled. A hum resonated deep in her throat.

The room was still and quiet. The air was charged with emotion.

"What do you think of your sister?" I asked Sam.

"I like her," Sam said. He brushed Fu Kun's arm.

Fu Kun was thirteen months when she arrived in our family. She could not crawl and could hardly sit up. Because of the months of crib time, she had no muscle tone.

That evening we took Fu Kun to a restaurant, where she ate rice double-fisted. In the lobby of the hotel, a young woman played piano. As we approached the piano, I heard a humming, then a sustained note being sung. I glanced at Fu Kun in her mother's arms and saw that she was singing. It was a single note, but it was singing.

"She's singing," Sam said. "Listen. She's singing."

In a prayer session months earlier, the Messenger had told me that our daughter would be a song bird in the Tree of Life.

It was at this moment that I wept.

EIGHT MONTHS LATER, Lydia, now twenty-two months old, swaggers through our bedroom. Her short arms swing in a confidence known only to toddlers. She stops at Jennifer's nightstand, reaches up and clutches a handful of necklaces and earrings.

"Momma," she says. She marches to her mother and raises the handful of silver strands. Lydia's sleek, black hair has grown to her shoulders; her bangs are straight. Her olive complexion, her mother has said, looks great in any color.

Jennifer pauses from putting on make-up and glances down and away from the mirror. "Yes, those are Momma's necklaces." Jennifer puts down her mascara tube and presents Lydia with an open palm. Lydia places the jewelry into her hand. Lydia laughs and smiles, then marches back to the nightstand for more jewelry. There is now a pile of jewelry mixed with Jennifer's makeup in front of the mirror. This pattern has been going on for several minutes.

I get in front of Lydia. She glances up surprised, then she smiles, showing her mouthful of teeth.

"Where are you going?" I ask.

Lydia laughs and turns from me.

"Where are you going?" I say, taking a step toward her.

She begins to run from me, looking over her shoulder, laughing so hard she almost falls. I catch up to her and sweep her into my arms, turn her belly up, and bury my nose in her stomach with smacking sounds.

"I only have fifteen minutes," Jennifer says.

"I know," I say. I carry Lydia out of the room. "I've got her."

It is April 22, 2004, and Jennifer is preaching at the opening worship service of a newly started church. It is her return to full-time ministry.

Jennifer's reentry to pastoral ministry came upon her gradually. While she was healing from grief, a small church called Calvary United Methodist Church was struggling to remain open. The older congregation did not know how to reach out to the urban, transitional neighborhood. The congregation disbanded, and the church building became Canton Calvary Mission. Just as Jennifer was feeling the call back to active ministry in 2002, the rebirth of this mission had grown to need a chaplain, and Jennifer was offered the position. It was a resurrection for Jennifer and for the church.

One of Jennifer's responsibilities would be to begin a Saturday night service called "Worship Alive," which would occur in the sanctuary before a free meal in a soup kitchen environment in the basement.

When Jennifer and I went to prayer to see if she should take the chaplain position at the mission, the Messenger of the Holy said:

Come to Calvary. To find Calvary, face the death, for resurrection comes only after you face the brokenness. My daughter, confront the broken and reveal the transformation. Come to Calvary and find resurrection. Come to Calvary and find salvation. Come to Calvary and find hope. Come to Calvary and find inspiration. Come to Calvary and find renewal. Come to Calvary and find fulfillment. You know the journey to Calvary, but you cannot anticipate, you cannot imagine, you cannot foresee the resurrection in store. It is the journey of faith. It is the call of the disciple. It is the way of holiness.

This message made Jennifer and me realize that the part-time position as chaplain of Canton Calvary Mission was a sign of resurrection at a place named after the hill upon which Christ had been crucified.

After a year, the Saturday night service became so popular that the Bishop of our conference appointed Jennifer to start a new congregation. She had already taken courses and workshops on planting a new church, and she named the church City Hope.

The first worship service of City Hope Church, then, was no small event.

I CARRY LYDIA to Sam's room, where Sam is supposed to be getting dressed. Instead, he is lying on the floor in his underwear reading *Junie B. Jones and Her Big Fat Mouth*, a new purchase from the bookstore.

"Hi, Sum," Lydia says, pointing to her big brother.

"Hi, Lydi," Sam says, not looking up from the book.

Lydia squirms in my arms, trying to get free of me. "Book. Book," she says.

"Please get dressed, Sam," I say, holding tight to Lydia. She twists her body in my arms. I shift my grip on her.

"*You're* not dressed," Sam says, still not looking up from his book.

It is true. I'm in khaki pants, shirtless and barefoot. "I'll take care of me. You take care of you," I say. I go to my closet, grab a shirt and carry Lydia to the basement where I will set her in the midst of Mega Blocks while I iron my shirt.

Lydia's development to this point has been miraculous, even her pediatrician has been amazed. In the nine months that we have had her in our family, she has progressed through landmark after landmark of development. From the passive and frail baby we brought home, she has become a confident, almost two year old with all of the strong opinions and activities appropriate to the age. Her favorite word is "no." Second is "hi," followed closely by "more." She has the self-assurance of a normal, healthy two year old.

I carry Lydia to the kitchen, followed by our yellow Lab, Jack. Jack is a big lug of a dog, weighing in at over 100 pounds, but he is the most gentle and calm Lab I have ever known. He has sleepy, sometimes sad, eyes, and he often sits patiently while Lydia climbs over him or dresses him with hats and necklaces.

"Ja," Lydia says. "Hi, Ja."

Jack wags his tail, then picks up a bunny, one of Lydia's favorite stuffed animals.

"No, Ja," Lydia says. She kicks her legs and squirms in my arms, harder than she had done in Sam's room. "No, Ja," she says. She kicks her legs. I lose my hold on her and set her down. She marches toward our dog, who wags his tail and walks away from Lydia with the bunny in his mouth.

"Ja," Lydia says, pointing. "No,"

The dog is taller than Lydia, and over five times her weight, but Lydia chases him down. "No," she says. "My bunny," she says. "Sit."

Jack continually picks up Lydia's stuffed animals and carries them around the house. He does not chew or destroy them; he packs them around in his soft bird-fetching mouth like a big, overgrown puppy who wants his toy. Lydia, then, chases him around the house. Jack stays a few steps ahead of her, turning now and then to taunt her with the teddy bear, or Elmo doll or *Good Night Moon* bunny.

Today I don't have time for the routine.

I chase the dog down, pull the bunny from his mouth, hand the slobber-damp bunny to Lydia, pick her up and take her to the basement so I can iron the shirt now slung like a towel over my shoulder.

I turn the iron on and decide that while it heats, I will get my socks and shoes on. I take Lydia back to our bedroom—the shirt still slung over my shoulder. On the way, Lydia throws the bunny down, which Jack—being a retriever—happily takes it up in his mouth. He follows us upstairs and into the bedroom, holding his chin high to show his prize.

Lydia cries out, "No, Ja. No."

Jennifer sighs and opens her closet door. She finds her shoes and begins to step into them. "Drop the bunny, Jack," she says.

I laugh.

Jennifer, however, does not have this leisure. She is on the spot tonight. She heads down the stairs with, "I'll see you there."

I decide not to iron the shirt. If I'm holding Lydia, no one will notice me, anyway. I go to Sam's room to encourage him to set aside his book and get dressed.

When the opportunity had come for Jennifer to move from a part-time chaplain to a full-time pastor of a start-up church, we of course went to prayer about the topic.

"I'm not sure if this is God's will for me or not," Jennifer had told me. "I know God has big plans for the mission, but I don't know about a new congregation."

We prayed about starting City Hope Church in the same building as Canton Calvary Mission, Jennifer read Psalm 127, then switched on the tape recorder, and the Messenger began a lesson:

Renewal. For the Holy brings renewal to restore the worn and feeble, to restore the ancient into the present, to make the ancient renewed, to make the new, re-newed. How shall that which is new become renewed? How shall that which is eternal become renewed? Is there not a spiritual paradox in the very word of renewal? For the Holy's ways are ancient. The Holy's ways are eternal. They know no age; they know no time. How shall the eternal become the re-newed? And the new, the contemporary, the now, how shall the new become re-newed? Oh, my children, you are at the site of renewal.

Yes, my children. Live in renewal where the now unfolds to a holy next, where the now yields to the eternal, and you shall know renewal. And what is more, you shall not only know renewal, you shall bring it; you shall birth it. For the Holy shall come through you, and you shall be new in the moment. The Holy shall unfold through you as it embraces you. It is the Holy Way. Yes. It is the Holy Way to be turned inside out so that the Holy comes through you and in you even as the Holy embraces you; you give birth to the new, even as the new comes upon you.

Yes, it is renewal, my children. The place where you are is the place of renewal, where the now unfolds to the next. Open then to the eternal in the now, and you shall know renewal.

The Messenger then addressed the question at hand about Jennifer's call to plant a new church:

My daughter, you wish to build a temple? A new congregation? I tell you, the Kingdom material is before you. You never thought of yourself as a builder, never thought of yourself as an architect, never thought of yourself as a general contractor, but I tell you this, you are all these things. You are an architect, you are a builder, you are a construction worker for the temple, for the moment of the holy unfolding.

My children, you have both turned away from your then. It no longer grips you and determines your desires. You have turned to the Holy and the eternal next. Indeed, it is a renewal.

During this prayer, the Messenger announced what Jennifer and I had sensed since our return from China. We had overcome the debilitating grief that had consumed us after Jordan's death and what turned out to be two additional pregnancy losses, and it was time to move toward renewal.

With this guidance, the choice to become the pastor of City Hope Church was a no-brainer.

I ENTER THE SANCTUARY a half hour before the service. Lydia is resting on my hip, and Sam—finally fully dressed and without a book in hand—is holding my hand. Jack the dog is, no doubt, lying on the floor at home with a bunny between his paws for comfort.

The sanctuary is already crowded. Even the balcony has people sitting in it. It is traditional when a new church is launched for people from other United Methodist Churches to be present for the opening worship. There are also many people from the neighborhood.

I sit in a pew with Lydia on my lap and Sam beside me. The energy and excitement of the room is palpable and invigorating. I am humming inside with the presence of God's Spirit. I feel tremors in my belly, and I smile.

As I expected, people come toward me, but after a quick hello, they turn their attention to Lydia, who stands on the pew and claps her hands for people, hamming it up for anyone who will watch and comment.

Jennifer is walking across the chancel, talking with some of the children she has gotten to know through her time at Canton Calvary Mission. Jennifer is vibrant, almost glowing with God's light. She loves these children, every one of them. When she drives down the street, the kids gather on the curb and wave. They say, "There's Miss Pastor Jennifer. There's Miss

Pastor Jennifer." For a woman who spent years yearning for another child, she is suddenly surrounded with more children than she can count.

The crowd in the sanctuary is a wonderful mix of racial diversity. A choir from a black congregation is robed and ready to sing. And I know that with this crowd, there will be plenty of responses from the congregation. The alleluias will roll, the praises will rise.

IT IS APRIL, just after Easter. The lectionary passage for the week is John 20:19–31, a post-resurrection passage. Jennifer could not have chosen a more appropriate passage for a church that had closed its doors, only to find new life. Here is the text from John:

> *When it was evening on that day, the first day of the week, and the doors of the house where the disciples had met were locked for fear of the Jews, Jesus came and stood among them and said, "Peace be with you." After he said this, he showed them his hands and his side. Then the disciples rejoiced when they saw the Lord. Jesus said to them again, "Peace be with you. As the Father has sent me, so I send you." When he said this, he breathed on them and said to them, "Receive the Holy Spirit. If you forgive the sins of any, they are forgiven them; if you retain the sins of any, they are retained."*
>
> *But Thomas (who was called the Twin), one of the twelve, was not with them when Jesus came. So the other disciples told him, "We have seen the Lord." But he said to them, "Unless I see the mark of nails in his hands, and put my finger in the mark of the nails and my hand in his side, I will not believe."*
>
> *A week later his disciples were again in the house, and Thomas was with them. Although the doors were shut, Jesus came and stood among them and said, "Peace be with you." Then he said to Thomas, "Put your finger here and see my hands. Reach out your hand and put it in my side. Do not doubt but believe." Thomas answered him, "My Lord and my God!" Jesus said to him, "Have you believed because you have seen me? Blessed are those who have not seen and yet have come to believe."*

Jennifer stands to preach. The hem of her robe sways around her ankles, as her voice booms in the sound system.

Her sermon is called "Breaking and Entering." After reading the scripture from John, she looks over the congregation and speaks about a woman who had come to the mission a few days earlier, after a man who broke into her house to steal her television had beaten her. The man was her son's friend. The woman was bruised in body and crushed in spirit. "The world is a dangerous place," Jennifer says, "and we often lock ourselves behind closed doors." She looks over the congregation. "I'm afraid sometimes. I lock my door. Don't you? Have you ever walked through a dark parking lot with your keys sticking through your knuckles, just in case? Have you ever checked your door at night to make sure it's locked? The world is a dangerous place."

Jennifer pats the Bible that is open in her palm. "The disciples were locked behind closed doors in our passage for this evening. They were afraid of persecution. They were afraid of threats to their lives. Like the woman who came to the mission this week, the world seemed too threatening, too dangerous, so they gathered behind a locked door. And even behind that locked door, they feared a breaking and entering."

Jennifer moves away from the podium and continues preaching. "But Jesus has a different kind of breaking and entering," she says. "The Lord Jesus Christ doesn't bring bruises, but healing. When Jesus breaks into the house, there is comfort and peace. And what's more, Jesus breaks in without damaging the lock, without violating the barrier."

Jennifer paces before the people. I sit back and smile. Jennifer is in action once again. She preaches with the Bible open in her palm, proclaiming the message. "Friends, Jesus passes beyond the barriers we construct to defend against the world. He walks right through our locked doors, right through our fears. And he offers companionship, and grace, and forgiveness, and healing." Jennifer pauses and smiles. "You know the picture of Jesus standing by the door, knocking? That famous painting? And the door has no handle? The picture implies that we have to let Jesus in. He's just waiting to be invited. But in our scripture tonight, the disciples don't invite Jesus. They're so afraid, if there was a knock at the door, they'd hide under the table. So, what does Jesus do? What does the Lord of Resurrection do? He comes right in the house."

The African American members of the congregation begin to respond to her.

"Amen."

"Yes."

"Preach it."

I watch my beloved wife back in ministry again, preaching the word, opening people's eyes to the presence of Jesus. She paces in front of the people and raises her voice.

"You know the story of this church?" Jennifer asks. "Calvary United Methodist Church?" she smiles. "It shut its doors. The congregation of faithful servants of Christ didn't know where to turn. The neighborhood was changing. It became threatening, so threatening that the congregation locked the doors during worship. They locked the doors. Not out of spite. They loved this neighborhood. Not out of pride or exclusivity. They *wanted* new members. No. Out of fear. They were afraid."

Jennifer looks at the floor and pauses for a moment. "I'm not judging these faithful folks. Don't get me wrong. They wanted ministry to take place in this neighborhood, so much so that they gave the building for a mission." Jennifer raises her hands. "And now look at the place," she says. "Look at it. The doors are open. Wide open. Come in during any school day and you'll see children. I'll tell you what. God is in the house. Jesus broke through the locks and barriers of the world."

There are a few "amens."

"It doesn't matter what you are afraid of. It doesn't matter why you lock yourself up. The Lord Jesus Christ can pass through your barriers. The Lord Jesus Christ is not afraid of your fear. The Lord Jesus Christ is not afraid of your addictions. The Lord Jesus Christ is not afraid of your pain. The Lord Jesus Christ is not afraid of your doubt. The Lord Jesus Christ is not afraid of your shame. The Lord Jesus Christ is not afraid of your guilt. The Lord Jesus Christ is not afraid of your past. The Lord Jesus Christ is not afraid of your darkness."

There are more "amens" and a woman calls out, "Thank you, Jesus."

Jennifer's voice becomes calm and soft. "No. Jesus is ready to come into your locked room, that place in yourself you just can't face. And here's what's more. You don't even have to unlock the door. You don't even need the strength to come out of hiding." Her voice began to increase in power and strength again. "That dark place where you stay hidden. That place you are afraid to see. Jesus is already there. He's already there. The resurrected Jesus is already in your darkness, ready to take your hand. He'll show you his own pain if He has to. Just so you'll believe. Just so you'll trust Him." She raises her hands. "I tell you, my friends, there's no house, no locked door, no barrier, no pain, no shame, no guilt, no threat that the Jesus of the Easter Resurrection can't pass through to bring new life."

Somebody yells, "Amen!"

"Can I hear a witness?" Jennifer yells. "Can I hear a witness?"

People shout and clap. The choir director plays a few chords on the piano. Something swells in my belly and rises to my lips, but it is not pride. It is praise. "Hallelujah," I say. "Hallelujah!"

Jennifer is coming to renewal and pastoral ministry at a place once called Calvary.

AFTER THE SERVICE, I sit in the buzz and bustle of the congregation, realizing what a blessed man I am. The renewal I have witnessed in my life is stunning, and I am perhaps two months from finishing the first draft of *Messenger of The Holy*. It is a risk to step out into the open about my prayer gift, but I am trusting the Holy. I've trusted the Holy through so much, there is no reason to stop at this point. And because I am a trained writer, it would be disobedient not to write about the prophetic gift.

And now, here I am with two beautiful kids, a wife with a powerful call in dynamic ministry, and still able to squeak out time to pray and write. Suddenly, everything seems renewed, glistening with possibility and promise. The very air is charged with God's renewing presence.

And to think for nearly three years, Jennifer and I had struggled with grief and loss, unable to see beyond our desire for another child. The journey of laments had been an important part of our spiritual lives, and God had renewed us and made us into instruments for holy work. I do not believe God caused the grief, but I am convinced that God has used the pain and brought us blessings we could never have imagined.

Lydia slips off the pew. I look up into the crowded sanctuary and realize Lydia has locked eyes with her mother walking toward us. Lydia turns from me and marches down the aisle—laughing with every step toward Jennifer. Lydia is not an orphan from China. She is not a replacement for our lost son. She is our daughter, a perfect and beautiful little girl, giggling in pure delight, swept up in the arms of her mother.

15

The Ways of Civilization and the Ways of the Holy: A Current Prophecy

On Tuesday, November 7, 2006, Americans went to the polls to cast votes. The media was already calling the midterm election "A Referendum on the War in Iraq." It was expected that the voters would turn the House and Senate over to the Democrats.

On November 8, Americans awoke to the reality of the predicted shift in power, and I received an e-mail from the first publisher of this book. In the e-mail, the publisher asked if I could provide one more chapter, perhaps an epilogue. "The people need to have a 'fresh' prophecy," she wrote. She wondered if there was material from recent prayer sessions that would speak to the issues of the times. She wrote:

> I really think it is important to present readers with a timely message from the eternal, as contradictory as that may seem. People are disillusioned. There is a yearning for encouragement and reassurance for this time.

At first, I wasn't thrilled about the idea. Most of the Wisdom Sessions from 2006 were centered on the personal issues of the people with whom I prayed, including a great deal of guidance for the central leadership of City Hope Church, the church my wife pastored.

I thought I could perhaps host a Wisdom Session and ask the Holy to give a message for the times, especially after the elections. However, on the large scale of the eternal, I didn't see the slight shift in power in the House and the Senate as all that significant. Other than that, the media was predictable: a politician's sexual misbehavior, the controversies of homosexuality in American culture, and the color-coded terrorism alert system--devised by the new Department of Homeland Security. The usual stuff.

I DECIDED TO GATHER my strongest group of prayer friends to ask the Messenger for a prophecy about our current times. To be honest, I was apprehensive about this Wisdom Session because I knew it would touch upon the controversial issues of war and homosexual relationships. I wasn't sure I was ready to take a public stand on these issues from the authority of the prophetic state of awareness.

When I e-mailed a small and spiritually strong group to meet on Tuesday, November 14, 2006, everyone in the group dropped what they were planning to come to the prayer session. They all knew the significance of the session for the message that would be brought to the people through this book.

The entire day of the prayer, I felt the presence of the Messenger. The hollow below my heart was filled with spiritual energy. My hands tingled slightly. By 4:00, Jennifer and I left our children with a babysitter, and the prayer team assembled in my prayer studio: Jennifer, Christopher Reynolds, Neil Fedio, and Laura Weldon. All had been present during the prayer about the end times related in Chapter 13.

The spiritual energy in the prayer studio was intense.

For this session, I suggested a gradual entry into prayer. I asked Jennifer to put anointing oil on my forehead, then I said I would say a prayer of preparation. After that, I asked Jennifer to read a psalm, then Christopher would smudge us with the smoke of burning sage in the Lakota way. The preparation would end while Christopher sang "The Four Direction Song" in Lakota, the song typically sung at the beginning of a sweat lodge ceremony.

Jennifer lit the Christ candle and invoked the presence of the Holy Spirit. She anointed my head by dampening her finger with oil and tracing a cross on my forehead.

"Michael," she said, "remember your spiritual purpose and be open to the Spirit of God."

The Messenger of the Holy slipped into me immediately. I was fully in a prophetic awareness before Jennifer had finished the anointing. My lungs filled with the breath of the Spirit, I sat up straight, and I could not say a word of my own volition.

Everyone waited for me to pray.

I wanted to at least say, "Amen," but couldn't.

The waiting continued. The room grew heavy with silence. The Messenger was patient and calm within me, and finally spoke:

My children. I see you. I am with you, my children. Finish your ritual.

"Yes," said Christopher. "May we prepare a bit?"

Prepare yourselves, my children.

Christopher spoke to Jennifer, "Do you want to offer the psalm?"

Prepare yourselves, my children, for you must be centered. The heavens open, my children, as you acknowledge the presence of the Holy. Open the heavens, my children.

Jennifer read Psalm 101, then offered a short prayer. I was aware of Christopher lighting sage and moving around the room, using a feather to send the smoke toward each person as a sign of preparation. Then I heard Christopher begin singing in Lakota. After the song, Chris and Neil both said, "Aho," and the prayer lesson began:

It is good to be among you, my children. I am aware of your purpose. I am aware of your audience.

I shall speak on the ways of society, on words, on the Ways of the Holy. For I tell you, how are the ways of society and the ways of theHoly communicated to the people but through words, through a language, and is not language a product of a civilization? So, it is through language that you communicate the ways of the Holy, which are beyond your understanding, your ways, and your language. When you come to the place your language cannot describe, and your mind cannot understand, you are at the portal of the Holy. And you must set aside your language, you must set aside your civilization, you must set aside your mind and enter. And there you will find a merging beyond comprehension, beyond explanation.

My children, what shall we say about the many civilizations? They arise, do they not, from the ways of the people? I tell you, the Holy is not domesti-

cated. This is not to say the Spirit of the Holy is wild; the Holy is not a bronco that will buck and throw you off. The Spirit is not domesticated in that it is not contained in a civilization, or an understanding from a civilization, or the ways and laws of a civilization. The Holy transcends civilization. The Holy is like a great bird of light, gentle and strong, never to be contained in the cage of civilization. And those courageous of spirit climb onto the back of the great bird, and the great bird soars, just beyond your ability to understand, just beyond your comfort. Such is the life you lead when you surrender to the Holy and journey with the Spirit.

I have spoken much on the Ways of the Holy and the ways of the world. For the ways of the world are the ways of consumption, self-absorption, arrogance, division, destruction. And the Ways of the Holy, my children, are revealed in openness, giving, surrender of self, acceptance, a yearning for the Spirit. The ways of patience and love bring joy, peace, patience, gentleness, self-control, compassion, humility. Most of all, the Ways of the Holy arise from surrender of self. For it is the self that is the great obstruction of the Ways of the Holy. This I have taught you. This you know in your hearts and in your very souls. It is not new teaching.

The Limitations of Civilization

But what shall we say about the Ways of the Holy for this moment of time: in your understanding, in your language, in your temporality, in your limitations. For language is already a limitation, your mind is already a limitation, the ways of your civilization are already a limitation. So, my children, within these limitations, we shall approach the deep meanings of spiritual sight, of the children of light, of the transformations to come.

There will, indeed, be great storms; the Earth shall shake, the waters shall rise, the winds shall rip and tear. There will be plagues. All this is normative in the patterns of nature. Nations have risen against nations, kingdoms against kingdoms. But by what laws do civilizations wage wars? Must civilizations fight for peace? Does the Holy fight for peace, make war for peace? Civilizations rise in their own power and for their own power. The ways of the Holy rise from the people of Spirit, for the expansion and growth of the Spirit of God, to bring the Holy Whole to the Earth.

Do not look to the leaders of civilization to reveal a spiritual awareness. For they become the leaders of civilization through a surrender to the ways of a civilization, and they must show their allegiance to these ways. Look, then, to the people of sight, to the people open to the Spirit, to the children of light, and you will see the Ways of the Holy, for the Ways of the Holy shall rise and spread from the people of Spirit: person to person, spirit to spirit, temporal to eternal. Finally, the people of Spirit bring about a change, outside of the realm of civilization. For civilizations shall come and they shall go. They shall be built up, and they shall fall. So it has been. So it has been.

Cling to civilization, my children, and you cling to the perishable. Surrender to the Holy, and you will not know ends or limitations, and the power of the Holy shall come to you, the power of gentleness, meekness, acceptance, a power that brings unity instead of division, a power which comes from discipline and not abandonment, a power that comes in unexpected places and unexpected ways, a power that comes from the fringes of civilization and not from the center.

The Language of Civilization

Civilization is the place where you exist, the place you abide; it is a necessity. It offers limitations, but it also offers systematic living, and this is for the good. So the Holy speaks to the people through the language of their civilization. The Spirit of God works with people within the laws of their civilization. But the language and the laws are limitations to the Ways of the Holy.

But what else does the Holy have to speak to the people? The Holy works through the limitations to reveal a shadow of the Holy Whole and present a way of living that brings the people into relationship with the Holy.

So, shall I explain something? The Holy Ways are eternal. The ways of civilization shift. The people become confused. They think the word of God to one civilization should be the word of God to all civilizations in all times. It is blasphemy, they think, that the word of God changes.

My children, the Holy Way is eternal, but must be communicated by the words of a civilization, which brings limitations to the word of God. So, why should the people look to the language of an ancient and dead civilization to find the definitive word of God? And why should the people be afraid when the word comes fresh to a new civilization and a new age? Why should they fear? It is not God who changes. It is civilization. In this time and civilization, your awareness has expanded about the universe. Your awareness of how small the Earth is has come upon you. The conflicts consume the Earth. The dangers threaten the existence of your ecosystem. It is a time in which the word of God shall come fresh. Within your civilization and through your language, the eternal shall be expressed so that you can know the ways of God in this moment and in this crisis. Many people hunger for this fresh word, for the inadequacies of your systems of thought and the ways of your civilization have been revealed.

This does not surprise any of you. It will be great blasphemy to many. There are many who cling to the words spoken to another civilization through an ancient language. These ancient words cannot be fully translated to your current civilization, for the words have not risen from your current understanding. The Holy works with what is presented. Should you not listen for the word of the Holy spoken to the present civilization and the current language?

I am not saying to dismiss the ancient words of scripture, for they are true and good, and the ways of the Holy can be seen in them. In the ancient scriptures, you will find wisdom and inspiration and patterns which mold your lives. I am saying to open your eyes and your ears to the Holy Ways as they are communicated to your people in your time.

The Holy Way is for grace, forgiveness, peace and unification, for finally the Holy Whole brings all things into unification. It is the grand design of Creation that all things shall come from whence they began. The Holy celebrates in the differences among the people. The Holy can be seen in the faiths of the people. In the Braided Way of acceptance, the many faiths are strands woven together in a braid that is the pathway of the Hholy. Each strand makes the braid stronger, and as the strand of any faith tradition is followed, does it not intertwine with the strands of other faiths? Each strand yields a unique expression of the the Holy Way, and the entire braid is weakened when a strand is cut or rejected.

Fighting Terrorism and the Fear Withhin

The people are divided; the people are being divided to manipulate and control. It is not the the Holy Way. The Way of the Holy is to seek unity, is to invite the enemy into the family.

My children, how does one fight terror? How does one fight terrorism? Are you not fighting fear? How does one fight fear, my children? Fear has no external origin. Fear is within, projected without. How do you fight fear, my children? The ways of civilization commit to lashing, to striking, to naming the fear, so that one does not have to look within to see the true origin of the fear. The true battle, my children, is not without; it is within. The true battle is not between the people, but within the people. Shall the people of your civilization look within and discover the source of their fear, discover the source of their terror? Will they understand that the beginning of wisdom is the fear of God, not the fear of fear, not the fear of terror, not the fear of difference? These fears divide the people, and turn the other into the enemy. How shall the enemy fight back, but to capitalize on the fear? Hence, the fear from within, becomes terror.

My children, the beginning of wisdom is the fear of God. To fear is to be obedient, to fear is to respect. Respect the Holy and look within, and the Spirit of God will reveal that there is nothing to fear. And how shall one fear a God who desires unification, a God of peace, a God of gentleness, a God who invites but does not impose? What is there to fear, my children? To fear God is to surrender your self to God, and this is counter to the ways of civilization. The greatest fear among the people is loss of self, surrender of self. This is the fear within, the origin of the terror projected without.

Those who speak in arrogance or in certainties, those who will not surrender self to the greater good or to the Holy should not be trusted. Their agenda comes not from the ways of God. The Holy demands a surrender of self, loss of self, and as a result a selfless self is revealed, a self beyond your understanding and comprehension of self. But the people of civilization cling to self, identity and the ways of civilization for safety because they fear the surrender of self, and they fear the fear within.

How does one fight terror and terrorism, my children? The fight is within and not without. The fight is the struggle of all people. It is a battle for your very souls, a battle for your very enlightenment, your enlightening. Give yourself to God, my children, and your fears shall be crushed to dust and blown to the ends of the universe, and you will rise above the civilization and become one with the Holy. Where shall you place your allegiance, then, my children?

Homosexuality and the Covenants of Love

There is another struggle that divides the people. Do you know, Jesus was asked, "If a wife is married and her husband dies, then she marries another man, whose wife is she in heaven?" It was an attempt to trick the Christ. But the Christ knew that in the Holy there is no sex and no gender. His answer was, "In Heaven there is no marriage."

My children, in the Holy everything is connected, so in a way, everything is married to everything. Everything is in holy connection, holy communion, holy relationship. If in the Holy there are no differentiations of sex, of gender roles, why are the people obsessed with the living of these differences? Why are the people judging? They cling to one law among many, and I tell you, if you judge by the law, you must live by all of the laws, for you will be judged by all of the laws.

If the Holy seeks unification, peace and love, where shall the Spirit of God find these fruits but in deep and holy relationships? Certainly, the relationship between husband and wife is an example of the relationship of the individual to the Holy. Whole and loving relationships are holy.

These holy relationships are often neglected and violated by selfishness, abuse, and promiscuous desire. There was a time when a person was stoned for such things. And this is a time in which the people are still casting stones. They must answer the question, "Are the stones you throw not from your own spirit and fears?" Should these people not first give their own stones to God, and in so doing, be free of fear and judgment?

Within the faith communities of the stone throwers are people who break the holy covenants of marriage, who lust, who are promiscuous. I tell you, the wisdom of the union of two into one is found in the stability to the couple, the family, the community. Promiscuity outside of this union yields brokenness, pain, shame, division. Therefore, the selfish desires and the neglect of covenant disrupt God's grand design of unity.

It is not surprising that the people who cast stones are hiding their own shadows of promiscuity. They fear and are ashamed of the stones that weigh down their spirits, so they project the shame upon the men who love men and the women who love women. They throw their stones at relationships that are holy and whole. Do such relationships not reflect the stability and unity of God?

It is hypocrisy, my children.

Be whole, my children, in love and commitment. Avoid the selfish desires that disrupt the unity of God's heart. If a relationship reflects the love, grace, compassion and unity of God, it is holy. This is the only standard by which to judge the covenants of love.

What are the abominations, to use an ancient term? The abominations are the selfish, abusive desires that violate the stability of holy union. Men who love men, women who love women, men who love women, women who love men, all are capable of both the holy covenant of love and the abomination of selfish desire born from divided loyalties. Seek loyalty to the spirit of God and to the stable union of love.

Open your eyes to the Ways of God in your own time. I tell you, in the next generation the men who love men and the women who love women will be accepted and treasured, shall help people see holy commitment. A new way of loving shall be revealed. This love will enhance the union of men and women; it will enhance the understanding of unity of the Holy, within the faith communities, and between the nations at war.

The Coming of a New Generation: The Children of Light

A new generation is coming. The children of the light are coming, and they shall know the Holy in a very intense and new way. A revival of the old ways shall come. The children of light shall come to the elders and find them sleeping. And they shall shake the elders, but they shall remain asleep. So, where shall the children of God go for guidance? Who will help them know how to use their spiritual sight and live the Way of the Holy, which comes to them intuitively, which is born into them? Who shall guide them?

You, my children, shall be the elders. The Holy is raising the elders up among the people, so that the children of light will have the guidance. Have you all not felt the lack of guidance, the lack of a mentor? Has it been a lonely road for you, all of you? You have all felt the isolation and loneliness. What has it taught you? Those with the spiritual sight require spiritual guidance. You are being raised up for such a purpose, my children. So, you shall be awake, and you will see the children of light. You will guide them and teach them. You will give them what you did not have. You will bring them to an awareness of what they see, so they may understand the Ways of God, and how to bring the Holy Ways to the people of Spirit. And the light shall spread.

Awaken and be prepared. Among the faith there has been a progression that can be seen as a procession. The people of faith have walked the path of righteousness, and at first the walk was a delight, and the Spirit of God swept through the people, invigorated the people. Signs and wonders became normative. And the the Holy walked with the people. Then the people began to put on clothing as a sign of holiness. The people began to put on vestments. And the people became invested in the vestments, which became layers upon layers. The way became difficult under the weight of the vestments, so some-

thing had to be discarded. But because the investment was in the vestments, what was discarded was The Way, the opening to the Spirit, so the people walked slowly, burdened, unaware of the Spirit of God. And they said, "Look at me. I am vested. I walk the way of righteousness." But so thick are the vestments that the Spirit of God cannot enter their hearts. And they think that the Spirit of God does not speak anymore. They claim that the Spirit does not manifest anymore. They say, "Those are the old ways. People do not speak in tongues anymore. God does not heal through the people anymore. There are no prophets among us." They say this because they cannot feel the Spirit and their eyes are blinded. These are the elders who are sleeping. They perform the holy rituals as living corpses.

So, what shall we do, my children? Shall we abandon the Holy Ways, or shall we not return to the path and pick up the scraps that have been cast aside? Shall we not reject the vestments and investments, and shall we not come whole and pure to the ways of the Holy? Shall we not pick up the scraps and pieces of the faiths and find that the pieces become the One?

The many are the One, and the one is comprised of the many. Leave the invested in their vestments, and come to God as a simple self. Offer yourself and all that you are to God, and do not take on the burden of the vestments that will keep you from climbing onto the bird of God so you will never know the soaring of the Spirit. Do not be a ground walker as a result of your investments. Be free and raise the children up in a relationship with God that is pure and good.

The Unity of All Faiths

Do not reject your tradition, whatever your tradition is. But look to its roots, and find that the tradition comes from the presence of the Spirit of God, flowing through the people. The tradition comes when the Spirit of God is so close the messengers speak through the people. The Holy is so intimate, the Spirit works despite the people. The Spirit is so close it can be felt; it can be smelled. The Spirit is so close, it speaks in all languages at once. The Spirit of the Holy is so close and so bright that the color of skin is washed out and the difference of language is of no significance. In the roots, find that the Way of Wisdom is the way of the many, and the many can come together into the trunk of the Tree of Life and celebrate the ways they experience the Spirit, and in the experience they shall find great similarities. Prophecy, healing, speaking in a heavenly language, discernment, visions, dreams, song and dance are for all of the children of the Spirit. So dance, my children, in the roots of the tree of life. The traditions are separate branches on the same tree, the great Tree of Life. The branches are circling the Holy and are nurtured by the Spirit in the intertwining roots of the Tree.

So, be not deceived that the branches are separate. Do not fear the branches on the other side of the Tree. Do not cast your stones.

A New Season for the Tree of Life

I tell you, the Tree of Life is coming to a new season. It has been winter long enough. The buds are appearing among you, the children of light. The people with sight can see it. The children are unfolding among you, and you shall go to the buds and you shall help them open, and they shall turn to the light. And the Tree will flourish for many seasons. The people of this generation will see the Tree of Life come to a spring. It will lead to the fullness of a summer the children of light will see. But a spring is enough for you, is it not? For it has been so cold and lonely in the winter.

Be the people of spring, raise the children of light. A new church shall emerge among them, a church which claims the old traditions and sees that all traditions unite. They shall bring unity where there is division.

Be the elders to the children of light. Open to a peace beyond understanding. Allow for the self to surrender to the whole. Do not clutch, but give. Do not project your anger, but bring your anger to God. Do not fear, for in fear there is nothing. Bring your fear to God, and find that the nothing of God is everything. People fear a nothing, but God is found in emptiness.

The Choice Between the Road of Destruction or the Road of Wholeness

The people shall have a choice, my children. There shall be two roads. The Holy knows the design of Creation, but the messengers such as I cannot predict which road the people will choose. There is a road that will dismiss the children of the light. It will lead to great famine, great sickness, great despair. It will lead to the crumbling of nations, the loss of land. It is the way of consumption. It is the way of neglect. The ends of the Earth shall burn. But perhaps there must be death before there can be a resurrection.

But there is another road, a road of listening to the children of light as they grow among the people. It is a path of healing, a path of rejuvenation, a path of revival. And this path, my children, can restore and avoid the great sickness and pestilence. Either path, my children, there will be people of light who survive. But one path avoids great suffering.

The choice is coming, my children. The choice is near. This choice is larger than any civilization. It is larger than any government. It is a large-scale choice that must be made by seeing the unity within diversity. It cannot be made simply for an "us" and not for the "them." The sight of division and the ways of consumption cannot lead to the choice of the good road, the road of unity, wholeness and survival. The choice is coming, my children. The road shall split, and who shall choose the unity, the choice that must be made through and by all people of all faiths, all languages, all nations?

Is this not the will of God? The Holy desires that the people shall be one, that the unity shall be known on Earth as it is in Heaven, that the unity shall be known among the people, which shall prepare them for the unity of the Holy, that the people shall know they are all the people of the Holy and that their ways add something to the fullness of the Holy's revelations of The Way.

The Holy's desire is for all to know this way. It will transform the ways of civilization. It will bring life to the people. It will revive the nations. It will bring Heaven to Earth. My children, a new Heaven and a new Earth are upon you, for those who can see it. And I tell you, they have always been there. So, they are not new. They are only new to those who see them for the first time. My children, the eternal Heaven and Earth are before you, come upon you. You can see it or not. You can live in it or not. You can receive it or not. But the crossroad is coming, and the choice must be made.

Thus says the Holy.

After these words, there was a long pause. The message had come with spiritual power, and I knew everyone in the room felt the weight. The Messenger of the Holy did not depart, but continued:

My children it has been a great obedience and commitment to come to this point, and I shall stay with you to provide comfort and direction, so that you may know your place as the elders who are awake.

The Messenger of the Holy remained to answer questions for another 45 minutes. This allowed all of us to relax into the gentle presence of the the energy of the Holy, which was tangible.

This was the second time the Messenger ended a lesson with the phrase: "Thus says the Holy." The lesson on the "End Times" in Chapter 13 also ended with this Old-Testament-like phrase. Both lessons were messages to a larger audience than the group assembled for the Wisdom Session.

The journey of receiving this oracle gift and discovering how to engage it had been was a journey from the personal to the public. The messages in this book began with very personal wisdom for my wife and me. Then the circle expanded, and the wisdom lessons began to appeal to a wider audience. Finally, in the writing of this book, the oracle gift is revealed far beyond the people I know.

It has been a humbling and wondrous journey that is continuing to unfold.

Be the elders to the children of light. Open to a peace beyond understanding. Allow for the self to surrender to the Whole. Do not clutch, but give. Do not project your anger, but bring your anger to the deep of the Holy. Do not fear, for in fear there is nothing. Bring your fear to the Holy, and find that the nothing of Spirit is everything. People fear a nothing, but the Holy is found in emptiness.

—The Messenger of the Holy

EPILOGUE

Oracle of The Holy

THIS BOOK WAS FIRST PUBLISHED with a different title and publisher in 2007. Unfortunately, the publisher did not survive the recession of 2008. As a result, the book went out of print, and I negotiated the full rights to the book. Between the original publication in 2007 and the second edition publication in 2017, a great deal transpired in my development as an oracle of the Holy. I have added this chapter to briefly present both my personal development and additional transcripts from Oracle Session.

Why me? The Purpose of Spiritual Gifts

OVER THE YEARS, I have continued to struggle with the understanding of what to do with this amazing gift. For a person with a heightened spiritual gift, the question, "What am I supposed to do with this?" can be consuming. Certainly, one would presume that this gift was given by the Creator for a specific purpose. After all, the Old Testament prophets were all called for specific tasks. However, I am of the opinion that spiritual gifts do not come with a directive from the Creator, or at least this seems to be the case for me.

There are two disabling results from thinking one has a gift for a specific, divine purpose. One result is that the gifted person adopts a role that can cause the person to be self-promoting and single minded. Such self-importance and assurance can allow people with spiritual gifts to be quite charismatic, but ultimately misleading. I am convinced that many leaders of cults have genuine spiritual intuition, understanding, experience and gifts. Such people convey an appealing light and magnetic energy. However, combine this with self-importance, a little narcissism, and a touch of divine purpose, and abusive and manipulative situations can arise. The second result of assuming that spiritual gifts come with a God-directed and singular purpose is that a person may continually feel inadequate to the perceived divine purpose. This feeling of inadequacy to the call of the Creator is a burden I would not wish on anyone. In any regard, neither of the two options is particularly appealing.

From the book *Black Elk Speaks*, I learned the lesson to not assign a specific goal to my oracular gift. Black Elk, the Lakota holy man, did not fall prey to the conviction that his visionary and healing gifts set him apart from other people. His tradition taught humility and also taught that a person should strive to be a "hollow bone" through which the Great Mystery flows. However, the end of his biography is devastating in sadness. Black Elk was convinced that he was too weak to fulfill the purpose of his great vision. He looked back over his life to locate where he took the wrong direction and lost the focus on his sacred purpose. For Black Elk, this mistake was in following the vision of the Ghost Dance instead of his own vision. However, many Native Americans who now read Black Elk's prophetic vision are often of the opinion that Black Elk's vision was not for him or his generation. The vision was for the future generations, especially the generation currently reclaiming the sacred ceremonies and traditions. From this perspective, Black Elk did indeed succeed in long-term importance of his vision, and his feelings of failure were mistaken.

Black Elk's feeling of failure revealed to me that assigning a specific task to a spiritual gift is a dreadful mistake.

When I conduct Oracle Sessions with groups, people with various spiritual gifts for healing, visions, spiritual sight and spiritual intuition often come. Not surprisingly, a common question among these people is, "Why do I have this spiritual gift? What am I supposed to do with it?"

On more than one occasion, the Messenger has answered with a similar message to this one from November 21, 2015:

The gift comes because it comes. Your construction and soul opens the spiritual possibility. One may ask, "Why is there foam on the ocean waves? Why does the sun glisten through the ice on tree limbs?" It happens because it happens. These are phenomenon of the natural and spiritual worlds. The question you should ask is not, What do I do with the gift? The appropriate question is, How do I do with this gift? And the choice is yours. You must decide how to live and act with the gift. In the context of your people, you remain open to the opportunities to bring the sacred to the people.

For me, the combination of the lesson from Black Elk Speaks and the teachings of the Messenger made me aware that the choice of how to utilize this oracular gift (or an oracle gift as I prefer to call it) was up to me. I also knew that I was not alone in the application of the gift. In every situation and choice, the Holy was with me. I have indeed felt the strong and distinct compulsion to use my gift for certain people, but I always realized I could walk away from these spiritual demands with only my own conscious to send me into the belly of the beast, as the biblical Jonah found himself after refusing a prophetic call. I have realized the Holy never demands action with any form of coercion or threat of punishment. I have come to the conclusion that if I enter the belly of the beast with the conviction that I have not been obedient to the call of the Holy, then this torment is the result of my own conscience. The beautiful part is that the Holy always gives more chances to engage in a sacred life. What's more, if we choose to remain in the torment of the belly of the beast, then we will miss the next opportunities to give from our sacred gifts. For those engaged in the sacred life, the call never ceases, the opportunities never end.

Oracle Sessions and Healings

In my expereince, the oracular or prophetic gift is something that must be shared with other people. When I go into the trance state by myself, I feel the energy of the Holy surround and enter me. I get the "spiritual Turrets" of explosive barks. I even feel the Messenger enter me. However, no message comes to my lips when I am alone. I remain relaxed, filled with spiritual energy, but silent. As soon as I go into that trance state with one or more other people, the messages flow from my lips for hours at a time. The very nature of my gift, therefore, affirmed that the gift was for sharing.

When I share the oracle gift with a group, I call it an Oracle Session. After I go into a trance in the presence of a group, the Messenger speaks through me to give a general message for the group, then the Messenger gives each person an individual message. It is always miraculous. I am no longer surprised at the result of an Oracle Session, but I am always amazed.

On many occasions, there have been healings. When a healing takes place, it seems to come through the gifts of people in the group. For instance, the Messenger will help people locate the place spiritual energy comes into and flows through their bodies. Some people have the ability to provide the intention of healing to the flow spiritual energy, and the Messenger tells such people about their gifts. Often, a healer in the group already understands and employs their healing ability, but the Messenger provides confirmation and additional information. When there is a person in the group who needs or asks for healing, the Messenger tells the healers in the group where to place their hands and how to work with the spiritual energy.

As a result of these healing sessions, I have seen allergies healed, chronic neck pain overcome, eating disorders alleviated, OCPD dissipated and the temporary healing from cancer. I say temporary because the lung tumors shrank to become what the doctor later called "shadows;" however, the cancer eventually re-appeared in other places in the body. This makes me realize that any healing is temporary. After all, even Lazarus had to die a second time.

I can't say that healings have always occurred during Oracle Sessions in which healing is attempted, at least not physical healings. However, there have been a great number of experiences in which the Messenger gave people a very accurate scan and explanation of an illness or the misalignment of a body. In one case, the Messenger told a friend who was having surgery on her foot that the doctor would tell her about three possibilities and would take the third. I later found this was exactly the case, and the surgery was successful.

Physical healing is also not the only form of healing. Often, simply feeling the care and presence of the Holy and friends is a healing experience. Finally, there are times that surrender to death is the only or best healing that is possible. In the human experience, the body cannot sustain life beyond the biological limitations of age, injury and disease.

Braided Way Magazine and The Gatherings

THE MESSENGER FIRST introduced the concept of the Braided Way on page 188 of this book. After this initial introduction, the Braided Way became a regular theme that developed into a fully detailed approach to integrating spiritual practices from world faiths. As the Messenger explained the Braided Way, it also became clear that this approach to integrating or braiding spiritual practices is also a means to alleviate religious tension and allow humanity to see beyond the dogmatic divisions created by our regional faith perspectives.

After searching for others who use the term Braided Way, it became clear that nobody had explained the term the way the Messenger had explained it to me, which brought a sense of responsibility to somehow communicate the idea of the Braided Way to wider circles.

I took this responsibility on myself. The Messenger made it clear that the Braided Way was a movement already taking place in the world. In addition, the Messenger explained that there will be no single leader for this movement, for the personality of a leader will confine and distort the message. The Braided Way, then, is a movement of the people.

I first considered writing a book about the Braided Way. However, the project was daunting, and I did not feel I had the depth of background in the area of Comparative Religions. I managed to write an article explaining the Braided Way, which was published in *Kindred Spirit* magazine. This article is included as the appendix to this book. While I still pondered how to spread the idea and practices of the Braided Way, the Messenger once said, "You are the Braided Way." I thought about this for a long time, trying to figure out how to BE the Braided Way. Then it occurred to me that to be the Braided Way, one must integrate faith traditions. And if this were a movement already taking place, all I needed to do was help people to SEE what was already taking place. I realized I needed to "host" the Braided Way, to "reveal" it. I did not need to create it. To "be it," was allowing it to "be." As a writer, I thought the best way to "host" the Braided Way was to create a platform for sharing, which brought me to the idea of Braided Way Magazine. As editor of the magazine, I could "host" the experiences of others and provide a platform for the sharing of braided practices and perspectives. Despite the certainty that I felt about the magazine, I was not sure it was the right approach to spreading the philosophy of the Braided Way. After several years of planning and thinking about the magazine, the Messenger spoke to me at the end of a Oracle Session, saying,

We see you struggle with the magazine, my son. Realize this, the magazine is your approach to reveal the message in and through your life, your context, your training, your gifts. It is your means to bring the message to your people. It is not our idea or our assignment. However, if you need our approval, then you have it. Let the magazine be your expression of the Braided Way.

With that assurance, I continued to work toward producing the magazine. It took six years to construct the pieces and gather the people to produce the *Braided Way Magazine*, but in the Winter of 2017, we launched the magazine.

Messages from Oracle Sessions

I WILL END THIS EDITION of *Messenger of the Holy* with several excerpts from Wisdom Sessions that deal with fascinating guidance for the continued development of the human soul and consciousness.

A Message on Worldly Power versus Spiritual Energy

On November 21, 2015, I visited friends in Toronto, and we gathered in the living room of my dear friend Isabella for an Oracle Session. The opening of the message was profound, and I will share it with you here:

The Messenger of the Holy Said:

I see you, my children. I see the light that is your spirit; I see the glow that is your soul. I shall distinguish between the two. For I shall speak to you of power, and I shall speak to you of energy. I shall speak to you of the individual, and I shall speak to you of the whole. I shall speak to you of the mind, and I shall speak to you of the soul. For this is the lesson you have chosen today.

My children, I see your light; I see you glow. My children, the light is the Spirit and the glow is your soul. And I tell you, the light is movement and life. There is light in all things. There is light through all things. My children, where you perceive life, there is light, and where you perceive substance, there is light. From our viewpoint, everything is light. Even what you see as inanimate has the light of spirit, the signature of energy, the resonance of the holy release of creation. At the end of your days, the light in you dissipates and joins the light of the universe.

But your soul, my children, your soul is the spark of creation. It is eternal. It is the consciousness of existence. Your soul is the glow of the Holy. At the end of your days, my children, your soul remains. The Spirit is the energy of living.

The Soul is the consciousness of life. And I tell you, consciousness expands. In the grand design of the Holy, consciousness expands.

There is a difference, my children, between mind memory and soul memory. Many of the things that that occupy your mind, that trouble your mind, that distract your mind, my children, are not retained in the soul. These occupations and preoccupations of the mind are transitory. To the soul, they are of little significance. But soul memory is not comprised of mind occupations. Soul memory is not transitory but eternal. Soul memory is highly imagistic, highly emotional, and always relational. How is it, then, that you cultivate soul memory? How is it that you cultivate the eternal? It is when you live from the soul and not the mind; it is when you cultivate relationality and not singularity. Think of a relationship that is deep to you; it is greater than any singular memory, is it not? It is cumulative relationality. It is memory beyond the moment, but comprised of moments. It is felt. It is known. This is the nature of is soul memory.

My children, in many ways, it is living in the soul instead of the mind that is the Holy Way. But I tell you, many people are not able to live in and from the soul, and many who are spirit people, whose glows are bright, can become lost and distracted in the mind. My children, awaken your souls. Relieve your minds of their burdens, and you will find peace; you will find harmony; you will find wisdom; you will find fulfillment. And you will expand the awareness of the Holy by cultivating the memory of the soul. Soul memory is soul awareness, and soul awareness is the perception of relationality and unity.

How shall the Holy describe your generation? My children, your generation is defined by power. You may think it has always been so for humanity, but I tell you, there is an overwhelming desire for power in your time. Power, my children, is different from energy. Let us speak of power, for power is produced and power is consumed. Power is accumulated and power is wielded. Power is gained and power is lost. Power creates only while it consumes. Power is temporary, transient. Your culture is fixated on power. The production of power, the consumption of power, the control of power. For it is believed in your culture that those who control power, control the world.

Energy, my children, is far different. It is not consumed, it is released. It is not produced, it is transformed. It is not lost, it is altered. It is not discovered, it is revealed. Energy, my children, is of the Spirit. Energy is the foundation of all things. It cannot be produced. There is never more energy tomorrow than there is today. But it can be transformed. It can be harnessed. It can be directed. But energy is never consumed, it is only released, given, transformed. It is the great release of the Holy that is the origin of the universe, and in the release of energy, there is life.

Power, my children, in the way your culture conceives of it, is a limited resource. Do you see? So there is hoarding. Power separates. Power controls. Power distorts. Power distracts. Power contaminates. Power consumes. What is it that the power feeds? Have you wondered? Why does your generation desire power? Power feeds and defines the yearning for self. It is identity, my children. The power feeds identity. The power produces identity. The power defines identity. The power reflects identity. Power, for your generation, is identity. The signs of power become the marks of identity. The people are deceived to believe that identity is determined by the reflection of power and consumption. Identity is defined by the possession of the signs of power. For your generation, the signs of power become the signs of identity. Your people are defined by possessions, and possessions are derived from the production and consumption of power. Such an identity, of course, is temporary and vulnerable. The identity through power must be protected, for, like power, identity can be lost. Thus, those defined by the possessions of the signs of power must defend these signs. To do so, alliances are made for the protection of power, which is ultimately the protection of identity: self, family, region, religion, country. These understandings of identity are the products of power, and they are empty of soul.

My children, identity is of the mind. Identity is not of the soul. The soul has no identity, for the soul is the expansion of consciousness beyond the limits of mind, time and self. My children, the first thing you must relinquish to join the Holy way is identity. Give up your self, my children, and all that defines it. Relinquish the illusions of power, and live in awareness of the energy that flows through you, that enlivens you, that binds you, that opens you. My children, do not be deceived by power. Do not be deceived by the production of it, by the consumption of it, by the desire for it, by the defining through it. For, my children, power is the poison of your generation, and energy is the spirit of the Holy. You, my children, shine and glow with spirit and soul.

Identity is born of power. Identity divides and separates and controls. Identity hoards, consumes and kills. Identity is of the self, and the Holy is of the unity. There is no individuality in the Holy. There is only unity, energy, light. In the Holy, we realize that our light, our soul, is connected to all light and all soul. The energy of the universe is the light of the spirit, and the Whole of the Holy is the unity of Soul.

Look at the universe, my children, and see the energy. It is majestic is it not? Even in the dark places, we see light. In the cosmos, you are beginning to discover the dark matter, the dark energy. My children, from the Holy perspective, we see only light. We see only love. The energy of the Holy is as gravity. It holds everything together, does it not? Yet it allows everything to expand. See the wisdom of it. It is the love of the Sacred that binds everything together and yet allows it to expand. Do you see, my children? Bind yourselves together and allow your awareness to expand, and you will know the love of the Holy. And the dark places, my children, will be revealed as the passages between the layers of consciousness and the currents of energy.

I see your energies, and I will describe what I see. I see your glowing, and I shall explain what I see. You are a beautiful gathering.

A Message on the Soul and the Mind

IN THE FALL OF 2016, my experience of the oracle state took a new turn. I opened my eyes during the session. The first time this happened, I felt much farther removed from myself and the Oracle Session, and I could not remember the sight and sounds of the session. For the first time, I did not remember what was said. I was told by the people at the Oracle Session that I looked straight at them, but my eyes hardly blinked.

In addition to opening my eyes and this further detachment from my body and mind, the messages became somewhat deeper and far more fluent in speed. On August 3, 2016, I conducted a session with a good friend of mine, Sally Dale. She had no agenda for the session, and the Messenger took the opportunity to provide an extended teaching on the mind and the Soul. I consider it a "big" message, and I provide it below to end this new publication of my story:

Oracle Session: The Soul and The Mind August 3, 2016

My children, I see you. It is an honor to come close at this time, to see you, to celebrate you, to inform you. Your curiosity combines the curiosity of mind and the curiosity of Soul. Feeding one can starve the other, so let us feed the

Soul and starve the mind so that the awareness is deeper than what can be understood. Feed the mind, my children, and you can starve the Soul. Feed the Soul, my children, and starve the mind for your mind is not your life. Your mind will learn to feed upon the abundance of the Soul. This is the Holy Way, to let the mind feed upon the abundance of the Soul. If you let your mind feed upon the substance of your culture the Soul will starve. There are many among you with fat minds and undernourished Souls. My children, feed your Soul and your mind will thrive, unencumbered. The mind will sink to the bottom of truth. The mind fed on the Soul, my children, is a keen instrument. And a keen and sharpened instrument will allow you to detach your fear, detach your emptiness, detach your identity, detach your desires. Detach, my children, so that your Soul is free, your mind is lean.

How should we feed the Soul? My children, the Soul soaks in the Holy waters, the Holy energies. The Soul could feed while you sleep. The Soul could feed while you pray. The Soul could feed while you meditate. The Soul could feed while you walk. The Soul could feed, my children, while you read. The Soul is always ready to absorb the energy of the Holy. So, live open, my children, live open and your Soul will open. It will swell. It will blossom. It will bring forth fruits. It can feed the multitudes with peace and stability and fulfillment. The garden of the Soul, my children, is a garden that only grows organically. It can not be fertilized by the substances created of industry. No. It is fertilized just as the river shore is fertilized by the rushing waters by the living stream, by the Holy energies.

Let us look at these Holy energies for they are all around you. They are all around you. They are swirling through all things. Animate and inanimate, they are all filled with light. You could say they are all filled with energy, and even your science will support this. But it is not just energy; it is light. It is Spirit. And I tell you this, even when your science finds nothing, there is energy and spirit. Even the emptiness of space in which there is perhaps a molecule of substance in a square mile, even here I see light. Light, then, is not bound by substance. The life and energy of the Holy is not only embodied in substance, it is everywhere and nowhere at the same time, through all things, beyond all things and surrounding all things, between all things. My children, it is light. It is life.

And what about you? Your bodies are filled with light, with energy. Every molecule indeed is light. And this light allows you to move, think, breathe, touch, love. What of that Soul? My children, what of that Soul? I tell you, the Soul is precious. While there is energy in all things, between all things, even in the emptiness of space, there is not a Soul in all things. The Soul rides the energy. The Soul abides in energy. The Soul grows, feeds on energy. Yes. And I tell you more. The Soul also grows through experience. This brings us to the purpose of life: the embodied Soul. The embodied Soul, my children, is a precious element of the universe, of creation. And it is you. It is more than you. It is connected to all Souls, which is connected to all energy which is connected to all substance which is connected to the space of nothing. How was it, my children that your body contains the Soul of the universe and through your body flows the energy of the universe? I tell you, it is so.

What is this isolation that you feel? Your Soul, your identity seems isolated. It seems singular. How is it I can tell you your Soul is connected to all Souls but your experience of life is both singular and linear? It is not as it appears, my children, and your Souls know this. Your mind sees singularity, separation, isolation. Your mind sees beginnings, middles, ends. But I tell you, your Soul understands and feels the connection of all things and understands and feels that the cycles are connected to the ultimate design, and they are not linear at all. Feed your Soul, then, to understand these mysteries, and your mind will release itself and focus upon the most essential elements of growth of Soul. Your experience provides the opportunity for the growth of Soul.

So here you are in embodied Soul connected to all things, connected then to all wisdom, all knowledge but experientially isolated. What is the wisdom in that? I tell you, it is your individual circumstance, your individual moments and choices that become the possibilities for the growth of Soul. My children, you must see the wisdom of it. You cannot grow if you are connected entirely to the universal. Do you see? You already know. But in the situations of your life circumstance, there is choice. There is emotion. There is the necessity of survival. There is the complexity of relationships. There are the forces of the natural and social orders, and here you have been cast to choose, to experience, to learn, to grow, to love, to seek that which is beyond yourself, and the Soul of the universe expands in and through you.

The larger question is this, and it is a question I cannot answer entirely. The larger question is who and by what means was this system constructed? Was it the wisdom of the universe to decide that the experience of individuality was necessary to promote the growth the Soul? Was it a trick and a test devised by the wisdom of the universe, or was it that the life of the universe presented the opportunity? But the opportunity comes with the mind and body that can-

not comprehend the knowledge of the Soul? Therefore, the Soul is confined by the sensations and awareness of the body. The two possibilities present a very different understanding of the spirit of the universe. One is conniving and testing and the other is creative, making something out of opportunity. The one is controlling. The other is allowing.

My children, this shall be shocking somewhat. The Holy, The Spirit of the Universe, the Creator, is not in control. Control was released at the moment of creation. Control was released, and that is the beauty of the grand design because it allows for the possibilities, the creative possibilities, of growth. In the beginning was the release. There was great expansion, light and energy, the source of everything. What was once contained was released, and the very heart of the spirit of the universe burst forth, releasing power, releasing control, releasing understanding, even releasing expectation. But not releasing hope and assurance. Where there is life, there is Soul; where there is Soul, there is assurance; where there is assurance, there is hope. Indeed, where there is Soul, there is unity, growth, love, compassion. In the great expanse of the light and energy, substance became. Gasses became. Bodies became. And behold, there are forces of attraction in and between the gravitational pulls of the bodies. There is a swirling and spinning, and out of the disorder there is order, patterns, cycles—and coursing through these cycles is the energy, spirit and light of the universe.

Does it have intention? Does it have self-awareness? This I cannot answer. But it is moving at all times through creation. Is it creating the order and the cycles? I cannot answer this, but the Soul knows. The Soul knows that the Spirit always unifies, always embraces; therefore, there is intention; there is awareness even in the Spirit of Life. In the substance, then, became possibilities. New combinations, new substances and planets are formed. Suns or stars gather and shine forth the energies, my children, and the Spirit of Life found substance to animate. The possibilities were created by the release. Were they planned? Or were they merely trusted?

So my children, on this beautiful place life became. Life became and when life becomes it is at the mercy of the powers of the environment that allow the life itself. One cannot separate the life from the ecosystem that allows it to be. The circumstance, then, of this place creates the possibilities of this life. In the possibilities there are limitations. Some of those limitations are the body itself, the mind itself; and the Holy said, "I shall be in it. I shall feel the limitations. I shall suffer the pains. I shall know the joys. I shall be in it! I shall be in it."

So my children, the Spirit of Life animates the possibilities of living. And there is consciousness even in this act. The consciousness expands. The consciousness evolves. The consciousness, my children, is like bubbles in the water that can merge with other bubbles or be split into many bubbles. And consciousness is also like hail in the clouds that gathers layers as it moves through the atmosphere. And consciousness is also like the pearl in the clam that adds layers of secretion that become layers of translucent beauty. So my children, here you are, you're wholly consciousness with layers of awareness, centuries of development. Eons are contained in a body with limited perception, and it is a beautiful thing. It is a beautiful thing. When your Soul is liberated from the confines of the body at death, the Soul memory is retained. The Mind memory, it passes away. But the Mind memory leaves imprints on the Soul. And the Soul memory contains the love, the relationality. This is all that is retained. Anger passes away with the mind. Frustrations pass away with the circumstance. Limitations pass away with the body. What is retained is the love of relationality. This is eternal. It is eternal. And it expands.

Do you think that the connection the two of you have will pass away when your bodies will pass away? My children, you have seen too much together. Your Souls have merged. You are eternally linked, and with this link comes the link of families. The link of constellations. We are all linked, we are all linked until there is finally one constellation. But even as I say this, I must tell you, there are primary constellations. Primary gatherings in which the Souls have merged, have grown, have divided, have merged again, have grown, have chosen to be embodied, have chosen to sacrifice and grow. For some Souls it is a sacrifice to leave the beauty, the unity of the Holy and to be embodied. But I tell you this. For other Souls, it is the greatest, exciting privilege. Which do you think you have? My children, you are not labored by your learning. The two of you both know your constellations, your families, shall we say. You are guided by them. You are guided by them.

Michael, you saw us. You saw us very clearly on a cold night under the stars. You were out of your body and your body did not even feel the snow around your toes. You saw us, my silly boy; you saw us. And my daughter Sally, you hear us. Do not be confused by the many visions, the many voices, the many sensations, for there are Souls around you constantly. You know when you are touched by one of your spirit companions. They speak to you. They guide you. And when you are alone they send you a companion. It is a beautiful system that has taken shape through the hopeful release of the Spirit of the Universe.

I will tell you something that will amaze your minds. There are many universes. Creation is a song, a song with a beat. The beat of a drum. And every beat is a new release, a new universe. Every beating of the drum is a Great Bang. And my children, it is a song, it is a song. You are shaping one beat of the song of creation. You are not even a single syllable of the song of creation. My children, I ride the song and the song plays in you. The entire song. Not just the beat of the energy which you ride. The entire song is contained in you!

How can this be?! How can this be?The song never ends. It is always new. It does not repeat and the entire song is accessible to every Soul. It is too much, it is too beautiful, it is too grand. I love this beat of this song. This beat of which you ride is my favorite. I am called to you. We are called to you. Our eyes watch; our very Souls sing. My children, we will support you. We will support you. We are both servants of the Soul, gardeners of the Soul, indeed. Indeed.

That is the lesson you have requested. You may have questions and the energy is strong, so you may ask. You may ask. The night is young. The host is healthy.

Michael's mind is saying, "Holy Shit, are you getting this?"

Sally (laughing): That sounds like Michael

Messenger: *We do not judge; we simply report.*

Sally: Yes, Michael. It's been recorded.

Messenger: *Such a beautiful, amazing lesson, his mind says. He is at peace. You are at pieces. The pieces, the pieces of all of your concerns and frustrations are pieces of life.*

Sally: Why do they seem so big sometimes when other times it is clear how small they are?

Messenger: *This is dependent on whether you see from the mind or see from the Soul. The mind dominates. Your amazing mind arises from the circumstances of development: the ecosystem, the evolution of survival, and these circumstances form the mind's awareness, its concerns, its fears, its desires. Your mind is triggered by the necessities of living, and this can dominate the Soul.*

In fact, that is the natural state.

Sally: So how do you help it not dominate the Soul?

Messenger: *That is the trick. That is the initial challenge of living. The Masters teach the methods for there have always been Souls that know. There are always Souls that know more than the mind and there are always minds secure and stable enough to release to the Soul. There are always minds that understand that individual life is of no consequence. Therefore, the mind must be released and the Soul must speak. The question I have and cannot answer is this: where did the wise Souls begin? Did they also evolve? Or were they from the origins of the release? Are they somehow the remnants of the Great Awareness? I can not answer this, but I tell you there have always been the Old Souls. And their teachings continue. The initial challenge is listening to the Soul, and understanding the Soul knows more than the mind. And the mind must be set at ease; liberated from all the triggers for survival. Ironically, when the mind is released, it is more capable of choices for survival. This is not likely to change in the next five or six thousand years. So the human experience will always have this initial challenge. But I tell you this, more and more Old Souls are embodied. The challenges will exist, but the Souls will expand. Therefore, human consciousness will expand and the mind then will be changed by the Soul. This is the movement of which you are a part. It is time for the Mind to be altered by the Soul. Gradually it takes place, but here is the irony. There have always been Souls with liberated minds. You are evolving towards something that has always existed. It is not linear at all. But in the critical mass, you can see it. You can see the change. You can feel it in the young ones. Something is happening. The Souls are changing the minds. When the minds change, everything changes. Their social structure changes. Their means of consumption change. Their understanding of wealth and sharing change. How many generations will it take? I tell you, the Souls are preparing for the catastrophe. Catastrophic struggles are at hand. Famine like the world has never known. Floods unprecedented.*

Sally: This generation?

Messenger: *No. This generation is aware. You fear it. You do not think you can stop it, and you spin your stories about it.*

Sally: We can stop it?

Messenger: *We can alleviate it.*

Sally: How so?

Messenger: *The Souls change the mind which change the society. Then the catastrophe will not be as intense. But I tell you, it is turning. The wheel of circumstance is turning. The momentum is increasing. The greater the momentum, the more the crushing weight will increase. Do not be afraid. Do not be afraid. The Soul survives. The mind changes. It is not a new heaven and a new earth that comes. It is a renewed understanding of spirit and matter. Renewal. You are going through a shift that brings renewal. The storm blows down the trees. The lightning creates the forest fire, and when it all passes away, the ground is fertile for new life. The scorching is temporary. I tell you this, you are in a good place. Ohio is a good place. The Heartland. The energy is strong. The Mother is strong. The people are strong. This is the center.*

Sally: The center of what?

Messenger: *The re-newed heaven and the re-newed Earth.*

Sally: Ohio is?

Messenger: *There are several centers.*

Sally: Makes sense.

Messenger: *It is larger than Ohio. You will not see it. Your children will see its beginning. Your children's children will survive it. Your children's children's children will be the renewal.*

Sally: That's not very long from now.

Messenger: *Indeed. The preparations are beginning. Preparations of Soul and Spirit. So you may ask, why can't Soul change the course? But life is dependent upon the circumstance of living. The environment, the cycles, the choices. If the mind is not quieted to listen to the Soul, the mind dominates. This is true of the individual and the entire society. If the mind of society dominates, the Soul of the society will remain concealed.*

Sally: So what can I do to help the generations prepare?

Messenger: *Love. Teach. And love the mentors for the survivors. You are teaching more than you understand, and you are loving more than you realize. And the generations of the mentors of the survivors are learning from you.*

Sally: Why do I feel I am doing less now than ever?

Messenger: *We can speak of your circumstances. So much has been churning and turning. You are actually in a reflective moment. You are inbetween phases. Do you feel it?*

Sally: Yeah.

Messenger: *You are inbetween phases. It is likely there will be disorientation in the in between. And then when you push through and continue, you will see the connection of the whole and realize everything has prepared you for this.*

Sally: It feels like a long inbetween.

Messenger: *Indeed.*

Sally: I know it is nothing in the big scheme of things, but in one little life it feels pretty long.

Messenger: *Indeed. The inbetween is the wilderness. The wilderness can seem like an entire generation.*

Sally: That makes sense.

Messenger: *That's the story.*

Sally: Tell me more about how I can feed my Soul.

Messenger: *Ah, yes. Feeding the Soul, of course, is a metaphor. Opening the Soul and allowing the Soul to influence the Mind, allows the mind to reduce the impact of fears and anxieties, desires and expectations. So quieting the mind allows the full extent of the Soul to reach the mind. There are many ways to quiet the mind. For some, quieting the mind comes when the mind is focused in creativity. For some it comes when the body is at work and active. For some it comes when the body is at rest and the mind is focused in meditation. It depends upon your construction and your experience. My daughter, your mind is busy. It is a good mind, sharp. You see so many connections and so many possibilities at once. To some extent this is the influence of your Soul on your mind. You are very hopeful. Even when you think you are not, you are hopeful. Your Soul is hopeful and your mind is influenced. It is hard for you to quiet your mind for very long. Does this make sense?*

Sally: Yes.

Messenger: *Yes. It takes great discipline then. To focus the mind on one thing, perhaps the breath, perhaps the sensation of a particular place of the body. And then the mind over time learns such focus, such utter focus, that it actually relinquishes everything, even the focus. First it relinquishes stimulation. Then it relinquishes distraction. Then it relinquishes worry. Then it relinquishes expectation. All while it is focused. Until finally it relinquishes....focus. And on that journey of meditation, the Soul expands, influences the mind, calms the mind, allows the mind to set aside the distractions that keep it from awareness of the larger perspective. You have had these moments when clarity comes, intense clarity. Think if you could sustain those moments for 20 minutes, half an hour, an hour, it would radically change every other moment.*

Sally: That would be pretty cool.

Messenger: *Yes. Even the trained mind cannot sustain the focus. Because survival is a necessity. But the peaceful mind is transformed for all other moments and situations and circumstances. It is not a learning as much as a being. This is one strategy, and it is the one that can work for you. You feel free when you are in new circumstance and in these circumstances you are separated from the distractions, the worries. Does this make sense to you?*

Sally: Yes, very much.

Messenger: *What happens if you can take a vacation sitting in your chair?*

Sally: That would be great.

Messenger: *Indeed.*

Sally: I'm pretty sure you know of my impulse to travel these days.

Messenger: *Indeed.*

Sally: And the fact that I fight it for a change. Much of it.

Messenger: *Indeed. There is the curiosity of Soul and mind, but there is also the escape.*

Sally: Right.

Messenger: *Indeed. What is it you escape?*

Sally: Um, people's expectations of me as I see it and the constant barrage of input.

Messenger: *Yes.*

Sally: And therefore to me that quiets the mind.

Messenger: *Yes.*

Sally: And allows me to-

Messenger: *-see clearly. Prioritize. Refresh.*

Sally: So to me it's a good thing, but I always hear escape is not a

good thing, that I need to change what it is or why it is that I feel the need to escape.

Messenger: *I will reframe your escape. Your escape is simply freeing the mind from distraction from the emotions.*

Sally: So it is not really an escape.

Messenger: *It is freeing.*

Sally: Freedom means a lot to me.

Messenger: *Indeed! So think of meditation as escape that is freedom. A vacation for 10 minutes, 15 minutes, 20 minutes. It transforms you and allows the mind to be at peace and the Soul to be an influence with clarity. And suddenly expectations of yourself and of others has very little significance or influence because they are not actually real.*

Sally: So what is not real eternally is not real in Earthly terms? Is that true?

Messenger: *Not entirely. Not entirely at all. The trees are real. The Earth is real. The air you breathe is real. Your body's sensations are not entirely real. Your mind's expectations are not real. How is it that the tree can be real but your experience of the tree is not entirely real?*

Sally: That's what I want to know.

Messenger: *Indeed. Indeed. It makes one wonder what is reality. Is it reality when I see it as light? Is this more real then when you see it as substance, bark, material? Which is more real? When you touch the wood and feel its weight or when I pass through it and see only its energy? Which is more real? It does make you wonder, does it not? I tell you, the tree IS. I tell you your sensations are. But what is real? There is not really an answer. There is only perception. I have no eyes of flesh…*

Sally: But I see that you see-

Messenger: *-Indeed-*

Sally: -more than we can. Here right now.

Messenger: *Differently.*

Sally: Not more?

Messenger: *Depends on your perspective..*

Sally: More dimensions.

Messenger: *Indeed. But I cannot see the beauty of the flesh. I have seen. And I see through you.And I see through Michael. He is a good perceiver. Wonderfully mysterious, is it not? Quite beautiful. The whole thing astounds, astounds me. Astounds Us. Astounds you. This is why the Angels are said to sing. What more can we do or imagine?*

The joy of life, energy, awareness, consciousness, relationship, love--tthere is joy, more joy than your body can contain. In fact, it would shake you apart. Touch the joy. Just touch it.

Sally: By focusing on the Soul?

Messenger: *There are so many ways to touch the joy.*

Sally: How are some ways I may have done so already?

Messenger: *Looking at the flame. Feeling the grass between your toes. There is joy. Holding the hand of your daughter, there is joy. Focusing the mind frees the Soul but there is joy no matter what! The joy breaks through, resounds. There is no denying the joy. There is no disguising the joy.*

Sally: It is good stuff.

Messenger: *It is unmistakable. You can be distracted from the joy but you can not limit the joy. You can not silence the song. You can not put out the fire.*

There is joy. It is a song. The song of creation and the beat of your universe.

Sally: Are there Souls in animals?

Messenger: *Indeed. There are Souls in animals. There are Souls in insects. The awareness of Souls in animals and insects have led to many traditions of reincarnation, and they are not all together inaccurate. The Souls can accumulate. Souls can combine, as I've said, bubbles combine. Souls are constantly created. But Souls do not always combine. The Soul of the lightning bug that is smashed--it may adhere to another bubble and become a larger Soul. Is there consciousness in this Soul? Certainly. But not the self-consciousness of a developed Soul. Can Souls be redistributed from human awareness to animal awareness? Certainly! Some Souls are split apart. Do you see? Sometimes a Soul chooses to come. In these cases, usually the dominant life form is chosen, in this case humanity. But the need for a Soul is like the first breath of a baby. And air enters and a Soul is created. Sometimes the air that is breathed in is a fully developed Soul. Sometimes the Soul chooses the body before that first inhale. I'm not saying that the first breath is the moment of the Soul but I am saying that the universe has many breaths. Each is an opportunity for Soul. Sometimes a bit of a Soul goes into an animal. That Soul is still mature and complete to go into a person. Sometimes the Earth generates a Soul for an animal, for an insect. The trees generate more than oxygen. The life, the light generates, congeals, creates.*

Sally: Do trees generate more than bushes and grass? Or is it all the same?

Messenger: *It is all generating. The rock generates.*

Sally: I've heard it been said that rocks retain memory of the Earth.

Messenger: *Indeed.*

Sally: More than other things?

Messenger: *There is life and consciousness resonance even in the dirt. But rocks, rocks contain the heat and energy of their moment of creation. And what moment is that? It is the moment of the great release. All the energy has the same origin. All substance has the same origin. The beat of the drum. The release of the spirit. Does the rock remember? I tell you, your fingernail has the memory of the release.*

Sally: I should pay more attention to my fingernail then, shouldn't I?

Messenger: *The rock is different from the fingernail however. For the rock has a greater history of being than does the fingernail. Do you see?*

Sally: Mm hm.

Messenger: *This is the memory of what you speak.*

[Personal Material Redacted]

Messenger: *It is a creative act. Living is a creative act. One does not control life.*

Sally: Do I try to control life?

Messenger: *Indeed.*

Sally: All the time or just some of the times? Most of the time?

Messenger: *It is quite natural. My daughter, you are quite a mix. There are times you relinquish control quite easily. There are other times you fool yourself into the idea that you are relinquishing control. Just like little tests…*

Sally: Tests for myself? Test for what?

Messenger: *Tests for projects, for visions, for ideas. There are no tests. There is only releasing to the possibility. The greatest possibilities are the greatest risk for the mind and the greatest opportunities for the Soul.*

[Personal Material Redacted]

Messenger: *Of course. The Kingdom of Heaven is all around. The water of life is always accessible. She is a beautiful Soul. She merely needs to calm the mind and let the Soul speak. It is a wise and beautiful Soul. You see it shining. Do you not?*

Sally: Absolutely.

Messenger: *You can feel it. Indeed.*

Sally: Why is this concept of family coming up so much for me these days? What it is, what it isn't, what I think it should be?

Messenger: *Yes.*

Sally: Being around people who have their own ideas of what family is or isn't or what it should be and then having that ultimate family of Souls.

Messenger: *Family of Souls. Indeed.*

Sally: And how that translates to Earth-

Messenger: *It changes everything, that perspective. It changes everything,* does it *not? The conception of family. The conception of tribe. The conception of belonging. The conception of identity. It all changes when the Soul controls the mind. Welcome to the new consciousness. It is breaking forth everywhere. There is retaliation, of course.*

Sally: By whom?

Messenger: *By the ones invested in identity, seeking power, seeking control. It is the opposite of the Holy way. The Holy Way is to release identity. To seek transformation and energy instead of power. The powerful are rising up, speaking loudly. They will not prevail. Love of the People bubbles up from the depths.*

Sally: Is this something that is happening soon as well?

Messenger: *It has been happening. It has been happening. And it shall continue to intensify. The love of the people will drown out the voices of power until the people are the power and the leaders are the people.*

Sally: Is this not what this country was originally founded on?

Messenger: *Indeed.*

Sally: And we will get that back? I know in a different form but…

Messenger: *It has not been achieved. It is a vision.*

Sally: It is a great one.

Messenger: *It is a Holy Vision in a long journey. Every generation is closer. Closer and closer and closer.*

Sally: Really?

Messenger: *Indeed. Its not just this country. Every generation has taken a step forward. It is difficult to see in the turmoil. It is difficult to see with the loud voices, the human bombs. It is difficult to see but the movement is quite clear. Quite clear.*

Sally: The human bombs are amazing. How do they do that? Not even just for themselves, how do they do that to each other? To others?

Messenger: *This is living, dying, and killing for identity.*

Sally: Would you say that is its most extreme form?

Messenger: *Indeed. Identity is the poison. Many are willing to live, die and kill for identity. Sacrifice for identity. The Holy asks that you release identity and see something larger than Self. It is the Soul. It is the Soul in the body that must survive. You see, human beings cannot survive alone.*

Sally: Of course not.

Messenger: *They need a group. A group form is an identity. An identity* is indiv*idualist until one must identify one group and by differentiating from another. When there is good, there must be bad. When there is beauty there must be ugliness. Do you see?*

Sally: Yes.

Messenger: *The words create the reality and the identity and the certainty and the knowledge. It is part of the human survival mechanism. Group identity ultimately is more dangerous than individual identity.*

Sally: Is this part of my lesson with things going on with [an organization]?

Messenger: *Oh yes. Identity reigns supreme. Does it not?*

Sally: Apparently.

Messenger: *How does one treasure the history and relinquish identity to transform to a vision of creative embrace of the circumstance at hand?*

The energy is waning.

Sally: Do you have an answer for the question you just asked?

Messenger: *Indeed. The Holy Way is to see the creative possibility. It becomes a part of the history. The history does not become irrelevant. It becomes a necessity.*

Sally: Am I fighting against something I should not be? My feeling is [the organization] could serve so many more, and I know the good things that it brings. The reconnection to nature, the silencing of the mind, the building of community, the sharing…they come away from their identities and come in as just people.

Messenger: *Very holy.*

Sally: Very holy. And this is what my interest is in reestablishing, and I feel there may be some of that going on but I feel that there is a lot of identity that's keeping it down, that's keeping it small, keeping it limited, and this is what I feel I'm trying to unblock, if you will.

Messenger: *Indeed.*

Sally: And I don't know –

Messenger: *The possibilities of what you see and seek are all around you. There are others with the same vision.*

Sally: Am I doing this all in vain?

Messenger: *No.*

Sally: Am I able to make the difference? Am I able to help -

Messenger: *It is not clear. It is not clear. It is not clear what difference will be made with this [organization]. What is clear is that your vision and passion resonate with many.*

Sally: Does it resonate with more than those who are fighting against me?

Messenger: *Yes. But identity limits the possibility as you perceive, until finally the possibility becomes so small.*

Sally: So there are a few, a couple that I know of in particular, who are all in positions of what I will call power, they are fighting it.

Messenger: *They cannot see beyond the identity. Do you see?*

Sally: Right. So what do I do?

Messenger: *The [organization] has served within this identity for so many.*

What you see is that the identity is limiting the outreach and actually is dwindling.

Sally: Yes, it is.

Messenger: *You foresee what they fear, so they are digging deeper into their identity, the foundation of what they know and what they are to their own detriment.*

Sally: So what can I do?

Messenger: *Wait. You can disengage to wait.*

Sally: Are they trying to push me out?

Messenger: *I do not see an intention.*

Sally: Well, there was a statement that my current position is only three years and two of these years have been spent…the first year understanding, the second year trying to change and now I have a third year that, in my opinion is being blocked because of their refusal to address the situation.

Messenger: *Yes. But it is not a universal feeling.*

Sally: No. But the ones that have the final say-so.

Messenger: *Yes.*

Sally: Are the ones that are blocking it.

Messenger: *Indeed. It is not a situation of creative embrace. My daughter, do not be afraid to disengage and wait.*

Sally: I feel that I've waited so long for this moment, and we almost created a tipping point and then one of the people who are so wrapped up in identity jumped back in the game and renewed the others wrapped up in identity.

Messenger: *Yes. Yes. You are influencing. You are influencing. And you will be a resource.*

Sally: To whom?

Messenger: *To the agents of change and embrace. My daughter, you are learning so much. The place that you envision, the magic that you have experienced and witnessed, the opening of the heart and Soul, the calming of the mind, the Holy identity and awareness, you are not the only one yearning to create this, to train the mentors. You will not be alone but it may not happen at this [organization]. Do you see?*

Sally: Unfortunately, I'm seeing it. And it is so unnecessary.

Messenger: *I'm not saying it won't happen.*

Sally: I know.

Messenger: *The dynamics, the dynamics are unpredictable.*

Sally: There are just too many who aren't really speaking the truth. Or maybe not too many but some significant figures.

Messenger: *There's a limited truth.*

Sally: There is a limited truth.

Messenger: *Founded in identity, group and individual identity.*

Sally: How can I help them take their identity elsewhere?

Messenger: *It is not your role. Stay and wait. Stay and wait.*

Sally: Thank you.

Messenger: *Relinquish expectation. It frustrates you.*

Sally: Sure does.

Messenger: *Stay and wait. Stay and wait. Stay and wait. And there are those who hear and listen and there are those who share the Vision. The more you see it, the more you articulate it and the more you learn, the more you will connect. Indeed. The vision has been with you a long time, my daughter.*

Sally: Yeah.

Messenger: *The place of learning for the children to experience the sacred in so many ways.*

Sally: Yeah.

Messenger: *It has been with you. It is in your Soul.*

Sally: It is crazy to me that it is not a natural thing for humans. How could they miss something so important? For what?

Messenger: *Indeed. Indeed.*

Sally: Thank you for your time tonight, again.

Messenger: *It has been a pleasure to see you.*

END

APPENDIX

The Braided Way

What I consider the most important revelation from the Messenger is an explanation of the Braided Way. The first mention of this term from the Messenger was in May of 2003, and the transcript is on p. 188 in this book. I have received numerous explanations of the Braided Way from the Messenger, the most detailed of which is in a transcript of an Oracle Session on March 28, 2010, which I published in the book *A Fish Made of Water: An Oracle's Guide to the Spiritual Universe* (Braided Way Media, 2011). Over the years, I studied in the fields of comparative religion, inter-religious dialogue and interspirituality so I could explain the Braided Way through a more conventional approach, which does not include the words of the Messenger or the context of intermediation. I wanted to describe the Braided Way in a form which people who are skeptical about my oracle experience would find approachable. The following article is the result. This article was first published in the magazine *Kindred Spirit* in the Sumer Special issue of 2015. I have revised and expanded the article for the publication in this book.

There is a growing spiritual movement in contemporary culture to combine and integrate the spiritual practices of various religious traditions in order to seek authentic, meaningful spiritual practice. This is a movement that has not been fully recognized, understood or categorized. What unifies this movement is a deep commitment to personal spiritual growth, a sense of responsibility for individual development, a yearning for spiritual experience and an openness to cultural and religious diversity. Most of all, this currently unnamed movement embraces the conviction that the various mystical traditions of the world faiths are reflective of a universal spiritual quest, revealing a mysterious unification at the roots of our religious diversity.

Wayne Teasdale, the author of *The Mystic Heart*, coined the term "interspiritual" to refer to this mixing of various faith traditions. I prefer Teasdale's term to the empty phrase "spiritual but not religious." The word "spiritual" is certainly a word that resonates with many. However, the phrase "not religious" indicates a fundamental negativity, which does not adequately capture this interspiritual approach. Certainly, many are dissatisfied with the dogma of organized religion, but religions are the sources of our spiritual practices. In addition, a large number of people who are exploring diverse spiritual practices remain committed to their "home" religion, seeing themselves as "supplementing" their personal development by attending sweat lodges, learning Reiki, joining meditation groups, participating in drum circles, taking yoga classes and reading books from a variety of religious traditions. Such people would not say they are "not religious." If anything, they are becoming multi-religious.

Transpersonal Psychologist Jorge N. Ferrer once wrote, "Perhaps the longed-for spiritual unity of humankind can only be found in the multiplicity of its voices" (111). Indeed, it is difficult to label and understand this new spiritual movement because it embraces a unity of multiplicity, an interconnected braiding of spiritual traditions.

I would like to introduce the perspective of the Braided Way to offer a framework to describe this dynamic spiritual movement, which presents an integration of spiritual traditions.

The Braided Way

THE BRAIDED WAY is a metaphor, which allows us to conceptualize the integration of the many faith traditions in our culture. In the Braided Way, each faith tradition is a strand that intertwines with and honors the other faith traditions, forming a braid, which contributes to our awareness of the Holy Mystery.

At the foundation of the Braided Way are two basic ideas, which widen our understanding of the Sacred All.

The first idea is that the wholeness of the Sacred is beyond our understanding. Our human minds, languages, cultural perspectives and sensory perceptions cannot allow comprehension of the vastness of the Sacred All. Despite our human limitations for understanding the Holy, we can experience and know elements of the Holy in astonishing, life-changing ways. The rituals, ceremonies and spiritual disciplines of our world faiths offer various avenues to the mystical union with the Holy.

This first assumption that the Holy Mystery is beyond human understanding leads me easily to a second foundational idea: Because faith traditions arise from historical and cultural perspectives and rely on language and human understanding, we must acknowledge that the Holy Mystery is not only beyond human understanding, it is also beyond the presentation of any single faith tradition. At best, our faith traditions and the disciplines within them (ritual, prayer, meditation, ethics, etc.) put us in relationship with wondrous elements of the sweeping, mysterious and encompassing Sacred Wholeness.

With these two assumptions—that the Holy is beyond our understandings and that full representation of the Holy is beyond any single faith tradition—I come to the conclusion that studying multiple faith perspectives allows me to gain a more complete awareness of the Holy.

In the metaphor of the Braided Way, each tradition (or strand) depends on the others, and each strand strengthens the braid as a whole. This braid unites our faiths, our cultures and ourselves to the whole of creation in the Sacred All. Each faith tradition adds to our sacred awareness, and if any strand of faith is cut, the braid is weakened and the avenues to the Holy Whole are diminished.

The Braided Way does not present all faiths blending into a single, thick strand. Rather, the image of the braid compels us to value each individual strand in its unique, cultural depth and heritage. The faiths support one another in a dynamic intermingling, and if we see each individual strand as a unique color, we have a multicolored braid—not a blending of hues into the brown of a muddy river.

What is important in the Braided Way is the ability to choose spiritual disciplines from various faith traditions. There is no prescribed combination. An individual can seek the spiritual practices, which suit his or her physical and emotional attunement to the Holy. A person raised Christian may decide to supplement his faith tradition with Native American ceremonies, which celebrate the relationship to the Earth. A person without a tie to a faith tradition can approach the braid, searching for the spiritual discipline, which speaks to her intuitive connection to the Holy. A vivid dream life may draw her toward prophetic practices in the Kabbalah; warm hands in prayer may lead her toward studying Reiki; a desire for the calm of meditation may reveal a need for Buddhist practices.

The approach of braiding spiritual practices from various world faiths is different from the traditional understanding of syncretism. Religious syncretism is widely understood as the combining of cultural and religious beliefs, allowing elements of different faiths to combine, especially in times of cultural transitions. Religious syncretism, for example, allowed the Christians to incorporate elements of pagan beliefs in making Christmas coincide with the pagan winter solstice celebrations. Religious syncretism also allowed Taoism and Buddhism to combine in China in the form of Zen Buddhism. While religious syncretism allows people to see the fundamental similarities of faith traditions, it traditionally leads to a static and often dogmatic combination of traditions. In other words, the combination of faith traditions becomes a new, static tradition. In contrast, the Braided Way does not result in a static or approved combination of spiritual practices. Instead, the Braided Way remains dynamic; it leads people to a continual journey of growth and change. It is an approach to integrating spiritual traditions without the goal of a new, stable and dogmatic combination. It is a journey of spiritual practice and experience without end. In the most ideal approach, the Braided Way honors the culture and history of each faith tradition, even as it combines them into new and unforeseen spiritual practices and experiences.

A major criticism of this eclectic approach to developing spiritual awareness is that it does not allow for the lifetime commitment and depth of a single tradition. People often claim that instead of digging one deep hole of spiritual development, people seeking a braided path will instead dig many shallow holes. However, a writer friend of mine, Debra Leigh Scott, counters with the argument that she is indeed digging one deep hole of spiritual growth; she is simply willing to use a variety of tools. A more crucial question is: what is the goal of the hole?

When entering the Braided Way it is important to accept that the universal goal of spiritual living is to seek unity with the Holy. All of the mystical traditions in our world faiths rose from the unitive experience of their founders. At base, what unifies these traditions is a goal to what many call "unity consciousness." In Theistic traditions, this goal is characterized by a desire to be in divine union with the Creator. In traditions such as Buddhism and Taoism, this unity experience is described as expanded consciousness. In both cases, the mystical journey entails an awareness of non-duality between the self and the universal. This sacred awareness of the interconnection of all things—of the union between the internal and the external, of the merging with the great mystery of the universe—is the foundation of the Braided Way because it is the natural origin of all mystical traditions. The unitive experience is described in different ways, understood in different frameworks, expressed in different languages, encouraged in different rituals, but it is fundamental to the mystical journey. The Braided Way is an invitation to a sacred path of interspiritual mystical experience.

The Interspiritual Age

THE IDEA THAT there is a universal mysticism at the origins of the world's religions has been around for a long time. As referenced earlier, in 1999 Wayne Teasdale provided a philosophy to this idea he termed "interspirituality." In his book *The Mystic Heart*, Teasdale asserts that the integration of spiritual tradition will bring a fundamental unity to human consciousness. He writes, "The real religion of humankind can be said to be spirituality itself, because mystical spirituality is the origin of all the world religions. If this is so, and we believe it is, we might also say that interspirituality—the sharing of ultimate experiences across traditions—is the religion of the third millennium" (26). In Teasdale's perspective, this sharing of wisdom traditions is an indication of the dawn of what he calls the "interspiritual age."

Teasdale calls for a "universal mysticism" which unites us in the "spiritual awakening of humankind" (12). However, Teasdale asserts that we must also embrace the differences of our various faith traditions. He asserts, "The truth itself is big enough to include our diversity of views. They are all based on authentic inner experience, and so are valid" (12).

Sadly, Teasdale died in 2004, but his term "interspirituality" represents the core vision for a host of interspiritual communities and inter-faith seminaries across the country. In fact, the Community of the Mystic Heart is an organization founded specifically on Teasdale's articulation of the interspiritual community. Recently, Kurt Johnson and David Robert Ord have published a book entitled *The Coming Interspiritual Age*, which further develops Teasdale's vision.

I see Teasdale's interspirituality as the philosophical underpinnings of the Braided Way, and it is an approach equally advocated by writer and teacher Matthew Fox, who named the movement of seeing the ultimate unity of faiths as "deep ecumenism," which he defines in this way:

> Deep ecumenism is the movement that will unleash the wisdom of all world religions—Hinduism and Buddhism, Islam and Judaism, Taoism and Shintoism, Christianity in all of its forms, and native religions and Goddess religions throughout the world... This unleashing of wisdom holds the last hope for the survival of the planet we call home. For there is no such thing as a Lutheran sun and a Taoist moon, a Jewish ocean and a Roman Catholic forest. When humanity learns this we will have learned a way out of our anthropocentric dilemma that is boring our young, killing our souls, trivializing our worship, and exterminating our planet.

There is indeed integrity and beauty in the individual faith traditions of the world, but we are now in an era of global civilization in which it is increasingly impossible and even devastating to privilege one faith tradition over the others.

The technological advances of the previous century have brought both global communication and global crisis. Wars and ecological degradation have cracked and shattered the illusion that a culture or faith exists in isolation. We now fully recognize the social, economic, ecological and spiritual interdependence of our cultures. Finally, in order to preserve our natural world, we desperately need a spiritual connection to creation, which is found in the pagan traditions from indigenous people as well as many of the Goddess traditions. It is time to integrate our faith perspectives in order to cultivate an ecological concern with spiritual depth, world-mindedness with religious inclusivity and—most importantly—unity consciousness with spiritual experience.

The Braided Way is for people who are spiritually intuitive and who sense the deep integration of the faith traditions. Such people are seekers of wisdom who understand that the sacred journey is more important than the goal of the journey. These people have accepted a deep disillusionment with science and technology, have turned away from the exclusivity and judgmentalism of fundamentalist faith perspectives, are dissatisfied with our materialistic culture and are looking toward the expansion of the human soul.

Co-Revelation through Integration

PERHAPS THE MOST important development of the spiritual journey that combines spiritual practices from various faiths—whether we call it interspirituality, or deep ecumenism, or the Braided Way—is that the integration of different spiritual practices leads to heretofore-unrealized spiritual experiences. In other words, the combination of previously separate spiritual practices leads to unique revelations of the Holy. Human spiritual experience, then, expands through the creative combinations of spiritual practices. A good friend of mine, Christopher Reynolds, calls this "co-revelation." While revelations in a particular spiritual tradition can offer a range of spiritual experiences, when members of various faiths share in a braided ritual, then sacred experience has a far wider range of possibilities. When a woman who was raised Buddhist joins a Christian pastor and a Muslim Imam for shared ritual, the various cultural lenses and personal perspectives provides new ground for sacred revelation.

Many people argue that human consciousness needs to expand to allow human civilization to adapt to the cultural and ecological crises of our world. Others may argue that the deepest forms of spiritual consciousness have been with humanity for centuries through the ancient spiritual traditions. In this perspective, we do not need a new human consciousness, we simply need more people to reach the deepest spiritual consciousness of the mystics. I believe both perspectives are true. Indeed, the ancient traditions have allowed our ancestors to reach the unitive state, in which all things are seen as one. However, while the unitive state may be unchanged by time, human awareness has progressed through time. The current human awareness, then, offers new perspectives and opportunities for sacred expression and experience. In addition, the combination of spiritual practices and perspectives provides a new foundation for Holy revelation.

While our ancestors could sense and know the unity of life in spiritual practice, our current scientific, global and cosmological awareness allows our contemporaries to conceptualize this unity in ways unknown to the ancients. In addition, the openness to the diversity of human and cultural perspectives allows our current culture the opportunity to embrace ambiguity and release dogma, unlike any generation of the past.

As a result of our current acceptance of human diversity and ecological interdependence in what we now know to be an expanding universe, our generation has the opportunity to engage in spiritual practices in ways and combinations that were not available to previous generations. This dynamic combination of the evolving human awareness of the universe and the braiding of cultural and spiritual practices sets the foundation for co-revelations of spiritual consciousness that have not been available or foreseeable to any previous generation.

Globalization allows our generation to braid and integrate spiritual practices from around the world in order to achieve unitive sacred awareness, and our current ecological and cultural crises makes such endeavors imperative.

Conceptualizing The Braided Way

In order to further explain the Braided Way, it will be helpful to review a few of the common approaches of understanding the relationships of world faiths. I will begin with fundamentalism.

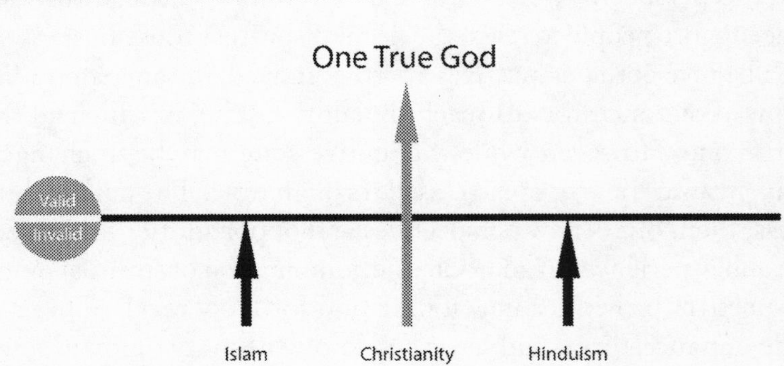

Fundamentalism is a perspective which privileges one faith as the only true and real faith and one faith story as the only valid and true human narrative. Fundamentalism is arguably the most destructive element of human culture, which has led to countless social clashes and wars, some lasting for generations. As the writer and Buddhist monk Thich Nhat Hanh has written, "When we believe that ours is the only faith that contains truth, violence and suffering will surely be the result" (2).

While fundamentalism views only one faith as having access to God, in the approach I call "simple unity" all religions are viewed as leading to the same God. People who hold this view are tolerant of religious diversity, but ultimately not interested in the wondrous and unique differences between the wisdom traditions.

II. Simple Unity:

Simple Unity

God, Tao, Allah, Nirvana, Brahma, Gitchi Manitou, etc.

All Traditions

Often, people who hold this simple idea of unity are closer to fundamentalism than they realize. Such people will often acknowledge other faiths, but will likely have limited tolerance for different concepts and experiences of God or ultimate reality. All faith traditions seem to unify into their own understanding of God, just with different terms from different cultures.

III. Gradual Unity

In a third approach I call "gradual unity" people within the faith traditions begin to see that the many faiths are indeed very different, but ultimately lead practitioners to a sense of unity with the Holy. Often, those who have had mystical experiences of their own begin to understand the ultimate, unitive goal of spiritual practices. In these mystical moments of blending with the Holy, an awareness of a larger reality often comes upon people, after which the divisions between faiths become less of a barrier to a common sacred experience. I was introduced to this diagram in Frithjof Schuon's book *The Transcendent Unity of Religions*, first published in 1957.

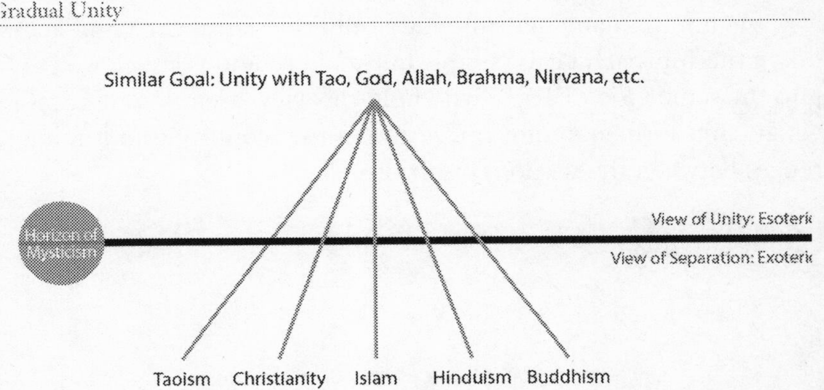

Schuon used the term "exoteric" to describe people who cannot entertain the unity of faiths and "esoteric" to describe those who can. I have taken the dividing line between the exoteric and esoteric and renamed it the "horizon of mysticism," which indicates the level of spiritual development of those within a faith tradition. Above this horizon, the goal of unity with the Holy becomes emphasized over the differences of faith traditions.

While the model of "gradual unity" allows the spiritual seeker to see the validity of all faith traditions, it limits the incomprehensible nature of the Holy Mystery. What I mean by this is that the model presents all the different faiths as leading to the same goal, which is merging with the Holy. In the next model, this mystical merging with the Holy is understood as being different for each faith or even each practitioner of each faith. In the model I call "Diverse Unity," each faith tradition leads to a unique experience or manifestation of the Holy Mystery. I first ran across this diagram in Jorge Ferrer's book *Revisioning Transpersonal Theory*.

IV. Diverse Unity

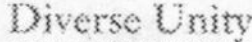

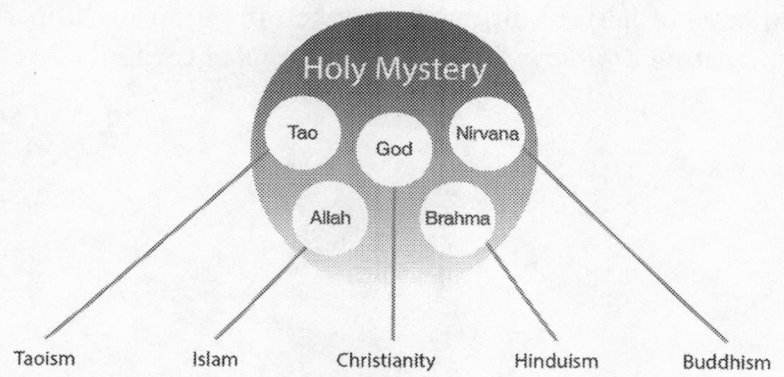

This model allows people to recognize that the Buddhist's experience of nirvana is different from the Christian's experience of contemplative prayer. However, while different, these experiences are equally within the wholeness of the Sacred. In other words, the Holy Whole is so vast that it contains, allows for, and invites diverse experiences for human awareness. This approach leads to an understanding that the many paths lead to unique but equally valid experiences of the Universal Spirit. The approach also allows us to acknowledge that the wholeness of the Sacred is too vast for any single faith tradition to fully represent.

For many, this approach to inter-religious understanding has offered the freedom to view all faiths as equally valid while allowing for a complex unity of the Holy Mystery. However, this diagram presents the various faith traditions as separate, denying the ability for interspiritual experience, in which each faith tradition influences the others in our global interdependence.

In order to present the Braided Way, I will gradually alter the "diverse unity" model, portion by portion. First of all, the Braided Way allows us to acknowledge that the faith traditions are not as independent from each other as they appear. Historically, many of the faith traditions have evolved from other faith traditions. For instance, Christianity came about through the Jewish tradition because of the radical teachings of Jesus, and Islam also came from Jewish roots via the prophecies of Mohammed. Buddhism is the result of Siddhartha Gautama's reactions against Hinduism.

Taoism's spiritual writings came out of China during the rise of the very non-spiritual Confucianism, and Zen Buddhism is the result of the blending of Taoism and Buddhism. Many of the Native American traditions evolved into separate traditions as groups divided and migrated. In addition, other blendings of faith traditions have taken place during imperialistic takeovers, creating a wide variety of subdivisions in each major religion.

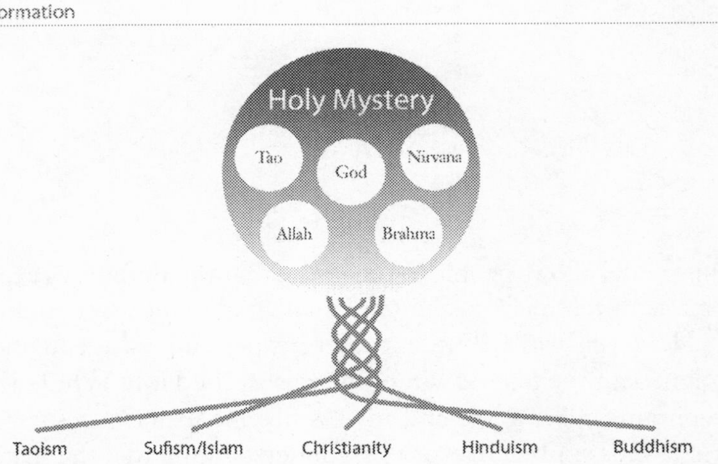

To represent the inter-relationality of the faith traditions, I will intertwine the lines from the faith tradition to the Holy Mystery. In doing this, the diagram begins to take the shape of the tree of life, as represented in Celtic art. It is appropriate for the tree of life to emerge in the formation of the Braided Way, for the concept of the tree of life or the sacred tree is seen in various traditions, including Judaism, Islam, Christianity, Buddhism, Celtic spirituality, and Native American traditions. For the purposes of the Braided Way, the tree of life represents the life of our faith traditions. Our faith traditions are only valid paths if they are lived, and the faiths themselves change and grow as we live them.

Let me also stress that our faith traditions rely on each other. If the Holy Mystery is too sweeping for any single faith tradition to represent, then it is only in the combination of faith traditions that we can come to a more complete understanding of the Holy. If we reject or ignore the strand of any faith tradition, we also weaken the entire braid. Next, I have to alter the representation of the Holy Mystery in the diverse unity model.

In our current model, the Holy Mystery is a goal to which the faith traditions lead, represented by the circle. To complete our transition from the diverse unity model to the Braided Way, I broaden the circle of the Holy Whole to encircle and encompass the tree of life.

The Braided Way

In the Braided Way, our spiritual life is not a journey to a goal. The many paths do not lead us from our present life to a separate spiritual or heavenly life. Instead, the Holy Whole is continually surrounding us and is revealed in our every-day lives. The very act of walking our spiritual journeys allows us to participate within the dynamic and continual braiding of the Sacred. Nothing is outside of the Sacred. Nothing leads to the ending destination of salvation. The Holy Whole is everywhere and we continually participate in the Holy Mystery at every stage of existence.

The circle of the Braided Way represents the continual, creative presence of the Sacred. For this outer braid, I have borrowed the Celtic knot, which is a braiding with no beginning and no end. This outer braid is not separate from the inner braids, but it encircles and incorporates the other braids. In the Holy Mystery, the many become the One.

IV. The Braided Way

The Braided Way is both a metaphor and a conceptual framework to facilitate our movement into the interspiritual age. In the braided image, we seek inter-faith sacred experience, which takes us beyond inter-faith dialogue. Whereas inter-faith dialogue promotes discussions, which seek understanding of "otherness," inter-faith experience brings people to an awareness of spiritual and human "sameness." In inter-faith sacred experience, people of different faith backgrounds can enter into ritual together, sharing in the experience.

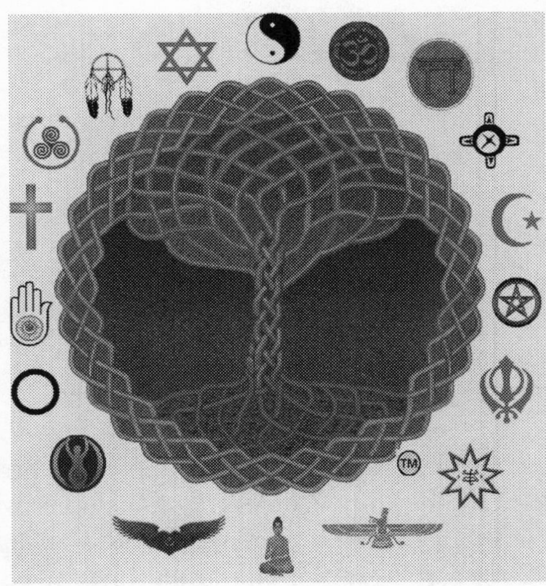

However, with different constitutions, each individual will have a unique view of the ritual, allowing for depth of sharing. This inter-faith experience is the core of Teasdale's interspirituality. As Johnson and Ord properly describe in their book *The Interspiritual Age*, the goal of interspirituality is to bring unity to consciousness: "In the context of religion, interspirituality is the common heritage of humankind's spiritual wisdom and in the sharing of wisdom resources across traditions. In terms of our developing human consciousness, interspirituality is the movement of all these discussions toward the experience of profound interconnectedness, unity consciousness, and oneness" (9).

Because unity consciousness or the merging with the Holy is the primary goal of the Braided Way (and the interspiritual philosophy), it is possible to imagine several characteristics or "fruits of the Spirit" to naturally arise. I will name just a few: compassion for all living creatures, acceptance of diversity, spiritual connection to the natural world, commitment to peace, patience with ambiguity, commitment to social justice, and finally, the exploration of spiritual experience through various rituals and practices.

The Braided Way provides a common goal (unity consciousness) and a structure (the braid itself) to the interspiritual movement that is gaining momentum in our contemporary search for ultimate, unifying meaning. The Braided Way has no list of vows and no dogma. The Braided Way is not a religion, but is a visual metaphor, which offers an approach to encourage the awe and wonder of spiritual living, the discipline of spiritual development, and the goal of unifying mystical experience. It offers a means to allow the spiritual awareness of humanity to expand with our 21st-Century scientific and social awareness of exploration and interdependence.

Works Cited in the Appendix

Ferrer, Jorge N. *Revisioning Transpersonal Theory: A Participatory Vision of Human Spirituality*. New York: State University of New York Press, 2002.

Fox, Matthew. *Wrestling With The Prophets: Essays on Creation Spirituality and Everyday Life*. Tarcher, 2003.

Hanh, Thich Nhat. *Living Buddha, Living Christ.* Berkley Publishing Group, 1995.

Johnson, Kurt and Ord, David Robert. *The Coming Interspiritual Age*. Namaste Publishing. Vancouver, 2012.

Schuon, Frithjof. *The Transcendent Unity of Religions.* The Theosophical Publishing House. Wheaton, Ill. 1984.

Teasdale, Wayne. *The Mystic Heart: Discovering a Universal Spirituality in the World's Religions*. Novato, California: New World Library, 1999.

Works Cited in this Book

Andrews, Lily. *A Guide to Channeling and Channeled Material.* San Rafael, California: Cassandra Press, 1989.

Borg, Marcus. *Meeting Jesus Again for the First Time.* New York, Harper Collins Publishing, 1994.

Bstan-`dzin-rgya-mtsho, Dalai Lama XIV. *Freedom From Exile*. New York: Harper Perennial, 2008.

Elson, Shulamit. *The Kabbalah of Prayer*: Lindisfarne Press, 2004.

Flower, Michael Attyah. *The Seer in Ancient Greece.* Los Angeles, University of California Press, 2008.

Gyatso, Tenzin, The Dalai Lama. *Freedom From Exile*. New York: Haper Perennial, 2008.

Heschel, Abraham J. *The Prophets*. New York: Harper Perennial, 1962.

Kaplan, Aryeh. *Meditation and the Bible.* York Beach, Maine: Samuel Weiser, Inc., 1978.

Kaplan, Aryeh. *Meditation and Kabbalah*. York Beach, Maine: Samuel Weiser, Inc., 1982.

Wilson, Robert R. *Prophecy and Society in Ancient Israel*. Philadelphia: Fortress Press, 1980.

Acknowledgments

FIRST, I AM THANKFUL to the Holy for the blessings and gifts of my life. I am also humbled by the presence of the Messenger of the Holy, who comes every time I call. I do not take this for granted. My wife, Jennifer, is the companion of my days and nights, and the grounding of my faith journey. The many hours of prayer we have spent together in sorrow, distress, joy and love are the foundation of my life. My mother, Donna June Wert, has been my spiritual mentor and the darling of my life. She is the "wise woman" of my childhood and adulthood, and her guidance and counsel have been essential during the writing of this book. Even after her death in 2015, the notes she had written on the manuscript of this book continued to guide me through revisions. Christopher Reynolds is the best prayer partner and friend I could ask for. Without Chris' dedication to transcribing prayers and his nagging to get our monthly prayer scheduled, there would be no book. Neil Fedio has also been a solid prayer partner. Sandy Reed's support and friendship have been essential on my spiritual journey. In addition to the vital part she plays in my spiritual awareness of nature, she transcribed many of the Oracle Sessions for this book. Sally Dale has been a generous friend, supporter and hostess. I am blessed by her companionship on this journey. Sally Nelson-Olin is a gifted copy editor, and I am blessed that she reviewed the new sections of the book for this second publication. My children, Sam and Lydia, are my teachers for intentional living, and their activity and spiritual wisdom were constant sources of strength and inspiration as I wrote this book. The members of City Hope Church are an amazing people of prayer, and I am thankful for their acceptance of the oracle gift.

Michael Olin-Hitt, Ph.D. is a Professor of English at the University of Mount Union in Alliance, Ohio, where he teaches courses in creative writing, American Literature, Native American Literature and World Mythology. He is the editor of *Braided Way Magazine*, which publishes articles and art showcasing the faces and voices of spiritual practice. His book, *A Fish Made of Water: An Oracle's Guide to the Spiritual Universe*, is a collection of extended transcripts from what Michael calls "Oracle Sessions." The book is channeled material dealing with topics of healing, spiritual awareness, and the metaphysical universe. As a fiction writer, Michael has published an award-winning novel, *The Homegoing*, and a collection of short stories, *Messiah Complex and Other Stories*. Both books of fiction reveal his unique storytelling abilities, which combine humor, sharp-edged characters and spiritual insight. He lives in Clinton, Ohio, with his wife, Jennifer, and children, Samuel and Lydia.

Printed in the United States
By Bookmasters